REBECCA CHIANESE

unspoken

Let us go forth with fear and courage

and rage to save the world.

~Grace Paley

REBECCA CHIANESE

unspoken

MNP
Mt. Nittany Press
an imprint of Eddy Publishing

Lemont

Published by Mt. Nittany Press, an imprint of Eifrig Publishing,
PO Box 66, Lemont, PA 16851.
Knobelsdorffstr. 44, 14059 Berlin, Germany

For information regarding permission, write to:
Rights and Permissions Department,
Eifrig Publishing,
PO Box 66, Lemont, PA 16851, USA.
permissions@eifrigpublishing.com, 888-340-6543.

Library of Congress Control Number: 2020952202

Chianese, Rebecca
  Unspoken
    / Rebecca Chianese
      p.   cm.

Paperback: ISBN 978-1-63233-277-6
Hardcover: ISBN 978-1-63233-278-3
eBook: ISBN 978-1-63233-279-0

    1. Novel
I. Chianese, Rebecca II. Title.

25 24 23 22 2021
5 4 3 2 1

Printed on acid-free paper. ∞

For my grandmother
Sima Leah Molofsky

To the waters and the wild
With a faery, hand in hand
For the world's more full of weeping
than he can understand.

~The Stolen Child, William Butler Yeats

Just like moons and like suns,
with the certainty of tides,
just like hopes springing high,
Still I'll rise.
~Maya Angelou

Table of Contents

ACKNOWLEDGEMENTS

The act of putting words on paper is a solitary experience, but getting a novel to readers is an effort of many people. Here is an attempt to thank all of you responsible for *Unspoken*.

To all of my readers, without you, I'm just a lady procrastinating in front of a computer screen at her kitchen table, so my deepest debt is to you.

To my friends who put up with my early draft, Carol Dawley, Jillian La Porta, Carol Lynch, Amy Bogusz, Ellie Becker, Emily and Greg Clary, this book is here because you believed in it. Your love and friendship mean everything to me.

To Patty Gillette, the first person who ever read these chapters, thank you for keeping me going, for your wise criticisms, and for your belief in these characters and their story. You carried this story with me from beginning to end. You are an important part of my life and my writing process and I love you very much.

To Laura Carraro, one of my favorite writers, without your support, and excellent eye for crafting words, I would have long ago thrown my computer into the Hudson River. Having you as a writing colleague has kept me going every step of the way. This story is better because of you. I cherish our marathon writing (and talking about writing) days more than I can express with mere words.

To Grace Clary, you understand more than anyone what

this process cost me, and you helped me believe in myself. Thanks for marrying my darling son, and for becoming my daughter.

To Alex Farina, when a writer who moves me the way you do says she likes a sentence, I abandon all my fears and push the send button! Thank you.

To Sandy Sackman, writing, dancing, and porch therapy in Avalon is why this book exists. Thank you for opening your home and being my confidant throughout this process. We write, we laugh, we cry, we dance, and we keep doing that until all of the words are written. We are partners in this life and probably many others, haha.

To Kimberly Goebel, my editor and friend, you are a spectacular editor, you made this a better book. *Unspoken* wouldn't exist in the world without you. Having you as a partner as well as a friend is something I will always be deeply grateful for.

To Laura Schaefer, *Scattered Books* in Chappaqua, New York, is a home for authors and readers and bunnies! Your warmth and commitment to books and community are the reason this book is in the hands of readers.

To Mallory Rock, you are the rock star of book cover art! Thank you, Jeff Altabef, you started this ball rolling and *Unspoken* and this beautiful cover wouldn't be here without your generous advice.

To Penny Eifrig of Eifrig Publishing, thank you for taking a chance on this story. Your commitment to readers is the reason books are in the world. You care passionately about the environment and people and community, and it is reflected every day in what you do. I hope every author is as lucky as I am to work with someone as smart and caring and supportive as you are.

To my husband Anthony, we started talking about writing the first time we met, and you have stood by me all of these years, both when I believed in myself and when I wanted to give up. You have inspired and encouraged me. To my first-born son, Anthony, Jr., you taught me how to be a mom, and it has been the most important thing I've ever done. You were a wonderful big brother and you're a wonderful husband, and I know you will be a wonderful dad to our little Sweet Pea. You also taught me new ways to see the world and I love you for that. To Arielle Scarpati, daughter of my heart, your smile lights up our lives, we share so much and you have brought us so much joy. Your dedication to nursing and to the tiny patients you care for inspires me to work harder and push myself (even when I want to throw my computer in the Hudson River.) To Joseph Michael Scarpati, my darling boy, you have been my writing champion all of these years! One of my greatest joys has been reading your work. Your sensitivity and sweetness and humor are a gift to everyone who knows you, and I can't wait for the world to read your work. To Grace Clary, daughter of my heart, this book wouldn't be here without your support. Your gifts and song make the world a shining place, even, and especially in, the darkest times. I love you and cherish you. And finally to my daughter, Leah Elizabeth Scarpati, my Lulu, I waited my entire life for you and when you came into the world 21 years ago, you brought power and energy and light and love to all of us. Your music inspires me, your commitment to your art inspires me, and I can't thank you enough for answering my ridiculous texts when I had "research" questions about cursing and music and things kids say, haha. I have been your lesson in patience, and you have been my great joy. I love you and will always cherish our midnight talks.

And finally, to my maternal grandmother Sima Leah Molofsky, you inspired this book. It is for you, and for all of the survivors. All of the survivors.

R. S.

Journal Entry

January 2017

If everyone has a secret, then I am his.

CHAPTER ONE
ALECIA

Late January, Alecia Calding believed, was the most difficult time of year. The sparkle of the holiday season had already dissipated, leaving behind a limp gray world. Alecia's method of mitigating the dullness was to do as her decorating guru suggested in one of his blogs, and be bold with color. Tangerine, she decided, was the perfect antidote for the lack of sunshine. Alecia imagined standing beneath a tangerine tree, looking up and seeing the bright orbs nestled in a bed of deep green foliage against a cerulean sky. The rich brown bark of the tree rooted them all to the ground.

Alecia was much more visual than tactile. So, while she bought 600-thread count organic cotton bedding, she did it because Everett was a stickler for the best. This made him quite easy to please, because all she needed to do was research the best of whatever it was they were doing, and execute it. Alecia was a master at executing, and she did it with the opportunity and confidence conferred upon her for being wealthy, well connected, and white.

When the jangle of her phone summoned its alarm each morning, Alecia allowed her self at least a full minute, sometimes 90 seconds, of gazing around her bedroom. On especially dreary mornings such as this one, she allowed her mind to wander one floor above to her daughter Hannah's bedroom.

It was, Alecia believed, a little girl's dream. Painted robin's egg blue with dove-white trim, it housed a white eyelet canopy-bed with matching window treatments, and the *piece de resistance* — a small mirrored vanity. Alecia had asked Hannah last night during dinner if she was ready to upgrade to a proper teenage room. They had exactly three months to the day to redecorate before her thirteenth birthday. Hannah refused. Alecia felt a brief flash of disappointment (she had carefully researched several exquisite options) but found it comforting that her daughter wasn't anxious to launch herself into her teenage years. Hannah was in some ways young for her age, refusing to give up her dollhouse, re-reading the *Harry Potter* series and eschewing any *Twilight* books or post-apocalyptic reads like *The After* series by Scott Nicholson that Hannah's best friend, Chloe Payne seemed to prefer.

Alecia's eyes widened as she remembered that tonight was book club. Throwing off the covers (a bit less gently than usual) causing Everett to grumble in his sleep, she placed her feet into her fleece-lined slippers and headed into her master bath.

Alecia's routine never varied other than seasonal demands necessitated. Her skincare products were different, but the regimen was the same. She had it down to a science and could complete it in 3.5 minutes. It took a few moments in her dressing room to slide out of her silk pajamas and into slim cut jeans, a bright yellow tailored button down, and a navy-blue cardigan. Like Gwyneth Paltrow, Alecia was a "spring" palette color type. Yellow had the dual function of flattering her pale gold hair and her light blue eyes. Alecia was aware that the other women in her book club admired her willowy body, and comparisons to Gwyneth from complete strangers were commonplace. It bothered her much more than she ever let on. Gwyneth had a reputation for being elitist, tone-deaf, and privileged. Alecia had grown up poor and tough, and resented the comparison, even if she did, perhaps unwittingly, cultivate it. No one, not even Everett, knew how poor she had been. It was something she had erased from her memory as effectively as bleach spray and a strong scrubbing brush erased mold from shower stalls.

Alecia descended her wide stairway, pausing as she did every morning on the middle landing. From this vantage point, Alecia could see a wide expanse of lawn from oversized arched windows soaring an entire story above the massive front doors. A sparkling chandelier showered the space in a prism of sunlight. Gleaming hardwood floors were covered in part by silk Turkish rugs in muted colors. With a slight turn of her head she could see the white and cream living room on one side; a 90-degree swivel of her body and she faced the grand piano in the music room, with a partial view of the formal dining room beyond that. Alecia took a deep breath in and waited for the feeling of calm she'd learned to associate with this moment, then continued to glide gracefully down the second sweep of stairs where she made a sharp turn to the back of the house. It was this space, her kitchen/family room, which drew the most ooohs and aaahs. Her book club friends preferred gathering here than in the stunning living room. Pale gray cabinets soothed the eye while the chartreuse silk dupioni wall coverings brightened the seating area, and oversized couches, and chairs beckoned you to settle in and read, with plenty of side tables in cheerful garden colors on which to perch mugs of hot tea or glasses of perfectly chilled wine. The entire room was automated, and with a single voice command music played, coffee percolated, water ran, and window blinds ascended to let the weak January light wash the salvaged wood breakfast table tucked under a bank of windows. The women would arrive at 7:30 this evening. Alecia had a long day ahead of her, and she genuinely wanted everything perfect for her friends. Perfectionism, Alecia knew, had many root causes. She made a distinct effort not to dwell on the obsessive aspects of her personality and focused instead on the pleasure she could provide for others. This, she knew, was her best character attribute — the genuine desire to make others comfortable and happy. Alecia, however, possessed enough self-awareness to understand the pitfalls — the terror — of coming up short.

Their book club was reading *Daisy Miller* by Henry James. Alecia was unhappy with the selection, she had argued for Virginia Woolf's *The Years,* but the others pointed out that she could choose that when it was her turn to select a book. The argument was irrefutable in its fairness, but it rankled anyway because she disliked Henry James and found *Daisy Miller* to be his most tiresome work. Alecia conceded that she might have been slightly dismissive and somewhat rude when Fiona Payne suggested *Daisy Miller*. She'd seen the bridge of Fiona's nose whiten and pinch, an annoying trait signifying hurt feelings. If emotions were a "tell," then Fiona would make a terrible poker player. Alecia felt strongly that the book selection and hosting should correspond, but the schedule was off, and it was too much for the others to sync back up, forcing Alecia to host during a book she was unhappy about. The saving grace was the continental fare she would be able to serve. Since Italy was a backdrop for part of the story, Alecia had carefully selected a lovely array of cheeses, meats, fruits, nuts, and Prosecco. The interior of Alecia's refrigerator was a careful assemblage showcasing form and function. There was no work of art, no sculpture, no painting, no hand sewn rug, ceiling mural, architectural masterpiece, no act of nature or God, (including the most spectacular sunset) that would rival a well-stocked, organized refrigerator. Alecia believed this with all of her heart. And it wasn't because she under-appreciated the list of wonders and beauty created by nature, God, or humans. It was the hint of memory, the knowledge of hunger, filth, and deprivation. It was necessity that drove her to see the beauty in her sparkling, well-stocked refrigerator. Alecia reached in and selected the ingredients for an omelet, pearl colored eggs, tiny bright red grape tomatoes, lush parsley, translucent violet colored shallots, and tender leaves of baby spinach. Soon the kitchen smelled of coffee and the table was set. It was time to call Everett and Hannah down for breakfast, but first Alecia picked up her iPhone and captured the perfection in a series of photos. After careful consideration, she selected the one where the eggs looked particularly fluffy and the flowers in the center of the table had a warm glow to them and off it went into the Instagram universe. Alecia couldn't help smiling as she typed #nofilter #breakfastanyone?

This, her daughter Hannah would think when she saw it later on the bus, *is why other moms hated her mom.*

CHAPTER TWO
IVY

Ivy Barnet sat on her deck overlooking the Hudson River smoking her only cigarette of the day. It was a Kretek, a clove cigarette, which was no better or worse than any other cigarette, but she'd developed a fondness for them during a backpacking trip to Indonesia in her early twenties. She allowed herself one per day. Her favorite time to have it was at 8:00 am with the boys off at school and James long gone, having taken the 6:40 train to the city, kitchen cleaned up, beds made, two loads of laundry completed with another in the dryer. After her third son was born, Ivy left the hard-won partnership at a white-shoe law firm (along with the 80-hour workweek) behind. She now volunteered pro bono for a local environmental agency instead, forgoing the enormous salary and keeping her insanity intact. While the decision had been agonizing at the time, she'd never looked back. She kept a few of her favorite tailored suits but donated the rest of her wardrobe to an organization helping low-income women get back to work. She joined the mom brigade and alternated between yoga clothes and her daily uniform of dark jeans and T-shirts. She traded her high heels for Doc Martins, cut her hair short and close to her head, no longer processing it, but letting it stay natural in tight tiny curls. She never wore makeup other than lip-gloss, so her morning routine was quick. Her one selection that varied day to day was her choice of earrings. She favored large interesting shapes in a variety of materials, silver, gold, wood, shell. Today she was wearing her favorites, large squares made of wood, each one fastened tightly to her earlobe with an onyx stud.

Ivy's gaze broke from the white-capped river to follow the back-and-forth movement of her cigarette hand, as rhythmic and relaxing as her inhale and exhale. Her sleeve covered part of her wrist, and the trail of leaves tattooed along her forearm twined over the dorsum of her hand ending between her pointer and middle finger.

Ivy looked down at her copy of *Daisy Miller*. She wasn't sure if she should brag or be ashamed that it was the 1987 copy from her junior year of high school. It was a ragged paperback with her 17-year-old self's handwritten notes in the margins. Ivy was surprised at how loopy and flowing her penmanship was; she was slightly alarmed to see her dotted i's were actually little round circles hovering above the words. She even found her initial entwined with a boy's in flourished script inside conjoined penned hearts on the bottom of a page. Twice she found notations further introducing her to her 17-year-old self. One stated *archaic social norms* underlined with three angry lines and a multitude of heated exclamation points, and *rampant sexism disguised as societal constraints* written in a firm hand with five floating circles dotting the i's.

Ivy knew if Alecia got wind that she still had her high school copy she would treat her to a by now familiar discourse on the magical benefits of Marie Kondoing (Ivy hated when people's names were turned into verbs, but apparently half the English speaking world had done precisely that with Marie

Kondo). Ivy would need to shut Alecia down with a *you do you and I'll do me* retort, which was the only thing that seemed to work once Alecia had gone down the path of inflicting the sparking of joy into everyone's life.

Still, Ivy was looking forward to book club with the ferocious hunger of a starved lioness. Book club consisted of four women, Ivy, Alecia, Thia, and Fiona. One of the reasons Ivy enjoyed book club is that although the women knew one another and each other's families intimately and for a long time, they didn't (as her Grandma Mimi used to say) *live in each other's pockets.* They each had their own separate circle of friends and while there was some overlap, as in any community, there was also enough separation that book club was something they shared only with one another.

Their book club had started four years ago. Alecia and Fiona's daughters were in the third grade, and they joined a mother-daughter book club, which Fiona said rapidly declined into a wine guzzling gossip fest. Alecia said the meetings began with fifteen minutes of awkward conversation before the girls meandered out of the room, leaving their mothers to sip Pinot Noir and engage in the competitive sport of talking about anyone who wasn't there.

Fiona hated the lack of interest in reading any of the classics, and Alecia abhorred the lack of real discussion about the books they read. So, they began a new book club for adults and cast a wide net on the local social media sites where neighbors went to sell old garden tools and dining room furniture, or have occasional brutal arguments about politics and missing cats. Within an hour of the first post, eleven women agreed to meet at Coffee Labs on Main Street. Fiona had a degree in library science and worked as the middle school librarian, and it showed in the agenda and guidelines she presented. Seven of the women backed slowly out of the door clutching cardboard cups of organic fair-trade coffee and looking wild-eyed at the depth and breadth of the recommended syllabus, the guidelines for discussion of which there were 20 mandatory questions to prepare thoughts on and 10 more optional suggestions. Anyone who did not finish reading the book (YOU HAVE AN ENTIRE MONTH was capitalized in bold at the bottom of the page) could not attend that month's book club discussion, and while not mandatory, the expectation was, whoever hosted would prepare food that corresponded with the theme of the book. Ivy liked the guidelines, the suggested syllabus, the fact that they each took turns recommending a book, the fact that it was a requirement to actually read the book, and that the guidelines were so dense that the only discussion they would have time for would be about the book. She also informed them that while she was happy to provide copious amounts of wine when it was her turn to host, as well as an exquisite charcuterie platter, there would be no circumstance under which, she would she ever, ever, ever, prepare corresponding theme food. Thia, eager to have her say in the negotiation process, stated she would happily provide take out from the restaurant of anyone's choice as well as the copious amounts of wine, but that her house was unruly. She had a big dog, three ill-behaved children, and a man-child husband, so when it was her turn to host they got what they got. She loved the syllabus and guidelines and asked if they could read Herman Hesse, because she was on a reading reprisal of Herman Hesse and no one would discuss Siddhartha with her.

Four years later they were going strong—which Ivy considered a big deal given the recent 2016 election and the fact that Alecia was the only member who voted for Donald Trump. They had all agreed during the campaign to agree to disagree. This was easy to do because Alecia refused to discuss anything political. She listened patiently to the other women when they discussed it (which they did if it pertained in any way to the reading), or sometimes at the end as they were gathering coats and handbags in the foyer of whoever was hosting. She never winced at Thia's pink pussyhat, or Ivy's button of a hissing cat that read, "pussy grabs back." Fiona only referred to the president as 45, which made Alecia blink, but any opinion she had about that, she kept to herself. Alecia made two declarations and asked the other women to respect them. The first was that she was voting for John Kasich because his politics lined up with hers and when Kasich lost the primary, Donald Trump got her vote. She believed it was better for the economy and always voted with her wallet. Also, Alecia added, last *she* checked, this was America and she had every right to do so.

Clearly, no one was changing anyone's mind and book club was too important to them to let the current political climate break them apart. Ivy was of the opinion that if the wreckage of November 8th hadn't broken them up, nothing would. What Alecia once told Ivy, in a rare moment of self-disclosure, was that her allegiance to the Republican Party didn't have as much to do with her wallet or politics as she let on, but more to do with the fact that her father had been an ardent vocal Democrat.

"Belicose political ranting reminds me of…a time and place I'd rather forget." Alecia confided after several glasses of Prosecco while they were sitting in Ivy's living room. Ivy saw a shudder move through Alecia, closing her features, vibrating almost imperceptibly through her shoulders and torso.

Ivy of course couldn't see the images flashing through Alecia's mind, the cramped filthy kitchen of childhood, fluorescent light casting a gray pall over the cracked speckled linoleum. Ivy now knew, after that brief whispered conversation, that the reason Alecia hated beer wasn't because of highbrow taste (of which Thia regularly accused her). Alecia hated beer because it conjured memory.

"Of your father?" Ivy had asked.

"Yes. Him. Always him."

Ivy saw the shutting down of Alecia's emotions and the placid mask of perfection she wore instead, and Ivy understood. It didn't make Ivy feel pity or even compassion, because Alecia repelled those sentiments as firmly as if she were swatting a fly. It did, however, crack Ivy's heart and make her love Alecia a bit more than she had before. Ivy never discussed it with anyone else, not even Fiona or Thia, and she never discussed it again with Alecia, but she never forgot it either.

Ivy's relationship with Alecia was more complicated than her friendship with either Fiona or Thia. Actually, Ivy thought, not for the first time, living in the white wealthy suburb of Westchester was more complicated than any of Ivy's white friends understood. To them, being Black in Westchester, New York, was no big deal, especially now that a Black family had lived (as recently as a week ago) in the White House. Westchester, her white friends often assured her, was colorblind. Ivy knew this was ridiculous. America was more color-seeing than it had ever been. And Westchester was no different. She tried once to explain that colorblind wasn't a goal for Black people. The goal was to be Black with equity and equality. Ivy caught Thia's surprised glance. Ivy understood Thia's confusion, but like a blister that never had a chance to heal, it irritated her. Ivy understood that Thia and her husband struggled financially to live in Westchester, and Ivy and her husband were well off. Ivy heard constantly how heterogeneous their village and school district was with a racially and socio-economically diverse population. Yet the wealth was almost exclusively white, Ivy and James were the anomaly, and that was a function of a long history of inequity. A notion that in 2017 Ivy didn't feel she should have to point out, these were educated women, they should know that from having seen it with their own eyes.

There were days, in spite of how busy she was, of how many interactions she had with her friends, her neighbors, various community members, that Ivy felt extremely lonely. She wondered if book club tonight would lessen that feeling or intensify it.

Ivy took a languorous drag of her cigarette and turned the pages of *Daisy Miller*. After a couple of chapters she found her first high school notation in faded blue ballpoint pen. Ivy had underlined the following:

> *The young girl looked at him more gravely, but with eyes that were prettier than ever.*
> *"I have never allowed a gentleman to dictate to me, or to interfere with anything I do."*
> *"I think you have made a mistake," said Winterbourne. "You should sometimes listen to a gentleman — the right one."*

In the margin, Ivy had written the following quote by Shirley Chisholm, *the emotional, sexual, and psychological stereotyping of females begins when the doctor says: it's a girl.*

Ivy applauded her 17-year-old self for finding and applying that reference and felt a wash of relief that her bubble dots and conjoined hearts didn't mean she hadn't been paying attention.

Ivy finished her Kretek and settled back to watch the swells on the river. Unlike in Daisy Miller's time, women now smoked, drank, cursed, had sex, wore sports bras and booty shorts to the grocery store without violating social mores. But Ivy was under no illusion. Women's bodies were still seen as chattel. Men in power declared the right to force a woman to host another body inside hers whether she wanted to or not; grabbing a woman by the pussy had been declared by the President of the United States of America as something he spoke of proudly. Furthermore, he declared it acceptable if you're a celebrity, and Ivy didn't think it was a stretch to think celebrity status also extended to the wealthy and powerful. Perfectly intelligent, good, kind men and women, while not *condoning* grabbing a woman by the pussy, and not *condoning* the remarks by the President of the United States, pointed out that everyone said stupid things privately, and it was a long time ago when the President was much younger, a mere 56 years old. So, while Daisy Miller may have died a fictional death long ago, while her rebellion may have been as simple as taking a walk with a man and no chaperone, perceptions about women were remarkably unchanged.

And the same was true for being Black in America. When Barack Obama became the first Black president, Thia and Fiona rejoiced. They believed things had finally turned. Ivy rejoiced as well. But she knew better. She knew the hate hadn't gone anywhere. It was churning beneath the surface, creating a force as mighty as the chop in the Hudson, which Ivy kept her eyes on momentarily before she went on with the rest of her day.

CHAPTER THREE
THIA

Thia Daniels began her morning in her usual way. Bolting out of bed, she hustled her three rambunctious children through their morning ablutions and oversaw an approximation of what passed for breakfast (handfuls of cheerios, hastily poured glasses of milk, segments of a shared Clementine). Next there was a chaotic and slightly violent hunt for the appropriate footwear. Schoolbags packed the evening before were somehow *unpacked* with their contents strewn about the mudroom, which created more opportunities for grabbing and fighting. There was the usual tussle over feeding and walking Brutus (their rescue Pit bull) and finally, a mad dash to the car.

By 8:15, Thia was back home to begin straightening and cleaning. She began by emptying the dishwasher from the night before and reloading it with the detritus from breakfast. The inevitable pots that had "needed soaking" overnight were scrubbed, rinsed, dried, and put away. Sink and faucets were washed then shined with a dishrag. Counters and table wiped free of breakfast crumbs, stains, and stickiness. Cabinet doors (every single one ajar from the morning chaos) had their rightful contents restored and their doors swung shut. Next she swept the kitchen floor then took the short cut of spot cleaning any spills with a rag and some Windex until she had time to properly wash it. Thia hurried through the tasks mindlessly and at moments impatiently (and if she were to be asked, she would admit resentfully), but there was a soothing rhythm to the routine. Thia inherited a wiry strength along with curly black hair, strong nose, large dark eyes and double rows of eyelashes from her father Alexander Geourgiou and her wide smile, full lips, and friendly nature, from her mother, Naomi Stein. This was all that remained of her parents' legacy. Thia hadn't seen her father since she was four years old. He'd literally told Thia's mother he was *going out for a smoke* and never come back. For years Thia thought her mother made the story up until her older sister confirmed it. Her mother had died when Thia was pregnant with her oldest child and left Thia in a strange state of ambivalence, feeling a loss that kicked at her insides every time her baby moved, and a terrible sense of relief that she could care for her baby without also having to care for her mother.

Thia was not a quiet person. She had a vibrancy and energy that hummed, she was petite but walked heavily, she was careful but banged objects when she returned them to their rightful place, she was deliberate in her actions but moved like a whirlwind, giving an impression of carelessness. She hummed, and sang, and moved around the house mumbling to herself. Yet there was a quiet intensity that Thia embodied to do things differently than her parents had. She and Eric were present in their children's lives, they established comforting routines, they were solidly middle class (albeit in a region that made middle-class income levels nearly impossible to live on), and they went to all of their children's various sports, dance, and musical activities with enthusiasm.

Thia may have been concentrating on the tasks at hand, mulling over the many activities in a long day ahead, but it was never far from her mind that she was essentially getting a do over. Living the life she'd longed for as a child, parenting herself along with her own children, loving Eric and catching the reverberation of his love back to her. Perhaps it was even more than love security she was basking in, letting it surround her along with the worn furniture, scuffed walls, and general chaos that she had the opportunity, every single morning, to sort. It was that tiny piece of knowledge, tucked into her consciousness that led Thia, while she might roll her eyes as she retrieved balled up socks from the kitchen table (which kid went to school without socks she wondered) to feel a sense of accomplishment she would never admit to.

Leaving the kitchen, she returned to fight club (otherwise known as the mudroom) to begin sorting (if sorting is defined by taking every single shoe, boot, soccer cleat, tap shoe, and ruby slipper, and throwing them into the giant bin in order to let the children's fight-to-the-death-games commence again 23 hours from now).

She continued the laundry cycle (there was no actual end to laundry ever). Then a wiping down of the most offensive residue left behind in bathroom sinks, toilets, and tubs. Beds were hastily made (or remade because her children were monsters and they made beds in a way Thia was certain might foretell something horrible about them — like they were destined to become serial killers.)

Thia stood in the tiny foyer of their cramped home with the scuffed pine floors and dingy paint job, and surveyed the worn furniture of the living room, her eyes scanning the seats and floors for miscellaneous toys, books, remote controls, underwear, or dust bunnies. It was all clear except for the various chew toys, which belonged to Brutus and littered the faded living room carpet like an obstacle course. Thia took a deep breath and readied herself to begin the part of her day that belonged to her. It was an allotted fifteen minutes, which nothing short of sudden death (either hers or someone imminently close to her) would ever interfere with.

The January air was particularly bitter that morning so Thia took the time to shrug into her jacket before stepping out of the kitchen door to the small garden. Even in January, the space felt magical to her. She knew where each of the bulbs lived beneath the icy ground, where the bed of moss beneath the Redbud Tree would show once the layers of snow and ice had melted. She knew what flower or leaf shape would grow on every bare branch or stalk in the garden.

Thia craned her neck up to the sky and recited her morning prayer. Thia (despite her Greek Orthodox baptism to please her father, and the nod to the Jewish traditions of her maternal ancestors, was still, like her mother, a practicing Wiccan.) *Gracious Goddess, O Gracious God, Lend me health, strength, and love. During this coming day, assist me with the challenges ahead. Share Your divine wisdom. Teach me to respect all things. Remind me that the greatest power of all is Love.*

Thia heard the whistle of the 9:40 train, signaling that she was right on schedule. Their home was a short walk up the hill from the Metro North railroad and the Hudson River, and the whistle of the train had worked its way into the fabric of her day. Thia allowed her feet to plant, to let the icy cold seep through the thin soles of her red converse sneakers.

Thia lifted her arms, palms to the sky in gratitude, feeling the stretch of pull between earth and air. Clouds moved and separated, brightening the day as Thia lowered her arms and turned back into the warmth of her kitchen. Retrieving a crude hand-woven basket from a shelf, Thia deliberately and efficiently arranged the objects on her counter — a perfect tiny cone of sage incense nestled in a brass plate as big as the top of her thumb, a thin sparkly silver candle whisked away from the box of birthday candles in the junk drawer, a cobalt blue dish of sea salt, and a sherry-sized pewter chalice that Thia filled with water from the tap. With a piece of white chalk, Thia drew a perfect circle around the symbolic objects of the four elements, sage for air, candle for fire, salt for earth, and the chalice for water.

The completion of this simple task allowed Thia to relax, to begin the release of the chaos of earlier, the letting go of the vestige of dreams she'd carried with her all morning. She had had one of those vague, anxiety-inducing dreams where she was trying to get to the children's school for pick-up and obstacles kept forming, traffic jams, one-way streets, and finally the steering wheel of her car coming loose, and then a sudden shift of location to a schoolyard empty of her children, teachers, or other parents, and a pit of dread that began in her stomach and spread like a rash throughout her body.

When the memory and sensation of the dream had evaporated completely and Thia felt her shoulders relax and connect to the blades of her back, she lit the incense, cupped her hands around the whorls of smoke, and recited the words, "with air I cleanse myself." She lit the sparkle candle and held it in one hand and passed the tip of her index finger on the other hand through the flame. "With fire I cleanse myself." Thia had learned many years ago to say the words with strength and clarity in her voice, rejecting the unsure murmur she'd heard her mother practice throughout Thia's childhood. After blowing out the candle, Thia pinched a few granules of sea salt and rubbed them between her palms, enjoying the faint scratching against her skin. "With earth I cleanse myself." Then she dipped her fingers into the chalice and rubbed the water between her hands. "With water I cleanse myself." Letting the stillness of the house settle around her, Thia visualized the burning of her fears, leaving behind the purity of ash. She visualized the exfoliation of shame and the washing away of any residue.

With her eyes closed, Thia called into the silence, "Any energy that no longer serves me, leave me now. Thank you for your presence, I am sending you home."

Thia stood in the middle of her kitchen and visualized the golden light from above shining down and filling her, radiating through her, a light eternal and shared with anyone willing to bask in it. "I ask to be filled with pure healing light." She waited for the familiar warmth to begin at the top of scalp then the tingle down her neck, through her shoulders, across her chest and down into her belly where it settled. Thia imagined a pool of light inside her abdomen, sending a healing and ease through her organs and limbs.

Thia smiled, gave a moment of gratitude to the God and Goddess, then carefully packed away the symbols of the elements and closed her circle, rubbing the chalk with her index finger, beginning in the West for Water, moving South for Fire, East for Earth, and finishing in the North for Air.

And just like that, Thia felt the lightness of her being rise up through the pain and muck of daily living.

Before getting into the shower and hustling to work (Thia, in addition to being a wife, mother, and practicing Wiccan, was also a dental hygienist who worked from 10:00 — 3:00 four days a week just ten minutes away in Tarrytown) she made one more plea, this time just to Goddess. "Please," she said, "let me get through book club with grace and patience tonight. No matter what."

CHAPTER FOUR
FIONA

Fiona Payne turned the flame beneath the hissing teapot off and waited for the water to settle. She'd been lost in thought about book club that evening and allowed the water to over-boil, causing it to deoxygenate and produce a less flavorful tea. Fiona felt a small stab of disappointment — she'd splurged on an especially delicate blend of Oolong tea, so expensive that she'd only allowed herself to buy an ounce of it, and she'd looked forward to sipping it in the quiet moments of the morning before Chloe came down and they rushed through breakfast and out the door to begin the day. Fiona shrugged it off, placed her tiny foil bag of Oolong back in the closet and took out the tin of hearty black tea, which would be unaffected by over-boiled water.

Fiona scooped the leaves into the well-used brass teapot she'd inherited from her grandmother, brought with her from Ireland in 1951. The dull sheen and small dents reminded Fiona that her grandmother had handled it countless times. Fiona wrapped her hand around the wooden swivel handle with the knowledge that her grandmother had touched it in the same place. Fiona was the only grandchild to have inherited, along with the teapot, her grandmother's red-gold hair, and she wore it just as her grandmother had, wispy red-gold curls, erratically shaping her face, which like her grandmother's was aggressively heart shaped.

Fiona steeped the tea and looked out the window. Morning had long broken, yet the light was dim, and the Rhododendron leaves outside her window, while not as tightly furled as they'd been on the coldest days, were standing straight up, causing Fiona to shiver just looking at them and instinctively wrap her hands around her tea mug. The tasks of the day flicked through her head. There were all the usual tasks plus a staff training for a new software system. Fiona felt confident that her presentation was in order, yet she needed to prepare herself for the inevitable moaning and groaning from her colleagues about having to learn yet another digital tool.

Fiona wished she could skip straight to book club. She was excited about discussing *Daisy Miller* in light of the surge of activism across the country and in many parts of the world. Chloe, her 13-year-old daughter, was taking far more of an interest in women's issues than she had previously, and Fiona wondered if that would be the silver lining for the times they were living in. The children had been shaken out of the state of apathy Fiona worried about, anesthetizing themselves with Kardashians and substances and computer porn. (Fiona was horrified by the ability of middle-schoolers to find porn sites with the click of a button and no manner of parental controls seemed to be out of their abilities to circumvent. She'd tried getting her friends to understand the issue, but they seemed unable or unwilling to believe their children would willingly expose themselves to watching people have sex on the internet. Apparently all of her friends forgot what it was like to enter puberty.)

Fiona sighed, then caught sight of the time. With a start, she realized she didn't hear Chloe stomping around getting ready. Chloe, unlike Fiona, had an unfailing internal body clock. Fiona knew that one of the many side effects from her divorce was that without her ex-husband to keep her grounded to time, her propensity to run late was exacerbated, and it was now Chloe's rhythms and constant prodding that herded them out of the door with only a minute to spare in the mornings. Fiona recognized that Chloe's need for punctuality was partially an internal drive and partially a result of having a perpetually late mother. Chloe did, however, share Fiona's hearty immune system and was therefore hardly ever sick beyond a sniffle or a 24-hour virus once in a great while.

Chloe had received so many "100 days of attendance" certificates that she simultaneously took them for granted and obsessed about them.

Fiona double-checked the time to see if she'd made a mistake—she hadn't. Setting her mug of tea down, she went to the bottom of the staircase. Their three-bedroom home was built in 1929; it was 1200 square feet, and creaky, impossible not to hear every sound. Fiona would know if Chloe was awake and getting ready.

"Chloe? Are you awake?" Fiona listened and heard only the soft sound of the radiator hiss.

Perhaps it was the silence, perhaps it was an unconscious knowledge Fiona hadn't known she possessed, perhaps it is an ancient frisson of fear that all mother's get, gripping the back of Fiona's neck, spreading across her shoulders and into her heart urging her forward, up the steps, across the narrow hallway, and into Chloe's room.

Chloe heard the frantic pace of her mother's footsteps on

the creaky floorboards, so she had enough time to close her eyes and feign sleep.

Fiona felt great relief at the sight of Chloe lying in bed, clearly alive based on the rise and fall of her chest. The relief was short lived when she realized Chloe was pretending to be asleep. Fiona would find it difficult to explain later, to her ex-husband and his new wife, to the book-club moms, to the doctors, to the police, to anyone who queried her about how and when she knew that something was very, very, wrong simply because her daughter stayed in bed and pretended to be asleep when she went to wake her up.

For Chloe, the pretense of sleeping was the only way she could think of to disrupt the daily routine of her life with her mother, to undo all that was familiar between them. Chloe needed, in order not to feel the impact of *it,* was to live without any memory of the before. The only way she could function without the images intruding at random times throughout the day, during lunch, or class, or on the walk to school, or at night when she closed her eyes, or in the morning when she opened them, was to do two things. First she relegated the images to one word *it.* Next she separated her life to before and after *it.* Now would always be the after. And it hurt too much to miss the before. So she needed to change everything. Live differently, without the memory of before, without her mother's small acts of kindness and care. This knowledge hurt much, much, more than the tiny cuts she'd made across the soft white insides of her thighs.

Last night, Chloe escalated to deeper cuts on her upper arms, which bled through the night and marked the sheets. Chloe didn't see the blood until it was too late; her mother had moved closer and was standing over her. Chloe heard the gasp, opened her eyes, followed her mother's gaze, and saw the bloody sheets sticking to the wounds on her arms. The deepening of the cuts had felt satisfying at the time, but now Chloe was faced with the unintended consequence of having alerted her mother and all that would entail.

CHAPTER FIVE
BOOK CLUB AT ALECIA'S

Ivy and Thia rode over to book club together. They lived closest to one another, and it helped Thia extricate herself from her unwieldy family.

When Ivy and Thia pulled up they were both surprised to see Fiona's baby blue Volkswagen Bug in Alecia's driveway. Ivy automatically checked her dashboard clock to see if they were late. Thia saw her do so and arched her eyebrows. They made their way to the massive front doors of Alecia's home while juggling handbags, books, and bottles of wine.

Everett opened the door in his usual gallant way and ushered them into the twinkling foyer.

"Ladies, you look lovely as always! Let me take your coats."

He kissed each of them chastely on their cheeks. Ivy registered repulsion at the warm dry scrape of his lips against her skin and instantly felt bad about it. Thia handed him the wine bottle, smiled, and winked.

"It's wine o'clock!"

Everett put his arm out to indicate they were to proceed through the house and said, "Your wish is my command."

Thia sighed. "If only I could get my guy to say that."

Ivy winced as she followed them both through the music room. She thought the world of Eric Daniels. Thia referred to him as her "man-child," but Ivy had always found him to be good natured and patient with his children and attentive to Thia in ways she seemed to take for granted, like bringing her a cup of tea unbidden or loping over and taking whatever packages Thia happened to be lugging at the time. She suspected that Thia envied the polish and grandeur of Alecia and Everett's home and the grown-up nature of their interactions as well as their social savvy. Ivy, however, always preferred book club in Thia's small, slightly battered living room where the scratched coffee table (sans coasters) made for an easy and comfortable evening. The pizza and wine they inevitably consumed was satisfying and took much less time and attention, leaving more energy for discussion. Ivy was aware that as effortless and gracious as Alecia's presentations seemed, she expected a considerable amount of praise that she could shush away.

Everett poured each woman a drink and waved. "Toodle-oo, don't do anything I wouldn't do."

Thia laughed and waved back and Ivy said thank you in a way she hoped sounded sincere instead of slightly embarrassed for him, which is how she felt. She watched Everett slip away through the back stairway, then followed Thia into the family room. It was evident from the way Fiona and Alecia spoke—deep in conversation—there was a reason Fiona wasn't the last to arrive as she usually was. In fact, so engrossed in their conversation, they didn't notice at first that the others had arrived. When Fiona finally did look up, it was immediately evident to both Ivy and Thia that something terrible had happened.

Everett escaped the book club by going up the back stairs just as Hannah descended the front stairs. She slipped unnoticed into the dim kitchen and saw before her the women turned toward one another, ringed in light, and hemmed into a composition by the furnishings. Hannah watched them carefully.

Fiona's face was pale and puffy and looked exactly like Chloe's after Chloe had been crying. Alecia stood with her arms splayed in two directions, clearly torn between comforting Fiona and welcoming the other two women. Hannah watched as Ivy's face registered surprise then settled back to her normal expression (slightly annoyed which Hannah knew was just Ivy's version of resting bitch face and didn't mean she actually was annoyed, although Hannah believed people's resting faces were an accurate reflection of their true selves). Thia, the woman Hannah liked the least of the women in her mother's book club, seemed the most concerned and had her hand on Fiona's shoulder in what seemed to be a kind manner. Hannah was suspicious of kindness in adults and perceived it as a form of manipulation at worse and insincerity at best.

Hannah found Fiona annoying, despite the fact that Chloe was Hannah's best friend and seemed to adore her mother, which Hannah also found annoying. Hannah found Fiona to be unnaturally skittish and frenetic, always worried about money or carpooling, or having to speak with her ex-husband or his new wife. Hannah found Fiona exhausting and didn't really care what had upset her this time. Except, Chloe hadn't texted Hannah to say she wouldn't be here, which was unusual, and Fiona's distraught puffy face seemed disproportionate to her usual complaints. Hannah began to wonder if something was up with Chloe. And *that* she did care about. She crept forward silently in the shadows so that she could listen.

Fiona was speaking. "I don't want to distract from book club."

"Is Chloe alright?" Thia's gentleness when she asked this question may have been Fiona's undoing because she began to cry again. Fiona's skin mottled and her features scrunched in a way Hannah couldn't help thinking was very unattractive.

Ivy knelt in front of Fiona, "What happened?"

Fiona just shook her head.

Alecia spoke and Hannah recognized the quiet, calm tone, as her mother's problem-solving mode. "Fiona, where is Chloe now?"

"With her father. "

"Okay." Alecia said, "So she's safe then."

Fiona shrugged, "Maybe… I, I just don't understand."

"Honey, what happened?" Thia's voice sounded almost hypnotic. "You can tell us."

"She's been cutting."

Hannah almost gasped out loud, which would have ruined all chances of finding anything else out. Suddenly the women were in a tight circle patting Fiona, handing her water and tissues, and asking too many questions for Hannah to follow. Hannah was shocked. She and Chloe were best friends and had been since kindergarten. How could she not have known this? That more than anything else angered Hannah. She felt tricked. The women were all talking at once, and Fiona was practically whispering. Hannah knew she wouldn't hear anything useful, just stuff moms said to each other to be supportive or sound helpful. Hannah went quietly up the back stairs and tried to remember how Chloe had been the last time she'd seen her. They didn't attend the same school so it had been over a week ago when Chloe slept over. Hannah remembered feeling vaguely irritated by Chloe that night. She'd been following her dad around asking him dumb questions about the solar system for a report she was doing. Sometimes Chloe could be such a nerd. Hannah's friends always fawned over her dad. He was funny and nice and spoke to them like they were adults instead of little kids. They also envied her house and parents. Many of her friends were like Chloe and had divorced parents or parents who worked all the time and were never home.

Hannah tried to remember if she'd acted irritated or annoyed with Chloe. Had she been mean to Chloe? Had she done something to cause this? Hannah tried to remember if she'd seen Chloe change into her pajamas, if she'd seen any wounds on her. She couldn't think of anything, could barely remember the movie they watched. Should she text her? But how could she ask about this without sounding weird? She couldn't. Besides Chloe's father was super strict about screen time, and Chloe probably didn't have her phone on her and Hannah didn't want to risk having Mr. Payne read any texts she might send. Hannah decided she hadn't done anything out of the ordinary to Chloe and that if she was cutting, it had nothing to do with her. Although, Hannah felt a moment of great unease, when she remembered the look that Chloe had given Hannah at the end of the night before bedtime. What had Chloe seen or thought to have given her such a look? Hannah couldn't be sure, but it seemed to have been a look of revulsion. Horror even. At the time Hannah thought it was because of the scary movie they had watched. What if Hannah had been wrong and that look of revulsion and horror hadn't been about the movie at all? What if it meant what she was afraid it meant? Hannah shook her head vigorously to eradicate the image from her brain, a technique, which often served her well. Then she returned up the back stairs.

When she reached the top of the staircase she paused in front of her father's study trying to decide if she should say good night to him or go to her room to finish the last of her reading. Deciding it would be better to say good night now, she knocked softly on the door and popped her head in. Her dad looked up from his computer and smiled at her. No wonder Chloe followed him around, Hannah thought. Her dad never did dumb things like limit her screen time or talk down to her. He understood kids in a way none of the other parents seemed to understand, even her mom, especially her mom.

"Hey, Hannahbanana."

"Hey."

"Everything ok?"

"I guess."

"Anything you want to talk about?"

"Nah."

"Wanna hang in here a bit? Finish your work?"

Hannah shrugged. "Okay."

Softly, she closed the door on the voices in the living room and all thoughts of Chloe.

CHAPTER SIX
EXCERPTS FROM THE NOTES OF
DR. MELANIE SCHAEFFER, PSYD

Patient is Chloe Payne, 13 yrs. of age, Caucasian female, presenting with Non-Suicidal Self-Injury (NSSI). Chloe is a pleasant and physically attractive girl with a shy smile and good eye contact. Chloe does not exhibit any characteristics of Borderline Personality Disorder (BPI), other than reporting two recent episodes of dissociation and the recent onset (last two weeks) of NSSI. Chloe denies substance abuse including the use of cigarettes. Chloe reports that she has never been sexually active. Chloe reports no incidence of physical, sexual, or verbal abuse. Until recently (last two weeks) Chloe has been an excellent student with perfect attendance. Until recently (last two weeks) Chloe has had no sleep disturbance and has maintained a regular and healthy diet, also has not started menstruation. Parents divorced with joint custody, Chloe lives with mom and visits dad every other weekend and has dinner with dad one weeknight a week. Chloe reports positive relationships with both parents with some trepidation about father's new wife (of 6 months), father's remarriage possible precipitating factor.

Recent changes in Chloe's behavior:

Unable to sleep

Weight loss due to decreased appetite

Loss of interest in former activities such as competitive swimming, reading, socializing with friends.

No decline in grades and school attendance with the exception of today's absence.

Self-harm in the form of cutting. Location upper and inner thighs. Preferred instruments, razor blade, and when unable to obtain razor blade, paper clip. Chloe states reason for cutting is to distract her from thinking too much. Refuses to discuss what she is thinking about, what feels like too much, or what thoughts she needs distraction from.

Contract with Chloe includes alternatives to self-harm:

Journal writing (on computer or phone so as no pens or lead pencils)

Taking a walk

Listening to music

Yoga

Snapping a rubber band worn on her wrist

Singing

Coloring (crayons only-no colored pencils, advanced coloring books made only with glue, no staples, or spirals)

All sharp instruments removed from her room and bathroom.

Locks removed from her bedroom and the hall bath, which is the bathroom she uses.

Onset of presenting problem appears to have occurred two weeks ago. Chloe reports no precipitating events. When questioned about what may have precipitated said behavior, Chloe becomes evasive, markedly uncomfortable, cannot maintain eye contact, and is clearly agitated.

Treatment plan: Ongoing evaluation. Weekly therapy sessions. Collateral sessions with each parent. Possible adolescent group therapy although Chloe is resistant to any type of group therapy setting. If incidences of self-harm continue or worsen, hospitalization will be considered. Currently no suicidal or homicidal ideation.

CHAPTER SEVEN
AFTER DAISY MILLER

When Thia returned home, Eric was waiting expectantly at the kitchen counter with a cold beer and the sports pages.

"Hey, Babe, how was book club?" When Thia didn't answer right away, Eric shot a few more questions at her, "So? Is *Daisy Miller* a feminist novel, or isn't it? Whose side was Ivy on? I know Fiona was on yours."

Thia rolled her eyes. "First of all, book club doesn't have *sides,* we *discuss* — we don't debate. Not everything is a competitive sport."

Eric wiggled his eyebrows, "No girl fights? Not even an arm wrestling contest to decide?"

"You're such a child." But she couldn't help laughing and Eric used her moment of weakness to pull her against him and kiss her.

Thia leaned into him, happy to let the events of the evening slip away. She kissed him again, enjoying the chill and faint taste of hops from the beer he'd been drinking. He moved from her lips to her throat, and she let her head fall back against his arm.

"Let's go upstairs," he whispered, "before I undress you right here."

She followed him up, holding her breath as they tiptoed past the children's room and locked their bedroom door before tugging at one another's clothes and stumbling in a clumsy hurried dance to the bed.

Later, when Eric's breath took on the rhythm of sleep, she untangled her legs from his and rolled back onto her side of the bed, letting the coolness of the sheets soothe the heat of her skin.

For a brief moment she thought of Fiona, alone and worried about Chloe. Thia couldn't imagine what drastic change had taken place in such a short time. Chloe's very being summoned sunshine; she exuded equal parts innocence and natural curiosity. Just two weeks ago Chloe patiently entertained Thia's daughter Lila for hours, so Thia could catch up on emails and household bills.

Imagining a healing circle of light, Thia placed Fiona and Chloe in the middle of it. She waited a moment, her eyes closed, seeing the radiance around them. Tomorrow, she would perform a true healing prayer to Goddess, but for tonight she would offer up this image as a wish for both Fiona and Chloe to feel surrounded by profound love. Thia placed her hand gently on her husband's back, flattening the space between his shoulder blades, feeling the rise and fall of his breathing against her palm until she settled into sleep.

Two hours after the women left, Alecia gave the counters a final swipe, the refrigerator handles a last polish with the dishcloth, and tucked the vacuum cleaner into the utility closet. With the breakfast table ready for the morning, Alecia was able to hit the light switch and make her way back upstairs with a clear conscience and a sense of peace.

Although book club hadn't gone as planned, Alecia was genuinely happy that she and the other women had been able to comfort Fiona — well they'd offered comfort, Alecia wasn't sure how much it helped given the circumstances. From the moment Fiona disclosed that Chloe was cutting, Alecia found herself lost in a cycle of worry and anxiety. It seemed so out of character for Chloe, who was truly an agreeable and seemingly happy girl. This led Alecia to contemplate the happiness and risk for her own daughter engaging in something so dreadful, and she literally felt her airways constrict at the thought.

By the time Alecia peeked in on Hannah, she was sound asleep in her room, the contents of her book bag strewn around the rug. Ordinarily, this would have triggered a compulsive need to immediately pick up and organize everything into the bag, but tonight she decided to let it go, recognizing the relative unimportance in the scheme of things that could be in disarray. She was too tired to stay on the hamster wheel of worry about Chloe and Fiona and, by extension, about Hannah and herself. She changed into her pajamas quickly and washed up, applying the requisite dots of eye and face cream before carefully blending them. Soothed by the evening ritual and the knowledge that Hannah was safe in her bed, Alecia walked into her bedroom surprised to find Everett sitting up with his reading glasses on, engrossed in his tablet.

"Oh!" She said, "I thought you were sound asleep by now."

Without looking up he said, "How was book club?"

Alecia frowned, wondering how much to tell him. Everett didn't like messiness. On the other hand, if he'd overheard any of their conversation and she didn't tell him, he would be angry. He'd consider it important information and would wonder why she'd withheld it.

Everett looked up from his reading and removed his glasses, "Lecia? Everything ok?"

"Yes, yes. The meeting was fine. We didn't actually discuss the book very much."

"Huh. Isn't that against your very strict self-imposed rules?"

"It's unusual for us not to—it's just—Fiona was upset and we spent the time talking to her. It was the right thing to do."

"What's she upset about? The new wife again?"

"No, no, she seems to have adjusted perfectly well to that whole thing."

"What then?"

Alecia rubbed hand cream into her skin paying special attention to her elbows. The winter air turned them rough and scaly and no amount of attention seemed to help.

"Lecia?"

"Oh sorry, well it's Chloe—she's been having some emotional problems."

Alecia didn't like the way Everett placed his tablet on the night table, how he carefully laid his reading glasses next to it before sitting up and turning his full attention to her.

"What kind of emotional problems?"

"It's personal, I'm not sure…"

"Alecia, Fiona and Bryce are my friends too and Chloe is Hannah's best friend."

Alecia didn't bother to dispute the fact that Everett barely spoke two words to Bryce or Fiona and had barely been in their company other than during a few birthday parties. She knew he was just trying to help. And believed he genuinely cared about Chloe.

"She's been self-harming, Everett."

"What does that mean?"

"Cutting… she has been cutting herself."

"My God."

They were quiet for a while but Alecia could see Everett formulating questions. She was so tired she just wanted to turn the lights off and sink into her pillow.

"Lecia — do you think — I hate to say it, but do we need to restrict Hannah's access to Chloe?"

"No. I don't think…they don't see each other as much now that Hannah's changed schools. I wouldn't worry. I'm sure it's just a phase."

"A phase!"

"Girls can be dramatic at this age and…"

"Exactly and I don't want Hannah caught up in it."

"Oh Everett, I don't think it's like that — they have her seeing a therapist."

Now he really looked alarmed, "A therapist!"

"Of course. They had to get her help! They couldn't just ignore it."

Everett reached over and moved a stray hair, tucking it behind her ear. When he spoke his voice was gentle, "One of the many things I love about you is your kind heart. You have compassion for everyone and I admire you for it but…"

Alecia waited.

"I don't think we can put our daughter at risk. This behavior is just so extreme."

"Let's wait and see. It will be weeks before we have book club here again, and I can put Hannah off if she asks to see Chloe, their schedules are both so full. But I don't think we should draw attention to it or make it obvious."

He nodded, "Agreed."

Alecia hoped the conversation would end. She really was exhausted and had a full day tomorrow. Everett smoothed her hair once more, his touch gentle. "I know it goes against your nature not to take care of the whole world, but in this case…"

Alecia nodded, "I understand."

"Good." He smiled tentatively. She could tell he felt bad and loved him for it. "Sleep well, my love."

She grazed his lips with hers and made a mental note to buy him some chap stick. Then, in the familiar pattern of a long-married couple, they reached over and turned their bedside lamps off with a near exquisite synchronicity.

CHAPTER EIGHT
THE MAN IN THE MOON

Fiona went to collect Chloe from her weekend stay with her father and his new wife. The weather had been unseasonably mild, which made Fiona feel slightly unhealthy, as though there was a festering in the air. Of what she couldn't be sure, but she longed for a clear cold night and a cleansing snow. She couldn't know yet that winter was going to make its way into March and extend the season with two more brutal snowstorms and a frigid spring. No almanac or weather pundit predicted this, and she herself had no prescient powers, which was just as well because Fiona was more terrified than she could ever remember being and didn't have faith or optimism that she would be able to make things okay. Even during the divorce, Fiona felt she could handle whatever came her way. She met the financial challenges of carving one household into two. She buffered Chloe's pain by bolstering her, guiding her, and modeling how adversity makes you stronger. She taught her daughter that illness builds your immune system, and hard work pays off. And she was *always* right.

The idea that her daughter, her sweet, happy, practical, daughter could be so unhappy, so disturbed, that she would take a razor blade and slice into her own skin, that she would find a release in watching her own blood bloom to the surface, was incomprehensible. Fiona needed to understand. Needed to make it better. And yet, she didn't know how. She would have to put all her faith in Dr. Schaeffer and wasn't sure that was enough.

Fiona pulled into the wide driveway of the McMansion at the top of Wilson Park Drive. It had taken two years to build and her ex, Bryce M. Payne had overseen every inch of the process that his new wife's salary (as a top performing divorce attorney in the city) had paid for. This marriage would have to hold if Bryce had any chance of staying in the home he'd painstakingly overseen, because his new wife had an airtight, kick-ass pre-nup. Fiona knew exactly how smart and fierce Valerie F. Shearling, Esq. was, because Valerie had done a kick-ass job representing Fiona during her extremely amicable divorce from Bryce. In fact, Valerie was way over-qualified, and far more of a shark than warranted for Fiona and Bryce's rather dignified and straightforward dissolution of marriage. But Val had been a friend of Fiona's from Club Fit where they took a kick boxing class together (Val because she loved kickboxing and Fiona because she was trying to reinvent herself). Val had in fact befriended Fiona in the Club Fit locker room when she'd unexpectedly found Fiona sobbing into a sweaty smelly fitness towel wearing granny panties and a stretched out grayish bra.

Val took one look at Fiona, who was so far gone into her crying jag that she didn't even care that the fittest, hottest, fiercest woman in the kick-boxing class was standing there watching her sob. "Hey there," Val said. "Knock it off. You're not the first woman to get divorced and you won't be the last."

With that Fiona looked up, her face puffy and blotched, her huge blue eyes that normally sparkled with clarity, were now swollen and red. "How," Fiona struggled to get the words out, her throat constricted from crying, "…do you know I'm getting divorced?"

"Isn't that why you're crying in the middle of a locker room?"

Fiona looked around. All the other women had cleared out as soon as they could. Nobody wanted to deal with a sobbing woman in her underwear. Val, Fiona noticed was wearing beautiful expensive-looking matching underwear. And her entire body toned, tan, and glistening with sweat. She was also impossibly tall, Fiona guessed six feet with no shoes on she was wrong, Val was only 5'8", but long lean legs and a slender torso made her appear taller.

"Yes." Fiona finally answered. "I am crying in the middle of the locker room because I'm getting divorced." And with that, Fiona smiled a slow, sly smile, lighting up her whole face before she burst into laughter. Which made Val laugh hard, from the belly, which was rare for her. Val snorted more often than laughed, and usually only extreme sarcasm or nasty wit caused her to do even that. Val was pretty sure that she had never ever in her entire life laughed from someone else's infectious laugh. But Fiona made her do that. Between the dopamine dump into her brain from the laugh, and the still swirling endorphins from the kick boxing class, she lost her mind, took out her business card, and pressed it into Fiona's hand. "I am going to represent you at a fraction of my usual fee, and we are going to use the savings to buy you some new underwear. So, strip that nasty crap off your body and throw it in the trash immediately. We're going to La Perla."

"But what will I wear home?

"Honey, go commando, and that bra is not lifting you by a millimeter anyway, so set those babies free."

Fiona found a friend, new lingerie, and a divorce attorney. Six months later, Bryce found a new girlfriend.

To be fair, Val and Bryce didn't marry for another three years. Two of which they spent building the McMansion three minutes away from Fiona's modest but very sweet home in Weber Park that she, Bryce, and Chloe had lived in since they moved from The City. Chloe could walk to school from both homes, although Chloe spent the bulk of her time at Fiona's. They were very "Modern Family." Chloe said her mom was Claire and Val was Gloria (duh), but Fiona quite frankly identified the most with Mitchell, which was slightly depressing.

Fiona had barely gotten out of the car before Val came out of the house and strutted (just the way Val walked) down the wide winter-brown lawn toward Fiona.

"Hey Fifi!" Val was the only person on the planet able to get away with calling Fiona that, and even the subsequent ending of their friendship and the attorney/client relationship they'd once shared didn't revoke that privilege.

"Hey Val." Fiona couldn't help being happy to see Val. The worst part of the hookup between Bryce and Val was the wedge it drove between the women. There was no way around it, and neither of them could pretend it wouldn't matter. But Fiona missed Val, and Val, when she thought about it periodically, missed Fiona. Nobody, not even Stephen Colbert, made Val laugh the way Fiona did.

"I wanted to catch you alone for a minute, Bryce and Chloe are finishing up a jigsaw puzzle."

Fiona nodded, waiting.

"She seems okay, a little quieter than usual, but okay. And there were no incidences. She kept the bedroom door open at all times and she was never in the bathroom longer than usual. Maybe the worst is behind us? What did you think of Melanie Schaeffer?"

"She seems knowledgeable. Her credentials are impeccable. I just…"

"She's the best, Fi. I promise."

"I just don't understand."

"Thirteen is a difficult age, you remember? And maybe she's taking this whole remarriage thing harder than we realized?"

"I honestly don't think that's it. She loves spending time here. I've wracked my brain. Did you — I feel bad asking this — but did you go through her phone?"

Val nodded. "Nothing out of the ordinary. Some stupid duck-lip selfies with girls at school, a few random texts about homework. Nothing worrisome."

Fiona bit a cuticle. A habit Val found repulsive. She had to restrain herself from smacking Fiona's hand as though she were a small child.

"Hmm." Fiona mumbled around her fingernail chewing, "I almost wish there had been something to explain this."

"Don't worry, Fi. We will get to the bottom of this. You did the right thing by addressing it head on."

As if on cue, Chloe came out of the house book bag in tow and her father right on her heels. Fiona searched for any signs. Chloe seemed paler than usual and her eyes didn't meet Fiona's, but her voice sounded chipper enough and Fiona tried to find solace in the typical Chloe behavior of getting the adults not to engage in drawn out discussions once she was ready to go.

"Hi mom. Ready?" She smiled, although it wasn't the usual bright smile Fiona had come to rely on from her daughter, and again, she wouldn't meet Fiona's eyes, but instead slung her book bag into the car, climbed into the passenger seat, and immediately plugged her music in. This was so typical of her teenage daughter that Fiona felt her shoulders inch down into their rightful place. Fiona waved to Val and Bryce and got into the car.

The short ride home was uneventful with Chloe giving exactly enough of a response to satisfy her mother without inviting more conversation than was necessary. Yes, she had a nice weekend, no nothing upset her, yes, she finished her homework, they watched three Star Wars movies, her new room is awesome but she prefers the one at their house, and she wanted her mom's macaroni and cheese with broccoli and carrots for dinner.

When they pulled into the driveway, Chloe, obviously relieved to get away as fast as she could, bolted out of the car and onto the porch. Fiona followed, grateful that Chloe had to wait for her to unlock the door. Once inside Chloe dashed up the stairs, "Call me when dinner's ready."

"Chloe, wait…"

Chloe stopped without turning around.

"You can't…I don't want you alone…"

With that, Chloe turned and walked down the stairs and looked her mother straight in her eye. "It's over mom. I did something stupid. I wanted to know what it was like. It wasn't anything. It didn't hurt and it didn't feel good. I'm done with it."

Fiona nodded and Chloe turned and went back upstairs. Strangely, Fiona believed her. And yet it didn't make her feel one bit better. Because whatever had caused Chloe to try it in the first place didn't 'just stop' and Fiona did not believe for one second that Chloe was just curious. She knew her daughter well, and that was not the form her curiosity took. Something was deeply troubling her child, and she had no way of discerning what that was.

Dinner was uneventful. Chloe answered her mother's inquiries in more than monosyllables and rolled her eyes and smirked in all the right places when Fiona regaled Chloe about her own weekend adventures including the book she was reading, the night out with friends, and her failed shopping excursion where she bought an ill-fitting dress in a hideous color which she now had to return. Chloe (more to show she was listening and grateful to have the focus off of her) demanded to see the offending apparel and was able to confirm that Fiona needed to get that thing back to the store as soon as possible.

Chloe was able to get into bed with a clear conscience and a sense of accomplishment of having successfully warded off any more serious conversations with her mother when Fiona knocked gently on the door. Chloe hesitated but gave the requisite permission for Fiona to enter, because she knew her mother wouldn't be able to sleep that night if she didn't, and quite frankly, Chloe couldn't handle another ounce of the crushing guilt she was collapsing under.

Fiona sat gently on the side of the bed. She moved once to touch Chloe, possibly to sweep the fine silky strands from her cheek, but thought better of it and placed her hand in her own lap instead. Chloe watched as Fiona took a deep breath before speaking. "Do you remember when you were little and you were afraid of the man in the moon?"

Chloe nodded, relieved that her mother wasn't bringing up the incident again and caught off guard enough by the question to actively listen. "Do you remember," her mother asked again, "why you were so afraid?"

"I thought he was following me."

Fiona laughed. "Yes. We were driving home one night and you were lying down in the back seat."

Chloe nodded, "Hannah showed me the face of the man in the moon."

Fiona nodded, "You were so surprised by it. And no matter how many times I explained that they were just craters that looked like a face, you were certain that it was a man in the moon. And that he was following you."

Chloe nodded again.

"When I was little," Fiona said, "I can remember thinking the moon followed me. And I remember my grandmother pointing out the man's face — and explaining they were craters that made the shape of a face."

Chloe went still while she listened.

"But," Fiona continued, "I was never afraid."

"Never?"

"Well I was afraid of spiders and rats — but not the man in the moon."

"I'm not afraid of spiders or rats."

"I know."

"And I'm not afraid of the man in the moon anymore."

"I know." Fiona's voice dropped. Almost to a whisper so Chloe had to listen even harder. "But you're afraid of something. I can tell. You have the same expression as you did when you were afraid of the man in the moon. I see it when you don't know I'm watching you."

"Please." Chloe whispered back, squeezing her eyes shut against the tears threatening to erupt. "Please stop watching me."

"Whatever you're afraid of, I can help you. Just trust me enough to tell me."

Chloe shook her head, eyes tightly closed, the tears spilling out anyway in hot angry streaks down the sides of her face.

"There's nothing. Please, just let me go to sleep."

Her mother sat there for what seemed forever. Chloe thought about the word forever and what that meant. Eternity. A concept she found overwhelming to begin with. Infinity was a mathematical concept that she was able to break down and puzzle over. Hell was a concept her mother didn't believe in. A concept, her mother once explained, devised as a form of social control, to get people to behave. To get people not to do things that would land them there. What her mother hadn't thought to explain, and now it was too late, was the kind of things people did to one another to land them a place in hell. Even if hell was just (as her mother explained) a construct, a story, there were certain actions that people could take that should according to those who believed in hell, land them there. Those were the secrets she must keep. Because there was no turning back once you knew. There was no unknowing. Finally, Fiona got up and quietly left the room. Chloe risked opening her eye into a slit so that she could make out the familiar form of her mother, the curve of her body, the shape of her hair around her head. Beloved. Chloe thought. That's what her mother was to her. Beloved. The word took shape inside Chloe's head, behind her eyes. It filled her ears and throat, her chest and stomach until she thought she would burst in pain. And she stayed like that, bursting with pain, until her mind took over and allowed her to escape into a dark, dense, dreamless sleep.

CHAPTER NINE
MAYHEM AND VIOLENCE

Monday morning broke cheerless and gray. Ivy had to forcibly eject her body from the warmth and comfort of her bed. The irony of just how warm and comfortable she was in these last few minutes before rising, compared to how uncomfortable she had been throughout the night, was duly noted. Unable to sleep, she spent most of the night lying rigid. James was a light sleeper, and she didn't want to wake him with her tossing, turning, pillow flipping, and general unease.

Ivy popped her head into the dressing room where James was fixing his tie. He blew her a kiss in the mirror and Ivy realized that he needed to be on the train in twelve minutes and she had less than that to shower and dress, before heading downstairs to fix breakfast and make lunches for the kids.

By the time she was taking her first sip of coffee, bleary eyed from lack of sleep and worry, the boys were pounding down the stairs.

Benjamin, her oldest, stopped short when he saw her, "You alright, Mama?"

"Just a little tired." Ivy lied while handing him his lunch. Ben looked at her twice but seemed to accept her answer. It was surprising how well he read her and she vowed to be a little smoother with her worries about Fiona and Chloe. A vow she broke immediately when her middle son, Bobby, took his lunch and leaned in for a hug the way he did every morning.

"Just wondering, have you seen Chloe Payne recently?"

"Duh. She's in my class." He narrowed his eyes at her and his mouth took on a twist of suspicion. "Why? What's going on?"

"Just curious. You used to be friends."

Bobby shrugged, "We aren't *not* friends. We just don't hang out. Gotta go!"

"Wait! Eat something."

Bobby grinned, grabbed a bagel, and ran out the door after Ben. Ivy looked down at Curtis, her youngest, who was staring at her with an appraising gaze that reminded her uncannily of her father.

For a moment, Ivy worried that Curtis had guessed that something was wrong, but he simply said, "I'll have Captain Crunch for breakfast."

"Absolutely not. We agreed that is in lieu of dessert."

"It has more vitamins and minerals than a bagel."

"That was a whole grain bagel baked fresh in an oven."

"A *store* oven."

"It has fiber, less sugar, and no preservatives or chemicals."

"Captain Crunch has more nutritional value when you add milk and account for the extra vitamins and minerals."

Ivy sighed. She was too tired for the fight and Curtis smelled blood. He waited.

"Fine." Ivy said not sounding fine at all. "But no dessert tonight."

Curtis went to the cabinet and took the box of cereal down without agreeing. Ivy sipped her coffee and watched two cardinals flit about on the lawn.

While Curtis chomped victoriously on his cereal, Ivy picked up her phone and sent a quick text to Fiona: *How are you?*

Ivy had a logical intuitive mind, which made her an excellent student of law and a successful attorney before she'd quit to stay home with the boys. It had been a wrenching decision to leave work when she found out she was pregnant with Curtis. She was on a partner track at a firm that was white shoe and demanding and she loved it, but she couldn't face keeping the same pace throughout her third pregnancy that she'd kept with her first two, working until the day she delivered then a hazy six weeks of maternity leave before pumping breast milk and putting her baby in someone else's arms to feed.

When Ivy found herself bereft of her job and in many ways her identity, and for the first time, home alone with a six-year-old, four-year-old, and a newborn, she had to lock herself in the bathroom for prolonged crying jags. Ben was at school most of the day and when he did get home he was surprisingly self-sufficient for a six-year-old, but Bobby was alternately sullen or full of mischief and refused to leave the house other than the three days a week of morning pre-school. The afternoons were long and in desperation Ivy would call Fiona and beg her to drop Chloe off.

Ivy loved Chloe because she recognized the creative mind of a dreamer. When Ivy listened to the children playing, it felt as though she too had climbed through the portal of Chloe Payne's imagination. Ivy fervently wished there was a way to climb through now, tear through the tangled root of Chloe's cutting and exact it cleanly and sharply, letting the wound heal over as though it had never been there.

Curtis cleared his cereal bowl and orange juice glass and hugged Ivy at the kitchen door. She squeezed him extra hard that morning, "You have all your homework?"

"Yep."

"Cause I'm not bringing it up there — remember the rule."

"Pretend you work in the city." With that he gave her a grin, his grown-up teeth too big for his little boy face, and ran to catch the school bus.

Ivy automatically checked the kitchen counter in case he'd forgotten his lunch. He hadn't.

Ivy then checked her phone, nothing yet from Fiona. She poured herself a second cup of coffee to fuel herself against her fatigue and began unloading last night's dishes so she could load the breakfast dishes.

When the doorbell rang, Ivy had the irrational thought that it was Fiona and nearly killed herself racing to answer it.

"Hey girl!" It wasn't Fiona. It was Ivy's neighbor Sally-Ann Montgomery.

Despite it being January, Sally-Ann was wearing heeled flip-flops (Ivy never knew there was such a thing as high-heeled flip flops until she met Sally-Ann). As usual Sally-Ann was wearing full make-up and a pink velour tracksuit Ivy could only guess was a holdover from the nineties. Sally-Ann's platinum blonde hair was in what appeared to be a haphazard bun the size of a bird's nest. However, Ivy had frequently watched Sally-Ann craft her up do in the front hall mirror of Ivy's own home. The hair pile was quite contrived and included many pins and a fruity spray that Sally-Ann whipped out of an oversized gold-lame handbag.

Ivy followed Sally-Ann into the kitchen and watched her pour herself a cup of coffee.

"I need some cookies or something, I've been up for hours and I'm starving—whaddya got?" she asked as she rummaged through Ivy's cabinet. "Jeez, you're boring, you have three boys in this house and not an Oreo or chocolate chip to be found."

"We have Captain Crunch." Ivy said helplessly.

"Shocking!" Sally-Ann considered it. "Nah, I need something to dunk. How do you have three kids and no cookies? You're such a health nut."

Ivy shrugged. "I think there's some ice cream?"

Sally-Ann rolled her eyes. "You think? Ice cream lasts one night in my house! No matter how much I buy. So, unless you went grocery shopping at the crack of dawn you should know if you have ice cream or not!"

Sally-Ann had raised four daughters, two of whom were married, one with a baby on the way, and two still in college, the youngest a freshman. Which rendered Sally-Ann a very recent empty nester. Ivy was the recipient of Sally-Ann's newfound freedom visits.

Sally-Ann opened the freezer door, gave a fist pump and did a happy dance at the sight of the ice cream carton, and proceeded to scoop fudge ripple into her coffee. "Mocha!" she announced before taking a noisy slurp. "Delish!"

Sally-Ann, Ivy noted for the millionth time, tended to speak primarily in exclamatory statements.

"What's new?" Ivy asked reluctantly, knowing the risk of a diatribe of Sally-Ann's youngest daughter's offenses as well as a thorough update of her oldest daughter's most recent visit to the obstetrician and quite possibly some sonogram pictures.

"Funny you should ask, Jenny just got back to school a week ago and already she's asking for more money! Hal won't give her any and he's forbidden me to. He thinks she's using it for beer! Of course she is! She's a college-student!" Sally-Ann shouted. "I say, 'if we don't give it to her she might turn to illegal activities to get it!' 'You're a nut-job!' he says. He'll see, when she's strippin' for beer money!"

"Maybe Hal's got a point. My parents had plenty of money and they paid my tuition, room, and board but I worked for my beer money."

"Yeah? What kind of work?"

"I waitressed in the summer and during the winter break, then I babysat in the school term."

"Well nobody's gonna trust Jenny with their kid, look at her! And she's too clumsy to waitress."

Ivy looked out the window. The cardinals were still there. The breakfast dishes were still in the sink and the dishwasher was still three quarters full. During her trial attorney years, Ivy was an extremely tough opponent. And she ran a fairly tight ship in her household. The board members she currently served with on a local environmental non-profit looked to her on difficult decisions about finances or board-politics. And yet, she was completely helpless against Sally-Ann Montgomery. Not for the first time, Ivy felt deep compassion for Hal as well as a tiny judgmental smidge of resentment toward him for letting Sally-Ann get away with such outrageous behavior. Yet, here Ivy was, completely helpless to get Sally-Ann out of her kitchen.

"Crap!" Sally-Ann yelled.

Ivy jumped and had to stifle the urge to smack Sally-Ann in the face.

"Crap! Crap! Crap! I'm late! I forgot I'm getting lashes today! My girl's gonna kill me!" And as suddenly as she'd stormed in, she was gone with a wave and a final, "See ya later, girl!"

Ivy allowed her body to relax and was in the process of

emptying the remnants of Sally-Ann's mocha concoction when she heard a loud bang, screams of terror and then, cries of despair.

The doorbell rang in frantic staccato bursts and Ivy rushed to open to find Sally-Ann, shaking, her eyes wild, and her finger pressed to the bell. She shoved a dollar-bill into Ivy's hand. "Quick! I'm retaining you! I need a lawyer!"

"She killed my baby! My baby!" Mrs. Henderson from across the way was on the ground sobbing at the wheels of Sally-Ann's SUV.

Ivy was ashamed of the revulsion and fear she felt at the thought of looking under the wheels, of seeing the carnage that was sure to be there. But someone needed to help Mrs. Henderson, who was 75 years old and had thrown herself onto the street next to the mess of blood and fur.

"He was off leash!" Sally-Ann screamed.

"Shhh!" Ivy said before manhandling Sally-Ann back into the house. "Stay here don't do or say anything, I'll be right back." Ivy saw Sally-Ann pull out her iPhone. "No texts! No calls! Just stay put!"

"But — my lash girl!"

"Give me that." Ivy took the phone and slid it into her jean pocket before heading out to help Mrs. Henderson just as she heard the first wail of the police siren.

Fiona saw Ivy's text come in just as she dropped Chloe off at the middle school entrance. A line of cars formed quickly behind her waiting to drop off passengers so Fiona couldn't sit and watch Chloe walk in, something she'd never had the urge to do before. She felt a snap below her left breast as she drove away, as if a piece of her heart had pulled away with her daughter's departure from the car. Suddenly everything was a danger, innocuous items found all over the school, staples, thumbtacks, spiked edge of a spiral notebook, pens, and pencils. More menacing objects were obtainable a short walk down the hill to the mobile gas station with the brand-new convenience store attached. Things for the traveler passing through, including razor blades for a few dollars. Should she start restricting Chloe's ability to carry cash?

Thoughts tumbled through her head with the ferocity of a hurricane, and Fiona nearly sobbed as images came unbidden of Chloe hurting herself. Despite the convincing promises Chloe had made last night, Fiona couldn't forget the shock of seeing the angry red marks on Chloe's upper and inner thighs.

By the time she parked she was nearly hyperventilating. She stared at Ivy's text willing her breath to deepen and her heart to slow. She wiped her palms on her corduroy skirt and focused on sending a response. With trembling thumbs, she formulated the lie, *good thanks for checking.*

By the time the text went through, Ivy was on the ground next to the crushed body of Mrs. Henderson's beloved dog, trying to lift the woman who was alternately hysterical and nearly catatonic, a psychological response Ivy hadn't known was possible. The sirens grew louder, then eventually ceased. Red and blue lights cast an eerie glow in the gloomy winter air. Ivy was ashamed of how relieved she was to turn Mrs. Henderson over to the capable hands of the responding officers. In a small town everyone knew someone, and one of the officers had grown up with Mrs. Henderson's daughter. Ivy wondered briefly who had called them. Looking around, she noticed her neighbor, Margie from across the street, standing in her doorway, her arms wrapped around her body, still in her pajamas. Margie gave a discreet wave and even from this distance Ivy could see she'd been crying. Ivy's mind automatically compartmentalized; there was the tragedy of the dog's death, Mrs. Henderson's grief, the relief of having the officers take over, the knowledge that law enforcement was on the scene, the fact that Sally-Ann was waiting inside for Ivy, and the knowledge that the peaceful little eco-system of neighborliness would never be the same.

Chloe used every ounce of will power she possessed to stay focused on her surroundings. She stood tall, her shoulder blades down her back, her ribcage separated from her waist as she'd learned in dance. She placed one foot in front of the other, holding her books against her with her arms wrapped around them, reminiscent of the way she'd once held her beloved American Girl doll. When she got to class she slid into her seat, rolled her eyes at the boy next to her when he spoke. Chloe didn't register his actual words but could tell from the other kids' expressions, that it required an eye roll. Once she was in her seat, she was able to focus on writing down her homework assignment. It was almost blissful to have the distraction. The lesson was engaging, and Chloe found herself able to listen attentively. Only once the vision popped into her head, his hand, his eyes looking at her, the horrible strangeness of his expression, something repulsive but unknown at the same time. Chloe was able to get rid of the image by willing it away and staring hard at Mrs. Rowan as she described the experiences of people during the Sudanese Civil War. As Mrs. Rowan elicited responses from the class, Chloe by rote nearly shot her arm into the air. She wanted to respond but didn't trust her voice; it felt rusty and swollen in her throat, as if she had spent her entire life trying not to cry, not to tell, to hide the human atrocities that were taking place against the Sudanese children. The topography of Sudan was alien to Chloe. She only had images based on photographs or videos. She couldn't imagine the taste, smell, or feel of the air there. Two weeks ago, she couldn't begin to imagine the terror, or lack of hope they felt. Maybe she still couldn't. There was one picture of a little boy, the look in his eyes — the terrible knowledge of what he had seen. She recognized it. So, when the other face threatened to take over in her mind, she focused instead on the face of the little boy.

Twice during math class, Chloe had to conjure the little boy's face to block out the other one. Once making the turn into the South Wing of the school, three times during history, three times during science lab because her teacher was a man and wore the same kind of shirt as the one wanted to forget, and not at all during lunch, recess, or physical education. By the time Chloe met Fiona at the end of the day to go to dance class she was in a pretty good mood. When she saw the gray shadows under her mother's eyes and the worried way she looked at her, all the hard work of the afternoon evaporated and she was right back to square one. Chloe swallowed the lump in her throat at the knowledge that things would never go back to normal, and that being with her mom made it worse. She wondered for the first time since her dad moved out if she should consider going to live with him.

* * *

At precisely 2:15, still in her dental scrubs (the candy-colored yellow top with a balloon print in primary colors, navy blue pants and bright red crocs), Thia headed over to the school in a full-on rage. Her usual morning ritual held no power over her autonomic nervous system. She didn't bother with her car, because the dental office was across the street from the kindergarten building. Usually a blessing in case she was running late, today the short uphill walk only fueled her heart rate, which had the unfortunate consequence of increasing her rage. Thia unleashed her rage on the poor security officer who was doing his best to put Thia's information into the computer before allowing her to cross the five yards past his desk and into the principal's office where Lila was waiting for her.

"This is OUTRAGEOUS!" Thia yelled, causing the security officer's fingers to stumble over the keyboard. In fairness, he was well-trained and able to keep calm in the face of an intruder, a drunk angry parent during a custody dispute unfolding at pick-up, a lock-down, a lock-out, and even a particularly brutal fistfight between two fathers in the parking lot. That incident was precipitated by the fact that one father's wife was the mother of the other father's newborn, all incidences that had occurred in the brief tenure of the security officer's time at the kindergarten. But an irate mom in dental scrubs for some reason turned his fingers to ham hocks and his insides to a pale formless jelly.

"All set, Mrs. Daniels," he finally said although of course he'd never verified her ID thanks to his ham hock fingers on the suddenly tiny keyboard, but he knew precisely who she was, which was the source of her completely overblown irrational irritation.

Thia took the time to throw him a filthy look before rolling into the principal's office in full on battle mode.

When Lila saw her mother storm into the office, the tears, which had been threatening, spilled onto her face. She'd never seen her mother look so furious, and the fear of punishment quickly dissolved into a sudden terror that her mother could withdraw her previously unfailing love.

When Thia saw Lila crying, her rage knew no bounds and the storm swirling through her shot out of her with all the magnitude of a category 5 Hurricane.

"*What* is the meaning of this?" Thia yelled, which in retrospect, she would find to be lacking authority, conjuring instead histrionic hyperbole.

In reality, her words held little impact compared to the aura of fury surrounding her. She may as well have yelled, "I'm going to hatchet you all with this machete."

Lila cried harder and Thia scooped her up, pulling her to her, letting that side of her body soften for her daughter while the other side grew mightier. "Hush, Lila, Mommy is here now, it's going to be okay."

Lila, relieved that her mother hadn't withdrawn her love after all but was there to defend her, burrowed her face into her mother's neck, breathing in the faint smell of cherry toothpaste, antiseptic, and the natural herbal shampoo which smelled a little bit like dirt and which Lila loved.

The principal, a kind, firm woman in her late fifties who was tall and solid, came around the desk and stood next to Thia, her hand reassuringly hovering without making contact, her body placed in a non-aggressive manner to Thia's side, all techniques she had learned in dealing with emotionally disturbed children throughout her career and which she'd eventually come to realize worked equally well with angry parents.

"Mrs. Daniels, please, have a seat and I can answer any questions you may have." The principal then guided Thia to a seat, allowing Lila to cling to her mother with the strength and fury of a barnacle making an ocean voyage on the bottom of a ship.

Thia sat and looked the principal in the eye, "Well?"

The principal squinted in an enquiring way, a technique that encouraged children to further develop their statements and also seemed to work well with overwrought faculty members and parents.

"Why…" Thia elaborated in a patient tone that implied she was at the breaking point of her patience and was actually not patient at all, "is *my daughter* the one in the principal's office, when it should clearly be that little cretin and his nightmare of a mother."

The principal somehow had enough discipline not to further enrage Thia by correcting her for name-calling, which was against the anti-bullying policy of the school. "Lila is here because we thought we could help her to learn an alternative method for dealing with her peers. As you must agree, Mrs. Daniels, violence is not an effective or safe way of dealing with one's peers."

"What a load of crap. From what I understand from her teacher, Lila was defending herself! What was she supposed to do?"

The principal looked at Thia with a mixture of disdain and pity, a serious miscalculation on her part, but even the most seasoned of educators could not always mask their thoughts, despite their belief that they were doing so. "Mrs. Daniels, Lila kicked another child off the slide, *physically* kicked him. He could have been seriously injured."

"But he wasn't."

"He is scraped and bruised and traumatized."

Lila pulled away from her mother and placed her tiny

hands on her mother's face turning her so she could look into her mother's eyes before announcing what she was burning to tell her, "He looked up my dress and told everyone he could see my pussy which is a *giant lie* because I have shorts on underneath. So, I did a Kill Bill move on him."

The principal gave Thia a triumphant look, an I-told-you-so look. What kind of mother let's a five-year-old watch Kill Bill? Thia felt nonplussed for a moment, "She has older brothers, and a lot of older cousins." Then she remembered why Lila had pulled a Kill Bill move on the slide. "The words that boy used were disgusting and vile. He should be the one in here."

"I assure you, Mrs. Daniels, we are addressing it." For a moment Thia saw the principal close her eyes, a fleeting moment of vulnerability. When she opened them again, their eyes locked and Thia read her thoughts as clearly as if she'd stated them, "What kind of world do we live in when a five-year-old boy hears the president of the United States say he grabbed a woman by the pussy?" And with that all the rage Thia felt at that little boy, at his mother, at the principal, all of it evaporated and formed a new storm of emotion at the President of the United States of America. She thought of Chloe cutting her own flesh. Of Lila shamed in the act of doing something as natural and innocent as climbing the steps of a slide, of that little boy hearing something so despicable and in some way identifying with it, a child as innocent as his mother who loved her son and (despite her overbearing ways and penchant for wearing school football jerseys everywhere) was really no different from Thia. They were all in the same boat and needed to row together or they were going to sink.

Thia turned back to Lila. "I understand why you did it. Do you understand why, you shouldn't do it again?"

Lila nodded, "Sticks and stones. But if anyone touches me

there, I'll Kill Bill him again."

Thia turned to look at the principal who just sighed.

"Lila, no one should touch you there, and if anyone does, you tell a grown up."

Lila nodded. "Ok. But if I need to get him off me, I am going to Kill Bill him."

The principal nodded, "That...is a good plan."

CHAPTER TEN
TAKING IT TO SOCIAL MEDIA

By the time Ivy sorted Sally-Ann it was nearly time to meet the school bus. The whirlwind of after-school activities, what passed for dinnertime in a household of three boys playing multiple sports, homework, baths, and bedtime, meant that it was after 10 PM before Ivy did anything other than a perfunctory social media check-in. Having settled into bed with a mug of chamomile tea, she was about to check the last of her emails when her phone blew up with texts from half a dozen people telling her to go on the local Facebook site, Manor Moms.

Ivy couldn't read fast enough, a familiar surge of adrenaline raced through her the way it did during a particularly messy deposition.

There were three hundred and eighteen comments in the thread with mini-fights going on in the individual comment sections and their subsequent replies. Ivy had to take a deep breath, move the waistband of her pajama bottoms, and sip her chamomile tea before she could zoom in with the laser focus required to see what kind of shit-storm Sally-Ann had involved herself in. Ivy treated the Manor Moms' online fight with the same respect and care she would give any evidence which might incriminate or help a client, all because of that crumpled dollar bill Sally-Ann had thrust into her hand after the tragic incident.

There were (Ivy counted) five admonishments by the admins warning that they would pull the post completely and that comments would be deleted if name-calling, which included *profanity* (i.e. sewer-rat, half-a-whore, and fat-fuck), did not stop. Additionally, invitations to "take it to the street" could result in the offending members removed from the Manor Moms Facebook group for good.

Despite the three hundred plus comments, a few people dominated the thread, Lisanne (Sally-Ann's 31-year-old daughter), Trudy (Mrs. Henderson's daughter), and Cara Carbunckle, the neighbor who lived between Sally-Ann and Mrs. Henderson. Cara had not witnessed the incident but was familiar with both parties. She knew all about Mrs. Henderson's insistence on letting her dog go off-leash and the driving habits of Sally-Ann. Ivy imagined Cara typing furiously, her beautifully manicured nails painted a deep plum color, hitting the keyboard with the fury and frenzy of the righteous. She could almost see the way Cara cast her eyes upward and to the side while she was thinking of the best, most fair, and strongest way to make her point. She imagined Cara's glossy black curls, shot through with silver, shimmering under the lamplight. Ivy — tempted to get out of bed and pull up the shade, sure Cara would be across the street, sitting in her office window the way she was almost every night, her magnificent Irish setters resting beside her feet, let the feeling pass. So far, Cara's comments seemed measured and thoughtful, but things had escalated rapidly since her last remark posted. Ivy imagined that Cara had been feeding and walking the dogs and had missed the full-on brawl. Sure enough, the little blue bubbles were appearing with fb's know-it-all message, *someone is typing a comment.* Just as she suspected, Cara's smiling face popped up in the little window right next to her comment: FOR FUCKS SAKE YOUR MOTHERS WERE BOTH CARELESS! THAT DOG SHOULD HAVE BEEN LEASHED! SHE WAS UNCONTROLLABLE DIDN'T KNOW HOW TO WATCH OUT FOR CARS AND POOPED ON EVERYONE'S LAWNS! THAT SAID, SHE WAS THE SWEETEST DOG IN THE WORLD AND WELL LOVED. A WOMAN HAS LOST HER FUR BABY WHAT THE HELL IS WRONG WITH ALL YOU HATERS!!! AS FOR YOU, LISANNE, YOUR MOTHER IS AN ERRATIC CARELESS DRIVER AND YOU KNOW IT! SO, GO READ YOUR KIDS A BEDTIME STORY AND GET THE FUCK OFF FACEBOOK! THAT'S RIGHT, ADMINS, I USED PROFANITY AND YELLED IN ALL CAPS! THROW ME OFF THIS STUPID FUCKING PAGE! PLEASE! I BEG OF YOU.

Ivy determined after an exhausting 35 minutes of reading, including the replies of members weighing in (most people siding with Mrs. Henderson against Sally-Ann, except for one woman who called her a "neglectful, murdering, fur-mother" for letting her dog run off-leash, which received thirteen replies back calling the woman a PETA freak and a POS). Ivy also gleaned that there were no witnesses, nor admission of guilt from Sally-Ann due to her daughter's prolific comments, and that despite the passionate outrage there was nothing that could harm or help Sally-Ann anywhere in the Facebook thread. It took Ivy twenty minutes more to turn off the attorney part of her brain, and she still had to watch the entire episode of Trevor Noah before she could turn off the television, unplug her phone, and settle in against James, who had been gently snoring for the past hour. Ivy tried not to think of Mrs. Henderson, alone and heartbroken without her dog, and the distinct possibility that she'd read the hateful comments posted about her. Ivy had long since given up the futile effort of wondering at the cruelness of human beings. She just accepted it as a truth as well known as the color of the sky. She was also accustomed to witnessing how in the face of true deep sorrow, people could resort to the pettiest of their natures. It was, Ivy believed, an evolutionary flaw, which she herself was as guilty of as anyone, given the dubious truth that the way she'd just spent the past half hour actually pertained to any legal matter and the much more likely fact that she had been indulging in a penchant for prurient gossip while spying on her neighbors, an activity completely sanctioned by their participation in a public Facebook thread.

Slightly sick to her stomach (chamomile tea was apparently *not* a panacea for adrenaline floods before bed-time) Ivy willed herself to focus on her breath, something Thia was always admonishing her to do. Eventually, her breath evened, and her mind settled into the limbo between consciousness and sleep. At the brink of sliding from one to the other, she thought of Fiona and Chloe and made a final fervent wish that they were all right.

CHAPTER ELEVEN
SOMEPLACE BEAUTIFUL

Alecia hovered over the send arrow for several heartbeats before touching it. She took one last look at the text. The words were innocuous: *be there in 20.* Alecia struggled with the ambivalence she felt. If she pressed send, she was committing Hannah to spend a couple of hours with Chloe, unsupervised. Whatever she did now she would either be turning her back on a friend or going against her instincts to protect her daughter.

Alecia had been dreading this moment all week, ever since Fiona surprised Alecia by showing up unannounced in the middle of the morning.

Fiona was falling apart. Chloe was spending most of her time at her father's house, seeing Fiona on Sundays, dinner on Tuesday, Wednesday, and Thursday evenings, but always returning to her fathers' for bedtime. Fiona had shown up on Alecia's doorstep last Monday morning in tears, having just delivered most of Chloe's winter clothing and all of Chloe's schoolbooks to her dad's house. Fiona completed the transfer with the new wife who made everything worse by being gracious and kind and assuring Fiona that it was just a phase and obvious that Chloe was closer to Fiona than anyone in the world. Yet, Fiona was turning her daughter over to Val in what seemed to be a very permanent way.

Alecia had never known Fiona to show up unannounced. As warm and welcoming as Alecia tried to be, she was aware that she put out a please-don't-drop-in-vibe. Alecia could have been in the process of sorting her craft room or cleaning out the attic, or worse, going over the myriad of spider webs in the chandeliers and light fixtures her maid never seemed to find no matter how many times she pointed them out to her. How could she behave graciously and welcoming with a dust mop in her hand, her hair covered in a snood, and no tea or refreshments prepared? The idea made her heart palpitate, and it was the stuff of one of many of Alecia's recurring nightmares if she neglected to take her Lorazepam before bedtime. Worse, what if Everett had not yet left for work and Fiona had shown up, her nose white and pinched, her eyes red and swollen from crying? He would have felt the need to be solicitous and possibly even missed his morning train. It would have thrown his whole day off, which would have thrown Alecia's whole week off!

As luck would have it, Everett was already half way to work, Alecia's closets and craft room were intact, and she had tackled all of the cobwebs the day before. She even had the kettle on because she was about to enjoy some freshly brewed Darjeeling herself and so she was able to whole-heartedly welcome Fiona in, pulling her into an embrace (which was big for Alecia since she wasn't a hugger), and guide her into the soothing sanctuary of her kitchen.

"Don't apologize," Alecia said while rubbing the narrow space between Fiona's shoulder blades, "I'm glad you came."

It was in the comfort and beauty of Alecia's kitchen, a mug of steaming tea warming Fiona's chilled, stiff hands, when Alecia agreed to allow the girls to go to the mall together.

"It's just," Fiona said in a small voice, "Chloe misses Hannah, she's withdrawn from her friends at school. What if I took them to the mall? They can go wherever they like and I'll go to Chico's."

"Chico's isn't at The Westchester anymore." Alecia managed to refrain from saying *Thank God*, just in time. "Why don't you go see my girl at Neiman's? She's wonderful and will set you up with some beautiful new ensembles. It will cheer you up! We could go together."

"Really?" Fiona's face brightened. "Do you think the girls would go for it?"

"Why wouldn't they?" But Alecia could think of a million reasons.

"Lecia, I can't shop at Neiman's. How about Anthropologie?" Fiona knew she would never buy one thing in Anthropologie and was just trying to impress Alecia. Anthropologie's clothes were also way out of her budget, and the few times she thought maybe she'd splurge, she couldn't find one thing to fit. Even the tops two sizes too large for her strained across her boobs. Fiona just wanted to be the *kind* of person who shopped at Anthropologie. She had seen a slender, chic woman in her late twenties walking around the store, placing candles and straightening mirrored pillows. Fiona realized that woman must be the one responsible for setting up the fabulous "home" area that looked like a cross between Jasmine's adult Disney bedroom and the magazine version of boho-chic. Fiona thought it looked cheesy, but also how fabulous it was, and she secretly wished she could hire that young woman to come over and redecorate her own home.

Fiona also knew that decorating her house like a catalogue wouldn't bring Chloe back. She believed Chloe appreciated their home as she did, the worn but good quality furniture, the paintings purchased from local artists that may not be valuable but were of excellent quality. Chloe also loved those paintings: the pastel of a house in a wooded area with a twilit sky, the gray steel columns and cables of what would soon be the old Tappan Zee Bridge. Yet Chloe's love of the paintings hadn't kept her from moving out, and Fiona was pretty sure that a redecorated adult Disney Princess room from Anthropologie wouldn't do the trick of bringing her back either.

Alecia considered Fiona's request to shop at Anthropologie. Alecia loathed that place with every fiber of her being, yet she understood what appealed to Fiona about it. She also knew Fiona wouldn't find a single thing there that looked good on her. Alecia was an expert at shopping. Having been born poor with impeccable taste and having garnered wealth as an adult gave her an insight into acquiring material things most people didn't possess. She sized Fiona up for a moment in a way Fiona felt was neither intimidating nor rude, but somehow comforting, as if she were in good hands. Alecia reached over and patted Fiona's leg quickly, firmly but with surprising gentleness. "We'll go to Bloomingdales. And the girls can go to The Westchester. They'll be fine on their own for a couple of hours, and it's right down the road."

Alecia always kept her word, and Fiona and Chloe were counting on her. So she plastered a smile on her face, hustled Hannah to the car, and pulled out of the driveway with dread covering the bottom of her belly like a familiar and unwelcome mohair blanket over fevered skin.

Chloe tried to read Hannah without letting her know she was looking at her. They had been friends since childhood. They knew everything about each other. Once, when they'd first learned about fingerprinting, they had studied the whorls in one another's finger tips so they would always be able to identify each other, just in case. In case of what, Chloe wondered now. What had they imagined in their 8-year-old brains? Innocence in children often led to macabre imaginings, because they didn't really understand the horror of their play. Chloe recognized that now.

But today, Chloe was having difficulty reading Hannah, and she wasn't sure which one of them had changed. Hannah seemed normal. She looked directly into Chloe's eyes when they spoke, didn't slide her gaze away the way girls did when they didn't want to be friends anymore or had lost interest in you. Her smile seemed real. Chloe knew Hannah's fake smile; it was the one she used with adults, even her own mother. She didn't seem remote or bored or creeped out by Chloe, which is what Chloe had prepared herself for. She just seemed like Hannah. Funny, pretty, bossy, confident, Hannah. So why did Chloe feel like Hannah was pretending, like she was *acting* like herself instead of *being* herself?

Hannah felt Chloe's gaze. Chloe either wasn't slick enough, or Hannah knew Chloe too well, so she turned to Chloe and gave her a sly smile. Which instantly made Chloe feel better. That was the Hannah she knew.

"How much money do you have?" Hannah asked.

"Twelve dollars."

"Let's go to Sephora."

Chloe followed Hannah into the scented glittering world of the store. At almost thirteen, Hannah had the panache and swagger of any of the top runway models. Chloe didn't have Hannah's interest in make-up but Hannah obsessed over it. From Hannah's 'finstagram' pics and everything the girls in Hannah's school posted,

Hannah had a veritable mini-Sephora in her school locker. She was known for making girls eyebrows look *exactly* like Gigi Hadid's and could apply winged eyeliner like a pro. Of course, Hannah's mother knew nothing of Hannah's love for, or proficiency with, make-up. Chloe asked her once why she didn't just tell her mother about her passion for make-up, and Hannah smirked and said, "I don't like that woman to know my bizness."

Hannah was also adept at blocking her parents from her finsta, while creating an illusion of pre-teen innocence on her Instagram account. Which Hannah's parents followed faithfully, liking every dandelion pic and homework grade she posted, Hannah's fake Instagram was, however, completely out of control, and Chloe knew Alecia and Everett would shut that thing down in a hot minute and ground Hannah for the rest of her life if they did catch a glimpse of it. Chloe's shoulders shuddered, and she automatically pulled her jacket tighter.

"Come here." Hannah pulled Chloe over to the counter and with feather light taps of her fingers began applying things to Chloe's eyelids. "Open." Chloe obeyed and could see Hannah's lips pursed in concentration and the beginnings of a black head on her chin. "There!"

Chloe looked in the mirror surprised that the pink sparkle was kind of fantastic. It made Chloe's eyes a deeper blue and they looked enormous in her face. "Take it off."

"One sec." Before Chloe could object Hannah had captured her eyes on film.

"Don't post it!"

"It's for my story."

Before Chloe could object, Hannah put it on her snap chat story. It would go into the permanent ether of the cyber world but would be gone in a moment.

They left without buying anything, but Hanna pocketed a bunch of lash wands and lip-gloss applicators, and they made their way out of the mall and onto the parking lot roof. They found a place to sit, away from prying eyes or security cameras. Hannah knew the security guards rarely patrolled the roof, and from here she could see them enter before they would spot the girls. Hannah pulled a one-hit from the pencil case in her bag along with a neon green lighter. Chloe watched the entrance while Hannah lit up. When Hannah offered it to Chloe, she shook her head and Hannah shrugged, "More for me."

After a while, Hannah got rid of the evidence, leaned back against the cold brick, and looked at Chloe, "So what's the deal?"

Chloe shook her head and looked out over the cars. "I'm not talking about it."

"So, it's true?"

"It was stupid. I only did it a couple of times."

"Why?"

Chloe shrugged, "I wanted to know what it felt like."

"Bullshit."

"Believe what you want. I don't care."

Hannah appraised her from hooded eyes. Chloe couldn't tell if Hannah was high or not. She herself had never gotten high, and so she didn't know what it felt like, and Hannah always looked at her like that even when Chloe knew for a fact she wasn't high. Also, her eyes weren't red, and Hannah bragged that she knew exactly how much she could smoke and would stop before she needed Visine. But she kept the bottle in her bag anyway. Alecia went through Hannah's backpack all the time, but Hannah had sewn a secret pocket into the corner where she stashed Visine along with the lighter. The one-hit was a risk, but Hannah was careful to only carry it when she knew she could keep the bag in her possession and hid it in a tree at the very end of her property when she returned home. She had even discarded a few of them despite the fifteen-dollar cost and slight difficulty in obtaining new ones. But if there was any risk that she couldn't get to her hiding place without detection, Hannah would leave the thing behind.

Hannah was also known to randomly leave her school bag strewn about because she knew her mom would pick it up and put it together. Hannah would say, "Alecia can't handle a mess," and empty the contents on her bedroom floor.

"Let the woman snoop; she won't find anything." Hannah had said the last time Chloe slept over. Chloe felt bad for Alecia, but she followed Hannah out of her room and downstairs to the "Media Room" where they had made popcorn and watched a scary movie. Hannah had left her alone for a while and Chloe, terrified, accidentally froze the movie on a bloody hatchet and went to find her. Chloe froze her thoughts at that point, just like the movie. She stood up and looked out over the sprawl of White Plains. It wasn't a beautiful sight. It didn't have a skyline like The City and it was in Central Westchester, so they couldn't see the river.

Hannah pulled Chloe back down and passed her phone over, "Read this."

"What is it?"

"Just read it."

It was a Snopes article. As Chloe read, she felt the cinnamon bun and Frappuccino they'd had earlier roil in her stomach, but she scrolled through the entire article and reread the worst paragraph, feeling Hannah's eyes on her the entire time.

A copy of the California lawsuit (filed on 26 April 2016) shared via the Scribd web site outlined the allegations, which included the accusation that Trump and Epstein had (over 20 years earlier) "sexually and physically" abused the then 13-year-old plaintiff and forced her "to engage in various perverted and depraved sex acts" — including being "forced to manually stimulate Defendant Trump with the use of her hand upon Defendant Trump's erect penis until he reached sexual orgasm," and being "forced to engage in an unnatural lesbian sex act with her fellow minor and sex slave, Maria Doe, age 12, for the sexual enjoyment of Defendant Trump" — after luring her to a "series of underage sex parties" by promising her "money and a modeling career".

Chloe looked up at Hannah, "Do you believe it?"

Hannah narrowed her eyes. "Why wouldn't I? This shit happens every day and nobody cares."

"But — he's the president — it can't be true!"

Hannah laughed, "That's exactly why it probably is true." She stood up and shook her hair behind her shoulders and down her back. "Let's go, ho. I've got the munchies."

Chloe automatically rose to follow her, but Hannah had stopped suddenly, and Chloe almost plowed into her. Hannah was looking up at the sky and pointing, "Look."

Chloe didn't see anything. Just a sky filled with different grays, and a stack of cumulus clouds. She looked at Hannah wondering if she was higher than she appeared.

Hannah spoke in a soft voice, one Chloe didn't recognize. "Did you ever just want to disappear? Go somewhere else?"

"Where?"

"I don't know. Away from here."

"Westchester?"

"All of it."

"Earth?"

"Yes."

"Like, be dead?"

Hannah looked at her. "Stop asking stupid questions."

Chloe's face burned red, "I'm trying to understand."

Hannah softened, which surprised Chloe. "Disappear to…some place beautiful."

"I — yes. I want to disappear."

"Is that why you did it? Cut yourself?"

"It didn't work."

"It wasn't beautiful?"

"No. It felt like…nothing."

"Huh."

Hannah started walking toward the roof top entrance to the mall. People were coming up for their cars and Chloe looked at her phone. They only had half an hour before it was time to meet their moms. She followed Hannah across the parking lot and back into the building, realizing she didn't understand anything and worried that she never would.

* * *

Despite the upheaval of Fiona's announcement during their last book club, the women managed to choose a book for February. With a solemn promise to one another not to let the discussion devolve around politics, but to discuss only the pertinent social issues, the women agreed upon Thia's choice of *The Handmaid's Tale* by Margaret Atwood. Alecia agreed that since it was becoming a series, it would be an impossible story to escape, and at least with the four of them, the discussion would be thoughtful and provocative.

What Alecia didn't mention was that the women at the country club were also reading it, and were probably equally horrified, but saw no parallel between the world in the book and the one they inhabited. Alecia knew that the fact that she understood the parallels — and voted for Donald Trump anyway — set her book club members' teeth on edge, especially Thia's, who believed that Trump apologists were even worse than Trump supporters, because they knew better. Alecia didn't care what the other women thought about her politics or whom she voted for, and wasn't uncomfortable with their disagreement. Her aversion to political discussions was simply that such discussions bored her. The emotions around it were overwrought and messy, and although she didn't particularly like President Obama and hadn't wanted him to win, she certainly hadn't cried over it for 8 years. Everett for his part was relieved that Trump was president, because he was hoping it would put an end to as he described it, *the PC nonsense.* He'd stated on more than one occasion that he and his golf buddies couldn't wait to get out on the links so that they could speak their minds without worrying they'd be overheard and censured. It had been on the tip of Alecia's tongue to tell him it made them sound like douche bags, but Everett despised profanity and she wasn't in the mood for a lecture. Everett and his buddies were looking forward to four years where men could be men and their wallets could potentially fatten under conservative fiscal policy. The "men being men" comment made her roll her eyes, but the tax relief issue was something Alecia sympathized with, and she bristled at the notion that it was selfish to worry about their wallets. Alecia knew it was a lack of humility to think like this, and she'd never say it out loud to the other women, but she was tired of their whining. She and Everett paid more money in taxes than all three of those families combined — well maybe she'd have to pull Ivy out of the equation to make it completely true, but it was pretty damn close. Alecia also felt that she and Everett were extremely generous to a multitude of charitable organizations in their community, and it hurt her feelings when the women carried on like she and Everett (and their choice of political party) contributed in any way to the suffering of others. She kept these thoughts to herself for two reasons. First, she knew it would cause a rift between her and the others, and she didn't want that. While these women weren't the ones she socialized with on the weekends, she liked and enjoyed them more than any of her other friends. Second, Alecia wasn't ashamed of her political beliefs, but in reality, was not particularly invested in them either. Alecia had observed from the moment she could remember conscious thought that the world was comprised of two kinds of people, ones who harmed others intentionally for their own benefit and ones who harmed others unintentionally. The only way to survive was to figure out how to get around the land mines other people buried.

Books, however, were orderly worlds, where the stories unfolded, and no matter how high the stakes were, no matter which character lived or died, the most important aspect of a book was the aesthetic — the cadence of the language, the progression of the story, the reveal of the characters. The ugliness or beauty of each book became the focus. The emotions and tangle of human beings — contained between the front and back covers — was what Alecia loved the most about them.

Since February was the anniversary month of their book club, they decided to meet at a restaurant to celebrate. The criteria for the venue consisted of three points: far enough away so they wouldn't be distracted by bumping into people they knew; quiet enough for discussion; and an excellent cocktail selection.

Alecia was the first to arrive, so she settled herself at the table, ordered a bottle of Prosecco and a few appetizers she knew the other women would enjoy. Thia came in shortly after, and Alecia noted her outfit with disgust before censoring the unkind thoughts immediately. Her first thought was, *where in hell does she think she's going.* The second thought was, *she looks like a trollop, and a scrawny one at that.* And her third thought was, *she doesn't appreciate or deserve Eric.* Her thoughts fired in rapid succession flipping between shame and remorse, causing her to jump up and give Thia an enthusiastic smile and hug — so uncharacteristic, that it startled Thia and led to an awkward embrace that included Thia kissing Alecia's ear by accident.

Fortunately for both women, Ivy and Fiona arrived almost immediately and the choreography of greeting one another smoothed over the ear-kissing mishap. Alecia even managed a tight smile when Ivy held Thia at arm's length looked her up and down and said, "Damn girl, get it!" Alecia wasn't sure what Ivy meant by that remark, but she assumed it was positive from Ivy's facial expression.

"You look ready for a hot date!" Fiona said, "Maybe you can attract some men my way."

"You don't need my help," Thia said. "But I'm happy to oblige."

Alecia was irritated. If they were going to have to put up with men catting around their table, Alecia was going to feign a migraine and go home. Although, it was her turn to pick the book for next month, so she had to make sure she did that first. She planned to nominate *Cutting for Stone* by Abraham Verghese. She'd wanted to read it for years and had never gotten to it. She was looking forward to reading it with the other women. She thought Thia in particular would enjoy it and wanted to hear her thoughts. Alecia imagined texting the other women while reading it, highlighting passages, and discussing them throughout the month. She felt an exquisite lightness just thinking about it.

As the women settled in and the Prosecco poured, accolades and heartfelt thanks given to Alecia helped to loosen her chest. For a moment, she actually believed her physical heart expanded. She could feel it. She wondered if this is what people meant when they described love.

It wasn't that Alecia hadn't loved before. Certainly, she loved Hannah. Yet it wasn't expansive. Loving Hannah started as an idea. *I'm pregnant.* Satisfaction that she would be a mother and do it right was the first identifiable feeling Alecia attributed to loving Hannah. Love was synonymous with satisfaction. Anticipation was the next phase of loving Hannah – imagining the tiny toes, the round warmness of the baby, the clean smell, the outfits. The outfits were a strong focus of her anticipation, outdone only by nursery furnishings and paint color. Alecia decided not to find out the gender of the baby ahead of time. What they didn't understand was that the anticipation of not knowing the gender of her baby enhanced the excitement. Alecia tasked herself with decorating and buying baby clothes in gender-neutral hues and tones. Onesies and receiving blankets had hundreds of baby motifs that weren't pink or baby blue. Alecia promised herself that once the baby was born she would buy wardrobes filled with little girl or baby boy themes. She would accessorize the nursery accordingly. She imagined walking with her child (boy or girl) along the riverbank, selecting dandelions, making wishes from fluff, pushing her (or him) on a swing. It was the closest thing to happiness she'd ever experienced, the possibility of things. Once Hannah was born, she loved her fiercely, protectively. Her heart didn't expand but shrank. Her world became as small and tight as a tunnel. Her baby needed to thrive, and Alecia had to keep any and all danger at bay in order to ensure that.

Falling in love with Everett had been easy. She'd described it many times for Hannah, or during book club discussions when the topic turned, as it inevitably did, to relationships and marriage. Alecia's memory of falling in love with Everett was that it was magical. He was everything she'd wanted in a man. Clean, tall, and well built, but elegant rather than powerful. His manners and speech were impeccable. He had a gentleness to him that was still manly. His financial success was truly a bonus. Alecia didn't care as much about that as people believed she did. She would have been equally happy in a modest home in a simple neighborhood as long as it was safe and well run. She could make anything beautiful on any budget, she was sure of that. Everett's financial success made life easier, because the anxiety about money wasn't there. Alecia felt extremely grateful for that as she had so much anxiety about everything else that she couldn't imagine adding money worries to the mix.

Everett hadn't so much swept her off her feet (which was never a concept which appealed to Alecia) as much brought her an exquisite synchronicity. They wanted the same things.

There was a delight in their early time together that continued and never dissipated. Thia in particular, when the conversation turned to husbands and marriage, lamented the loss of spontaneity, of passion. Yet Alecia recognized passion in Thia's relationship with Eric. She recognized it and knew it wasn't something she and Everett had ever shared, but she didn't have an ounce of regret, jealousy, or bitterness. She wasn't interested in passion. It was messy and it waned. Delight, however, was sustainable. The physical world offered so many opportunities for it and both Everett and she shared an aesthetic that knew no boundaries. The many shades of green in the foliage on the side of a highway could bring her happiness for hours. A cloudy sky had infinite patterns, textures, and colors. There were countless books to read, concertos to listen to. Life could never be boring, only dangerous. That was Alecia's primary goal in life, to keep the danger out and the harmony intact. What was so wrong with that? It was natural, and every one of the women at that table worked toward the same thing every moment of her life, even if they were too naïve to recognize it.

The Prosecco bottles replaced multiple times, a robust cabernet arrived for Ivy and Fiona, and the women decided to forgo entrees for another round of appetizers. With the exception of Alecia, who never drank more than two glasses of Prosecco, they were all a little drunk. Thia was speaking, and Alecia kept getting distracted by the fact that Thia was most definitely wearing a push-up bra with a low-cut blouse revealing her bony chest, which was not at all flattering. Alecia forced herself to raise her gaze, stop being a judgy bitch, and listen to what Thia was saying.

"I think it's interesting that this book feels more current and less futuristic than it did in 1985 — it seemed so far-fetched then."

"I don't know about that," Ivy said. "I read it in high school, probably 86 or 87, and it terrified me so much I was afraid to read it again."

"Yeah," Fiona agreed. "We would have been handmaids then. We'd be crones now. Our daughters would be…" Fiona's voice trailed off.

"Uh-uh," Thia said. "I'd get off that crone island and find them for you. Promise."

Fiona smiled, yet the constriction in her chest intensified. There was a time when her fears about Chloe were generalized, now the threat to Chloe's wellbeing seemed real, and Fiona couldn't shake the feeling that it was imminent. She forced herself to focus on the conversation.

"When I was in high school, we didn't have cash cards," Ivy stated.

"Obviously," Alecia said.

"Remember the beginning of the book?" Ivy asked, "When her card stopped working, and she never saw her husband again?"

"Yeesss." Fiona dragged the word out intrigued by where this was going.

"Well, that scene has haunted me since high school. Every time I use my plastic — and that is how many times a day? I think to myself — what if this is the time?"

"Wow." Thia said, "I'd expect that from any one of us but not you — nothing seems to scare you."

"You'd be surprised what goes on in my head."

"Me too." They all turned to look at Alecia. "I think that way. I didn't have the reference of this book. But I have thoughts like that all the time."

"Do you think Atwood was prescient?" Fiona asked. "Or were the signs there in the eighties and we just didn't know?"

"Well, it isn't literal. I mean, it's metaphorical — but yeah," Ivy said. "The signs were there."

"Yet," Fiona paused, "it's more difficult to ignore them now."

Ivy took a deep breath, as if she were about to plunge from a diving board. "The thing about this novel for me though, Atwood makes a single reference to race without really looking at the impact of the repression of Black and Brown women — it alienates me — where do I fit in?"

Thia turned sharply. "You said metaphorical, Atwood is writing about all women."

"No." Ivy said. "She isn't. She's writing about white women."

Thia took a gulp of her champagne, "I don't think she means to delineate women — why does this story — which is about the subjugation of women — have to become about race?"

Ivy looked at Thia for a long time, but not, Thia realized, in a *thinking-about-it way*, but more like a penetrating *I-see-you* way.

"Because," Ivy said, "when you're Black in America, race permeates everything."

"If I said that," Thia defended, "I'd be called racist."

Ivy set her wine glass down and sharpened her gaze. "For acknowledging that race permeates every element of society? For acknowledging that America is a racist society?"

Thia looked away, "I get it — the backlash against having President Obama, but the fact that we elected a Black president in our lifetime shows that we're capable of not being racist."

Ivy fought not to roll her eyes. Instead she caught Thia's gaze. "Having a Black president doesn't mean America isn't racist."

"That's true." Alecia said, and all the women looked at her. "America is racist. And we live in a racist society. And it permeates everything. And you and I," she looked right at Thia, "and Fiona don't have to *think about race* or *bring race into it* because we don't suffer the effects of racism."

Fiona nodded.

Thia could tell Ivy was surprised by Alecia's agreement. But Ivy just nodded definitively and picked up her glass of wine in that calm graceful way that Thia partially envied and fully loved. Ivy sipped her wine and looked at Thia right in the eyes.

Thia wanted to argue. She wanted to defend herself. She wanted to be the one on the right side of this argument; she couldn't believe it was Alecia who got it right, and she, Thia, champion of human rights, who had blundered. Thia looked defiantly around the table. Fiona was looking at her expectantly, that soft halo of reddish curls around her head, her freckles stark against her pale, white, skin. Alecia had made her declaration and was now helping herself to more Prosecco, and Ivy was still watching Thia as if she could read her petty, resentful bubble. Thia smiled in spite of herself. She *was* at times petty and resentful; it was a character flaw, one she worked on all of the time. She knew it, her husband knew it, some day her kids would know it, and all of these women knew it, and loved her anyway. And while *of course* she'd considered Ivy's points before, she'd never *really* thought about them in any more than a passing moment.

"Okay," Thia said. "Consider me schooled."

Ivy looked at her but didn't smile her usual sly smile back. And that wounded Thia. She'd felt humiliated and then been the bigger person. Ivy had to understand what that cost her.

"Sometimes," Ivy then said. "It's not about you, Thia."

That stung. Thia searched for a way to explain how much it stung.

Fiona placed her hand on the table, her fingers splayed out, as if reaching for Thia, but not actually touching her. "If we're going into the resistance, we need to do it for real. With everything we have. And it's going to hurt."

Thia nodded. This she understood.

"Yes," Ivy said, relieved that she'd brought it up, and made her point, and held her ground, now eager to make the other point, which had resonated with her so deeply about this story. "More than anything, this story is about resistance. It's also, I think about what happens to love in the face of resistance. Love is relegated to memory, and it becomes too painful to hold onto, but it isn't forgotten, it isn't absent."

Fiona and Alecia nodded.

Thia swallowed the rest of her Prosecco. She was still resentful, but she loved these women. And she knew that in the face of resistance it would be love that fueled her. "If we were in Gillead, I'd resist until death."

Ivy looked at Thia. She believed her. "No doubt."

Thia nodded, "Just so you all know."

Fiona laughed, "We know."

Alecia wondered what resistance meant to each of them. It seemed easier for the other women to grasp. A pink hat with pussy ears, clever chants, the unity of a cause. None of those methods of resistance resonated with Alecia. She believed her form of resistance was building a world with a veneer as impenetrable as a fortress. Her form of resistance was the insulation of wealth and beauty. She looked at the other women and though she felt separated from them, a state of being she actively cultivated (after all, it is impossible to insulate yourself properly if you allow others in), if their society really did devolve into a dystopia, if she no longer had the fortress of wealth and beauty at her ready, if they had to go to war, she would want these women fighting at her side.

Alecia was about to make a toast with some approximation of that idea, when the waiter came over with a round of pale pink drinks in martini glasses and handed them out in a flourish. "From the gentlemen at the bar."

The women turned to look over.

"Cosmos? Really?" Ivy asked, "Do they think this is a scene from *Sex in the City*?"

"*So* 2000," Fiona laughed.

"Now, now, be gracious." Thia nodded and gave a flit of her fingers and smiled at the men.

"Stop it. They'll come over here!" Fiona sounded panicked.

"So?" Thia said. "That's a good thing. Maybe we'll get you a date."

"I don't want a date with a guy who sends cosmos!"

"Beggars can't be…"

"Don't you dare, Thia!"

But it was too late. They were on their way over.

"This is why we can't have anything nice," Alecia said to Ivy, making her laugh.

Thia deeply regretted drinking that Cosmo on top of all that Prosecco. She went to bed with one foot on the floor to stop the room from spinning (something she hadn't had to do since her mid-twenties) and fell into a deep troubled sleep, filled with nightmarish dreams, and woke up with a pounding headache and a sore throat from snoring (the snoring detail provided by an unusually grouchy Eric when he pushed her arm to wake her up and told her the kids were already up and fighting).

Thia struggled to sit up and saw that Eric's good spirits were magically restored by her obvious pain.

"Someone had a rough night." He then had the audacity to wink at her and thrust his chin at the trail of clothes and one stiletto. "Too bad that wasn't what it looks like, but I'll let you make it up to me tonight."

Thia groaned and tried to swallow, but her throat felt like sandpaper. Eric grinned again, took pity on her, and handed her the glass of water he'd place on her bedside table, plus three aspirin. "Sorry I can't stay and help, but I've got an early meeting."

Thia nodded miserably and let him kiss her gently before he headed out the door. She wanted more than anything to sink back into the pillows and close her eyes against the dim but painful light. The sounds from the kitchen were alarming, and there was an ominous thud followed by some more screaming. Thia did however smell coffee, so she was able to rouse herself and go downstairs hoping her resemblance to a zombie apocalypse victim would scare the kids to death — or at least get them to shut up for a blessed second.

It didn't, but she did manage to get them to finish their breakfast and gave them each money for lunch (she knew if she even attempted to make a peanut butter sandwich her stomach would revolt). She got them out the door and forced them into the car, creating a giant carbon footprint by driving around the corner to the bus stop where she could hide behind her sunglasses (despite the dreary day) and the wheel of her car.

"Wow," the nosiest, most annoying bus-stop mom said, when she rudely stuck her face in Thia's car window. "You look like hell. Flu?"

"No," Thia said. "Hangover."

The woman pulled her face back like Thia actually said yes to the flu. "But it's a school night."

"Exactly." Thia said and revved her engine before pulling away.

"The bus isn't here yet!" the woman shouted.

Thia waved her fingertips out the window in a way that could be taken as a toodle-oo or a fuck you. She didn't care which. She knew her kids would make it onto the bus just fine, and it mortified them when she stood there waving good-bye to them. Lila in particular gave her a death glare from the window whenever she tried it.

Worse than the hangover was Thia's remorse at how badly she'd behaved at the end of the evening, pushing Fiona on those random guys, embarrassing Fiona and herself in the process. Alecia had been giving her the hairy eyeball all night but rather than slow her roll, Thia had amped it up and behaved as if she were a rebellious teenager. One of the guys was someone Thia had seen at the gym, and now she'd have to play it off like it was nothing every time she bumped into him. Maybe she'd freeze her membership and save some money in the process. She could run outdoors, and there was a yoga studio in town with a good deal. But Thia hated yoga, which seemed counterintuitive to everyone who knew her. She wondered if Fiona was even speaking to her.

Before she could talk herself out of it, she picked up her phone and texted Fiona. *Still friends?* She added the laugh/cry emoji then deleted it. She pressed send and watched with alarm as the response bubbles appeared almost instantly.

No. But there were three laugh/cry emojis, which instantly made Thia feel better.

Let me take you for lunch today. To make up. (heart eyes emoji face).

Only if you do the walk of shame and wear that outfit.
Ugh.
You owe me.
Fine. Horsefeathers?
I can get there by 11:50.
I'll order us cosmos.
No!
Haha

Thia felt relief, despite the knowledge that the early lunch was going to make her morning even more harried than usual. The tab from last night and a restaurant lunch was going to blow her weekly budget, but it was worth it, she told herself. She'd just have a little less to put into her Christmas Club account this month. The water, aspirin, and coffee were beginning to work, and her headache had almost dissipated when she went into the back garden to begin her prayers.

Twice however, during her morning ritual, once in the East and once during the South, an image of the guy from the gym flashed into her vision. Both times his face was too close to hers and she was looking into his eyes. Once they were smiling, once they were serious. Intense. Thia felt a terrible unease that even her ardent chanting couldn't dissolve. After she'd finished, she went back into the garden to try and recapture the peace she'd felt moments before. But it was too late. She felt a menacing presence. Something she hadn't felt in years, something that pierced the beauty of the morning.

CHAPTER TWELVE
THIA 1982

When Thia's older sister Ariadne went to college, she left Thia the dregs of her album collection (including some wayward marijuana buds forgotten in the creases). Ariadne had taken all the good ones (The Lurkers, Beastie Boys, GoGos, The Cure, DMZ, Blondie, Ramones, Talking Heads, The Police), leaving behind Kim Carne, Hall and Oates, and Rick Springfield. Ariadne packed all her of her clothes, except for a fuchsia sweater that was too tight, a pair of black stockings with a run in them, a stained T-shirt of their father's left behind when he moved out in 1978, an almost but not quite empty tube of black lipstick, and a pair of Doc Martins with a missing heel. She also left (by accident) a purple and gold feather-earring and a mood ring. There were large squares of less dingy white on the walls where Ariadne's posters of bands had hung. Ariadne hadn't taken the posters with her but refused to leave them, saying Thia needed to form her own identity. The posters were crumpled in a giant ball and stuffed callously down the incinerator shaft while 9-year-old Thia followed, begging, pleading, and threatening with all the might in her tiny body.

"Stop it," Ariadne had said, brushing past her smelling like glue and incinerator dust, "You're embarrassing yourself."

And just like that, the most stable force in Thia's life moved seven hours away from their boulevard in Queens to Buffalo, New York.

Whenever Thia thought about her sister, she imagined her in a place very much like the TV show "Little House on the Prairie," vast plains of golden wheat moving in the wind, distant hills the Technicolor green of a television tube. She imagined her sister taking classes in the same schoolhouse Laura and Mary took classes, feeding a wood stove so they wouldn't freeze to death on the prairie. Outside, on "the campus" a mysterious word bantered knowledgeably about by her sister and mother (when they were speaking to one another), Thia imagined a lone and mighty buffalo.

Thia obviously had never been to Ariadne's school. Her sister had applied by mail, received an acceptance, and said yes (sight unseen, since it was the most affordable option furthest away). Ariadne hitched a ride with a friend's family who had a station wagon and lived in Middle Village (in a lovely detached two-family home with a driveway — thereby making it possible to own a station wagon). Thia had waved good-bye long after the car pulled away even though Ariadne hadn't looked back. But before they had left their apartment, Ariadne had leaned down, hugged her tight, and whispered, "Don't worry, I'll be back for you as soon as I can." Even though the hug hurt a little bit, it was the best feeling Thia ever had. She breathed in the smell of Ariadne (patchouli oil and weed as Thia figured out years later) and hugged her back.

Thia went back upstairs alone, holding her breath with a superstitious belief that it would prevent the elevator from getting stuck, and let herself back into the apartment with her very own key. She was the oldest (well only) kid home now, and she had a new-found sense of responsibility. She tiptoed down the foyer to her mother's room. When she gently tried the doorknob and found it locked, she knew her mother was still asleep. So, she went to her room (hers alone now) and found the unintended treasures her sister had left behind.

An hour later her mother hadn't yet emerged, so Thia ate a handful of cheerios from the box (there wasn't any milk) and left the apartment, her key safely stowed in the pocket of her jeans. Beneath the jeans she was wearing Ariadne's stockings with the run in them. The feather earring dangled from one of her ears, the tiny gold stud she always wore glinted in the other. Thia had circled her pinky in the lipstick tube and carefully painted her lips. With the lipstick on, Thia thought she looked more like her sister than she'd previously realized. She wished she had found some eyeliner since Thia never saw her Ariadne without it. Perfectly ringed or smudged and messy, it was part of her sister's face. The sweater, though too tight for Ariadne, was much too big for Thia, but she didn't care and wore it proudly. The Doc Martins, however, were impossible; not only were they far too big but the missing heel made her limp. With great regret, Thia stowed them carefully in the back of her own closet and consoled herself with the Capezio's Ariadne had given her years ago when she'd grown out of them. They almost fit. And the bunched-up stockings took up some extra toe room, which helped. Daringly (because they were her only ones), Thia cut a small slit in her jeans with a kitchen knife, widened it a tiny bit with her fingers so the stockings would show through, took the stairs six flights down (no sense in risking the elevator twice in one morning) and let herself out onto the boulevard feeling grown up and very beautiful.

It was a warm September morning, and Thia was hot in her sister's clothes, but she championed through and wandered the boulevard hoping she'd see someone she knew. She noticed disapproving looks from the old people on lawn chairs in front of her building, but Thia didn't care about them. They were always giving her mother and Ariadne disapproving looks, and the pitying glances thrown her way made Thia want to spit. Her favorite old person, Mrs. Schwartzman used to give her candy wrapped in cellophane, butterscotch ovals, or bright fruit flavored balls in lime-green or raspberry-red. But Mrs. Schwartzman hadn't been there all summer, and Thia was worried that she'd died. A few times she'd almost asked her mother, but she realized she didn't want to know and preferred to think Mrs. Schwartzman had gone on vacation and would be back now that summer had ended. Thia saw the super of her building and noticed the double take he gave her. Maybe, she thought, he'd mistaken her for Ariadne, who was much taller, but Thia had pulled her hair into a high side ponytail and convinced herself it made her appear almost as tall as her sister.

Thia meandered up and down the boulevard for a while, looking in shop windows, sitting on a couple of stoops in buildings where her friends lived, hoping someone would appear. But she didn't see any of her friends or Ariadne's friends, and she was beginning to get bored. She thought about heading over to the playground, but she didn't like going there by herself. Sometimes there were fistfights or big dogs that frightened her. She wished her best friend Julie was around, but Julie, like most of her friends with divorced parents, had to alternate weekends, so she was most likely somewhere on the Lower East Side where her dad was a musician / druggie (as Julie referred to him). Thia had gone with Julie a couple of times. They'd shared the pull-out sofa in the living room. There was a handle built ingeniously into the iron, and when you pulled it a bed would emerge like a groaning angry beast freed from its cage in the couch. It took up the entire room and in order to go from one side to the other, you had to roll across the bed. That's how Julie's dad had to get to his room. If he had to go to the kitchen when the girls were already in bed, he'd roll across and Julie would yell and kick him. Thia sometimes worried he'd get mad, but he never did. He was a strange hybrid of an adult and a kid. Thia liked him and couldn't understand why Julie and her mom referred to him as Lonnie the Loser.

One morning when Thia asked where Lonnie's room was Julie gave her a funny look.

"His bedroom I mean."

"This is it, Thia. It's a studio."

"But — where did he sleep?"

Julie rolled her eyes and pointed. With a sinking feeling Thia rolled across the bed and peeked into the bathroom. Sure enough, he was fast asleep, curled in the bathtub with two pillows and two blankets. Thia was glad he had two of each.

She jumped back into bed. "What if I have to pee?"

Julie shrugged, "He won't care. Nothing wakes him up."

"I'll just hold it."

Julie shrugged already bored of the topic. "Let's go out."

"It's 5:00 in the morning."

"We'll watch the sunrise."

They dressed in under two minutes. Julie gave her a stick of Doublemint gum since they now had a plan and didn't want to risk waking Lonnie the Loser to get their toothbrushes.

As smooth as can be, Julie slid two Kools from her dad's cigarette pack in his jacket, filched some matches from a drawer in the kitchen, and ushered Thia out of the apartment. Thia watched as Julie expertly used her keys to tumble the multiple locks on the door. The girls ran down the four flights of steep steps, holding their noses against the stench of urine mixed with other people's cooking smells. Within moments they burst out of the narrow building and into the streets, just as day broke across the sky.

It was early summer so the heat wasn't sticky and the city had yet to grow as fetid as it would. Wandering an unfamiliar neighborhood, the girls bought warm bagels with cream cheese and two small cartons of orange juice. They found their way through some of the narrow alleyways into a courtyard Thia had seen from the kitchen window. It was larger than the other yards in the neighborhood, which were primarily small squares of cement surrounded by chain link fencing, and garbage pails or dumpsters servicing the corresponding businesses. This yard had a tree with roots breaking through the cement. All the apartments overlooking them had their shades drawn, and the girls felt relatively safe eating their breakfast. When finished, they wrapped the wax paper into balls and stuffed them into the cartons, planning to carry it all out. Thia watched Julie light the stolen cigarette. The smoke in the open air smelled good. Julie's lips were soft and pink. She drew the smoke in expertly and blew it out in a steady stream. Thia tried to do the same thing, but it burned the insides of her cheeks, her mouth, and her throat, so she wound up spurting it out of her mouth in an inelegant cloud with a scrunched-up face and watering eyes.

"Don't worry," Julie said. "You'll get the hang of it."

On the way back to the apartment, they were walking across grates and cellar doors testing their weight and playing what Julie called "Walking Russian Roulette." She told Thia about a girl who had stepped on one of the grates without testing it first and it had given way sending her straight to the bowels of the city, where rats fed off her face and made nests for their babies in her hair. Julie argued that they couldn't spend their lives in New York taking baby steps all over the city and they had to learn to walk with confidence and courage over the grates. She was making Thia go first and rating her. So far Thia had an F. The first two had been chickenshit according to Julie. For the next block, she'd walked with a swagger and courage she didn't possess, but it seemed to work as Julie nodded and said, "Better."

Thia turned back with increased confidence and walked into an old man. He smelled like mothballs and rubbing alcohol, but his grip was surprisingly strong.

"Sorry!" Thia blurted. Her face burned with embarrassment, and she tried stepping backwards to escape his grip, which tightened.

"You girls need to be more careful."

"We will." She stepped back again but was now leaning awkwardly toward him because he still had her shoulders in a claw-like hold. She finally looked up at him and saw the leer in his face, the delight. She was confused because she thought he was angry, that maybe she'd even hurt him. Then he ran his tongue around already rubbery lips, the loose jowls in his face swinging when he moved closer and whispered, "Do you have hair on your pussy yet?"

Thia could barely hear him, "What?"

"Do you...?"

But Julie had pried the old man's fingers off Thia's shoulders, pulled her by the hand, and they were running away. When they were around the block Julie slowed down and looked behind them. "Don't be so fucking nice all the time."

"I—"

"He's a perv. You gotta learn how to spot 'em."

Thia nodded.

Thia felt like she had learned a lot since then. Julie had shown her the social club on the corner and told her the men there act nice, but they're pervs, so don't go there.

Thia told Ariadne about what Julie said, and Ariadne nodded. Yeah. And the firehouse, don't walk past there.

"Why not?" That was one of Thia's favorite places to go. She loved looking at the trucks and getting peeks inside at the gear. You could even see the pole! Thia desperately wanted to climb up the pole and get a look at the entire set-up. She imagined it would look like the cottage that Snow White stumbled upon in the magic woods, with rows of beds and an efficient little kitchen. Thia knew it wouldn't be tiny, since the firemen were full grown men, not dwarfs. But the space looked small, so that's how she imagined it.

She'd mentioned her plan once, to bake some brownies and bring them by in the hope that they would show her the room. Ariadne's face grew angry and red, her eyes turned into the mean slits she used against their mother whenever their mother said something she didn't like, which was pretty much all of the time. "Listen to me, Thia!" and she shook her arm a little too hard. "You're a cute little kid now so they'll be nice, but in a couple of years they'll be cat calling you and trying to get you to talk to them. Stay away. Cross the street and if they say shit to you, look straight ahead like you can't hear them. Like they're air. Ok?"

"Ok." Thia pulled away and rubbed her sore arm.

"I mean it, Thia!"

"I heard you!" Thia stomped off to get her dolls; they were the only things she loved that weren't confusing (unlike Ariadne the asshole, who didn't seem to care one thing about her unless she was bossing her around).

But that warm September morning Thia would have given anything to have Ariadne and Julie bossing her around, giving her tasks, which she knew were some kind of test she would probably fail.

Thia had once heard her mother tell Ariadne that all children were born pure. The trick was to keep them protected before the world tainted them. She had herbs and incantations, crystals, oils, and talismans, designed to ward off the evils of the world. Yet Thia had managed to elude all of her mother's safeguards and was adventuring around the neighborhood, which seemed disappointingly placid that warm late summer morning.

Thia was just about to give up and had even started the journey home when she heard a low voice calling her name. She looked behind her but didn't see anything, she spun her head, left then right, but the street was empty. She heard it again. "Up here dummy."

Jeff McDougal. Ariadne called him Doogle. They were in high school together, and he had been at their apartment a number of times. He was always nice to Thia. He bent down to talk to her so their eyes met and she didn't have to strain her neck to look at him. One evening he'd spent an entire hour teaching her to tie her shoes by making two loops and tying them into a bow. Thia realized that must have been years ago, because she'd soon advanced to wrapping the lace around one loop and pushing it through with her thumb against her forefinger.

"Hi, Doogle," she waved.

"Where are you going all dressed up?"

Thia shrugged.

"Well it's your lucky day, I'm off work. Come on up."

"I gotta get back. My mom —"

"Don't be a baby. Come hang out."

Thia entered the cool dim interior of Doogle's building and waited for the buzzer to let her in.

Later that day, when Thia returned home, her mother took one look at her and knew something terrible had happened. Her mother didn't have the capacity to discuss it. Some truths, she believed, were too awful to put into words. Thia knew this instinctively. There were tricks, she knew, to handling bad things. You just went on as though they'd never happened.

Thia also knew, how much her mother loved her. The way she would cuddle her at night, sing her silly bedtime songs, stroke her hair from her face, even when she was tired from working double shifts at the diner. Thia also knew that when her mother's lips grew thin and her eyes crinkled, it was because she worried about her. Thia knew people only worried about people they loved. That's why Thia no longer worried about her dad. She hadn't seen him in four years, not since she entered kindergarten. One day Thia decided she didn't love him anymore. She could barely remember his face or his voice or the scratchy feeling of his whiskers when he put his cheek against her cheek and called her his 'Thiabear'. And because she no longer loved him, she no longer had to worry about him. About where he'd gone or when he'd be back. She'd watched her mother grow stronger. She'd stopped secret crying (although Thia could always tell), she'd started eating like a normal person, and regained the slight swell in her hips and tummy that Thia missed when she'd grown thin and sharp looking. One of the consequences of her father leaving was that her mother now had to work doubles and grew tired to the point of illness, so as Thia worried less about her father, she worried more about her mother. Consequently, as she loved her father less, she loved her mother more.

That evening, her mother supervised Thia's bath. Her mother ran the water and tested it carefully before letting Thia go in. Her mother scanned Thia's body with her eyes, and Thia saw the fear in her gaze give way to relief. Thia knew nothing would show. Some wounds weren't visible; they didn't stain or tear your skin. But they ruined the taste inside your mouth, much worse than the cigarette had. They burned your eyes so you never wanted to see again. They settled deep inside your stomach like a lining of lava before it spews from a volcano.

After her bath, Thia put on her favorite nightgown. It was white cotton with tiny pink roses in a tight pattern around the collar and hemline. Thia's mother braided her hair for her so it wouldn't tangle while she slept.

Then she took Thia by her hand and brought her into the living room where she'd drawn a white chalk circle on the rough parquet floor. Thia stood in the middle and closed her eyes.

"Visualize blue healing light surrounding you," her mother said in a soft voice.

"I see it."

"Good."

"Can I open my eyes now?"

"Yes."

Her mother was holding a gray candle and lighting a perfect cone of incense. The scent filled the room, and Thia associated it with the familiar, the safety, of home. At her mother's direction, Thia cupped her hands around the smoke and recited, "With air I cleanse myself."

Her mother held the gray candle, "Pass the tip of your finger through it like this." Thia gasped. "Don't worry," her mother said and smiled, "It doesn't hurt."

Thia was so happy when her mother smiled that she immediately did it and laughed with delight when it didn't hurt at all.

"See!" her mother laughed. "Magic."

Thia laughed too.

"Now do it again," her mother whispered. "And say, 'With fire I cleanse myself.'"

Thia passed her finger through again, feeling nothing. "With fire, I cleanse myself."

"Good, good." She took Thia's hand and opened it palm up, sprinkling salt into it. "Rub your hands together and say, 'With earth I cleanse myself.'"

Thia felt the scratch of salt against the skin of her palm. "With earth, I cleanse myself."

Her mother nodded, then held out the chalice. How Thia loved that chalice. Coveted it. Sometimes, when her mother was at work and Ariadne wasn't paying attention, Thia would sneak into her mother's room and remove it from its sacred place on the altar. She moved it around under the lamplight and watched the colors of the stones brighten against the soft pewter. It was the most expensive and precious thing her mother owned, and Thia didn't want to get caught touching it. Now, her mother was offering it to her. Thia took it carefully because there was water in it. She wondered if she should drink it.

Her mother must have known her thoughts, because she shook her head. "Dip your fingers in it." Thia did so and her mother reached for the chalice. "Now rub your hands together and say, 'With water I cleanse myself.'"

Thia did it. When she was through, her mother carefully erased the chalk circle then stepped into the space where it had been, hugged her, and whispered, "Thanks be God and

Goddess. Wrap thee in cotton, bind thee in love, protection from pain surrounds like a glove. Brightness of blessings surrounding thee this night, for thou art cared for, healing thoughts sent in flight."

"Mama?"

"It's all better now."

Thia hugged her mother and whispered, "Magic."

"Yes. Magic."

Later that night, when Thia was sure her mother was sleeping, she took her favorite doll off her shelf and whispered to her, "I can't have you anymore."

She removed her favorite nightgown and stuffed it deep into her drawer and slipped into shorts and an old T-shirt. Remembering to take her key, she held her breath as she tumbled the locks on her apartment door. She propped the door open with a shoe, held her doll tightly, and ran the few yards to the incinerator door. In one fluid motion, she opened the mouth of the incinerator and tossed the doll in before letting the door slam shut and running back to her apartment. She tumbled the locks back in place and got back into bed. She pressed the sooty dirty palms of her hands tight against her eyes to stanch the hot tears building. She told herself her penance was complete and she would never think of that day or Doogle or her favorite doll again. And it worked. By her tenth birthday she'd forgotten all of it. Except the magic, she kept the magic.

CHAPTER THIRTEEN
THE UN-LUNCH

As it turned out, Thia was able to put some money into her Christmas club account after all. The mild winter weather had lulled them into a false sense of security, but the forecast said a storm would hit on Friday. Fiona, concerned that she would be stuck indoors the whole weekend, decided they needed to forgo their lunch and walk the Aqueduct instead. She quickly ate a yogurt at her desk before leaving to meet Thia at the back gate on 448.

"Hey!" Fiona shouted when she saw Thia waiting just outside the school grounds. "You aren't wearing your outfit! That was part of the deal!"

Thia thrust a giant Starbucks at Fiona. "I went all the way to Ossining for this."

"Is this what I think it is?"

Thia nodded, "A Venti Green Tea double shot espresso with extra whip and two pumps of caramel syrup. Hot."

"I love you."

"I ordered that fucking thing and put my name on the cup so we are now officially even in the karma embarrassment universe."

Fiona took a sip of her drink. "Deal." Then struggled to

keep up with Thia's pace.

"You know, Thi, it wasn't that big of a deal. You didn't embarrass yourself as much as you think."

"I made you uncomfortable."

"It was funny."

"I don't know — I think I may have to change my gym."

Fiona looked at her, "That guy did seem pretty into you."

"It's not like I know him or talk to him or anything. I've just seen him around."

"Well. He's noticed you."

"Ugh."

"What do you think Eric would say?"

"Eric? He wouldn't think twice. He knows I'd never cheat on him."

"Do you ever think about it?"

"Hell no. He's enough to deal with. Who wants another one?" But Thia was lying. While she didn't think about cheating on Eric, and she certainly didn't want to with anyone around here, especially gym guy, she did find herself wondering what her life would have been like if she'd married someone else, or never married at all. She wondered about who she may have become. It made her feel guilty. She was lucky to have found Eric, she loved him, and he was a great dad. But at times it felt as if she had four kids instead of three, and he was one of them. She wondered what it would have been like to marry someone more mature than she was. Someone who handled the bills and the loans and all the myriad of household things that went wrong. Eric was great at fixing things; he said Thia kept a honey-do list a mile long just to keep him around on the weekends. But that was the problem. Thia had to keep the list. All decisions fell to her. And she was growing weary. Which made her feel like a giant asshole. Compared to what her mom had had to do when she was Thia's age, Thia lived in the lap of luxury with Prince Charming, and it still wasn't good enough for her. She longed for a bigger nicer house, a fancier car, more romance and spice in her sex life (although to be fair that had never been an issue between them, maybe it was just variety she was after). Did that make her an asshole, *and* a slut?

"Good," Fiona said, "because Eric's the best and I hope you know it."

"Yeah, yeah, whatever."

Fiona looked at her sharply, "Seriously, Thia. Don't ruin things."

"Do you wish you were still married?"

Fiona took a long drink of her concoction. Thia watched her, trying to gauge what was in her mind. "No. I don't. I'd rather be alone and lonely than lonely in bed next to someone."

"What about the practical side of marriage? In prior centuries, it was nothing more than a business arrangement."

"Yeah. Well in prior centuries we would have been chattel — but to answer your question — I don't wish Bryce and I had stayed married. But sometimes I wonder if I should have tried harder. For Chloe's sake."

They walked silently for a while. The air darkened beneath a cloud cover and an icy breeze blew in from the West. "How is Chloe?"

"She seems…better in some ways. But so much worse in others."

"How?"

"I believe her about the cutting thing being over. For now, anyway."

"Like a phase?"

"I guess, but whatever caused her to do it — she refuses to

talk to me about it. And I'm at my wit's end."

"What do you think happened?"

"I just don't know. I thought maybe the divorce — maybe she took her dad remarrying harder than we thought. But I don't think that's it."

Thia stopped. "I have to ask."

"Go ahead."

"Is there any way — something happened? Someone may have bothered her?"

"You mean molested her?"

Thia nodded.

"I thought of that. But who? When? She's always with one of us. And I've talked extensively to her about good touch / bad touch / secret touch."

"Yeah." Thia didn't know how to talk about it. How to explain that Fiona may have taught Chloe all those lessons, but it didn't mean Chloe would know how to apply them when faced with the manipulations of a predator.

"I was always pretty lucky," Fiona said.

"How so?"

"I was sheltered. I grew up with parents who loved each other, older brothers who protected me; I met Bryce my freshman year of college." She shuddered. "I mean there was an uncle of my dad's, we called him "Merv the Perv," but my girl cousins and I knew how to avoid him, you know, so he wouldn't be able to get all handsy with us."

"Was his name really Merv?"

"No. I can't remember what it was though." They walked silently for a while. "I couldn't bare it if someone hurt Chloe."

"It was probably a reaction to her dad's remarriage. She must have taken it harder than either of you expected. I'm sure she'll be fine now."

Maybe they both believed that. Or maybe neither of them did. As if they'd made a silent pact, they kept walking and spent the next 15 minutes discussing the Manor Moms Facebook page, unpacking whose fault it was that the dog was killed (both parties) and which of the daughters on the angry rant of a thread was the biggest idiot (a tie).

When lunchtime ended, they hugged harder than they would ordinarily have done and went back to work, telling themselves the worst was behind them.

Ivy saw Fiona and Thia going onto the aqueduct. She was rushing to get her errands done before meeting the school bus, but wanted to chuck her to-do list and catch up with them.

As she drew nearer, Ivy prepared to catch their attention, by beeping, opening the window, calling their names. Yet she silently rolled by, watching with relief as they disappeared onto the trail, keeping her gaze straight ahead in case one of them happened to turn and see her.

Ivy's hesitation caused her to miss the light and now she would have to wait at the intersection of Route 9 and 448, for what was arguably the longest light in the history of the world. Thia had told them once that she used every red light as an opportunity to practice her Kegel exercises, but that was just information Ivy wish she didn't have. In fact, most of the information she had about other people was information she wished she didn't have. Ivy had an analytical brain. She was a problem solver. She liked puzzles. Information that didn't help solve a puzzle, or increase her knowledge in a useful way felt burdensome to her.

Thia said two things during their discussion last night

that had rattled around in Ivy's brain at three o'clock in the morning: first that Thia believed that nothing seemed to scare Ivy, and second, that Thia would go and find their daughters and rescue them in the event the *Handmaid's Tale* proved prescient.

Ivy had sons whom she feared for all of the time — in ways that were different from what scared her as a woman. She admitted to herself, she wouldn't ever put her sons at risk in order to save Thia, Fiona, and Alecia's daughters. They were after all, her babies — her flesh and blood, but that secret knowledge made her feel like a coward and a fraud.

Ivy also imagined that during their walk, Thia and Fiona were going to discuss Thia's flirtation with that guy from the restaurant and Ivy didn't want to get involved. Ivy liked Eric Daniels and was impatient with Thia when she complained about him. Ivy thought Thia's behavior last night had been crass, and she was afraid she would say that out loud. Which would make her not only a coward and a fraud but a bad and judgmental friend as well.

The light turned green and Ivy made the turn onto Route 9. A moment later she turned into Philipse Manor and caught sight of the river. She paused at the hill on Kelbourne Road. There were no cars in sight, and she allowed herself to watch the silver and white foam under a metallic sky. The mild weather was ending and a cold front was coming in. Ivy felt it in her bones as she drove toward home.

When Ivy pulled into her driveway moments later, she had exactly enough time to unload the groceries, start dinner, switch over the last of the laundry, fold and put away the current load in the dryer, meet the bus, and get to Benjamin's basketball game. Ivy had bought all the ingredients for a beef stew, perfect for the impending weather. She looked forward to the mundane task of cooking, the vibrancy of the carrots against the cutting board, the scent of sizzling beef. She would play Edvard Grieg's Holberg Suite, Opus 4, to liven up the cheerless gray afternoon and lift her spirits. She wanted, more than anything, a couple of hours to be alone in her house, away from other people and the burden of fixing them — a trait she knew people desired from her and despised her for.

Ivy wrestled the last of the groceries into the garage and was about to close the doors when she looked outside and saw her neighbor sitting on the ground at the end of the driveway, sobbing. With a hint of shame, Ivy wondered if it would be possible to close the garage doors and go back into the kitchen to finish unloading the groceries without being noticed. She could pretend she'd never seen her. Even as she imagined going back inside, pressing the play button and filling the kitchen with music, unloading the groceries and beginning the stew, she was walking down the driveway, resting her hand gently on her neighbor's shoulder, then helping her up.

The woman leaned into Ivy. She was four or five inches shorter than Ivy and frail. Ivy placed an arm around her shoulders and consoled her while she cried. After a while the woman took a breath and said, "I can't face going home without my little sweetie."

"Come in, I'll make tea." Ivy guided her into the kitchen, settled her at the table, filled the kettle, and ignited the flame to bring it to a boil. She looked at her neighbor sitting with her hands folded in her lap. The sobbing had dissipated to a slight hiccup; pale winter light from the kitchen window made a perfect square in the center of the table. Ivy placed a tiny pitcher of milk and a bowl of sugar in the light and waited for the kettle to boil.

CHAPTER FOURTEEN
THE BEGINNING AND END OF A SESSION WITH DR. MELANIE SCHAEFFER

Chloe sat across from Dr. Schaeffer or "Melanie". Chloe was uncomfortable addressing her by her first name and solved that problem by never calling her anything. In her mind, she referred to her as "my therapist." Sometimes when she was in a sarcastic mood, she thought of her as Mel.

Mel, as Chloe was thinking of her that moment, was tilting her head and listening hard. Chloe registered it with a bite of cynicism, but it worked on her in spite of herself.

"I just," Chloe found herself saying, "want things to go back to normal."

"Why can't they?"

Chloe felt the heat of frustration build up inside of her. "Because."

"Because?" Head tilt. Concerned face.

Chloe closed her eyes and tried not to remember what life was like before.

"Chloe?"

"Because it can't!" With that she refused to say another word. And she hoped Mel was frustrated as fuck.

CHAPTER FIFTEEN
Snow Day

As it turned out, Thia didn't stop going to the gym. She didn't switch workout times, or days, and consequently bumped right into gym guy. Figuratively that is. They both stopped short in the middle of the narrow corridor between elliptical machines, so close to one another that the heat emanating from him burned her and she had to crane her neck up to see his eyes. Deep blue. Lines forming as he smiled at her. Four heartbeats went by. Thia watched the laughter in his eyes drain and desire seep in. She felt a corresponding pull inside her, a sensation across her skin. As though he was touching her. He wasn't. He was just looking at her. She watched him watching her. He saw the difficulty she had swallowing, the blush creeping from the top of her workout tank along her throat and cheeks.

His gaze sharpened, his lip lifted on the right side. "So, you girls were having a fun night out."

Thia leaned back, "My friend Fiona asked about you."

"Yeah? What did she want to know?"

Thia shrugged, "Who you are."

"What did you say?"

"That you work out a lot."

He grinned. "I do."

"Are you a fireman?"

"Nope."

"Cop."

He shook his head and laughed.

"Hmmm. Military?"

"No."

"Doctor?"

"Do I look like a doctor?"

"Not sure what a doctor is supposed to look like. I can't think of any other jobs that have the kind of hours that would let you be at the gym every day."

"How sexist."

"What? Why?"

"Well what do you do?"

"Dental hygienist."

"So maybe I'm a dental hygienist. And I'm *not* at the gym every day."

Thia narrowed her eyes at him. "So, what *do* you do?"

"Retired."

A flash of disappointment went through her. He laughed again. "It's not a euphemism for laid off if that's what you're thinking."

"I wasn't." She was.

He shrugged. "Sold my business. So…"

"What was it?"

"Boring stuff. Investments."

"Fiona's a school librarian."

"Ok."

"School librarians and hot retired guys make a good couple."

"You think I'm hot?"

Thia wished she had a bottle of Drano to drink and kill herself with. "Fiona thought you were hot."

"So, you *don't* think I'm hot?"

"Doesn't matter what I think."

"Does to me."

"Well. I think you're hot enough to go out with Fiona."

"What if I want to go out with you?"

Thia wiggled her hand. "Married."

"Happily?"

"Very."

He leaned closer so that his lips brushed her cheek, then her ear. He whispered, "You don't act like a very happily married woman."

"What's that supposed to mean?" Thia backed away but his lips followed.

"I don't think Fiona's the one that's interested."

"I've gotta go." She tried to leave but found herself trapped by the machine behind her. Suddenly she became aware of the two women a few machines away, watching them, openly curious, the guy lifting weights nearby, smirking at her. Could he have heard their conversation? Was there something in her body language giving her away? Thia felt her throat closing, the air thickening. She wanted to get away but didn't want to pass him.

"Hey." He put his hand gently on her hip. "I'm interested too."

"Get. Your. Hand. Off. Me."

He lifted his hand away and stepped back, "Easy."

Thia pushed past him and walked across the gym, which seemed the size of a football field, before she escaped into the women's locker room, her face and neck burning. She wouldn't be getting her workout in before the impending snowstorm after all. She should have gone for a jog like she'd originally planned. This was her penance for hoping, without admitting it to herself initially, that she would see gym guy here. Thia's hands trembled as she fumbled with her locker. She managed to open it, grab her coat and handbag, and get out of the gym without making eye contact with anyone. It wasn't until she'd crossed the parking lot and steadied herself against her car that the cold air calmed her and dispelled the burn from her skin.

Fiona had to stay late at work, so by the time she walked home the sky was violet and the light was fading quickly. The temperature had dropped significantly and she shivered despite her quick pace. By the time she arrived on her front porch, she was nearly desperate to get inside.

The house was dark and Fiona went from room to room switching on lamps, her coat still on and scarf wrapped tightly around her. Eventually, when she'd warmed up enough, she hung them carefully on the rack in the front hall and walked back toward the kitchen. Heat hissed from the radiator, and she took a moment to lean into it. Her phone pinged somewhere in the house, and, thinking it might be Chloe, she rushed to answer. It was a message from the school. The district's email declared a snow day because of the impending storm. Fiona immediately texted Chloe with hearts and snowflakes, their shared signal, and waited for Chloe's text back. It took a few minutes before the anticipated ping.

Yeah, saw that.

Fiona felt a pit in her stomach but she texted anyway.

Should I come get you to spend the night? Snow day pancakes tomorrow! Smileyface emoticon, Yum emoticon, hearteyes emoticon.

Fiona waited for Chloe's text and when it came, it left a hollowing in her chest: *staying here ttyt*

Fiona made several attempts to text her back but couldn't find anything to write that didn't sound desperate.

Chloe watched the bubbles form and disappear. Then she put the phone down and wondered if the pain of missing her mother would ever lessen. She didn't think it would. So, for now, she would try feeling numb. If that didn't work, she would just make one tiny cut, far up on her leg where no one would see it.

Fiona forced herself to heat a can of tomato soup and eat it. She also opened a lovely bottle of Cote de Rhone she'd been saving for book club. She carried her soup, wine, and her library copy of *Cutting for Stone* over to the living room couch just as the first snow began to fall.

Snow days for Ivy meant many children at her house (payback for all those years as a lawyer-mom making desperate calls to at-home moms for childcare). It meant wet floors, searches for snow pants (for God's sake, she'd think, when we were kids we played in the snow in our dungarees), many rounds of hot chocolate, and (it seemed to Ivy) a ridiculous amount of food preparation followed by a startling short consumption period followed by a long clean up period that led immediately to the next preparation period. It began with French toast at 6AM (their nanny had started that tradition twelve years ago and somehow Ivy had been guilted into keeping it). Ivy wondered why the kids were bounding into her room at 6AM on a snow day. Wasn't the point of a snow day to sleep in? Even Ben woke up early despite her having to shout his name up the stairs every school morning in order to rouse him. She could understand why Fiona enjoyed snow days — it was a day off, and Chloe had the appetite of a bird and made the exact same food choices as her mother. She thought about Alecia who loved snow days. Her house was like living in a snow globe of perfection. Ivy imagined Alecia and Hannah reading side by side; Alecia would be reading *Cutting for Stone* and Hannah would be rereading *Harry Potter*. Like a wind-up toy, Ivy imagined Alecia standing up in front of the bank of windows, the snow globe shakes of snow fluttering around her, crossing to the stove, and melting Belgian chocolate for hot cocoa. No scooping of processed sugary concoctions out of a pale blue cardboard package the way Ivy was doing, while her boys and four of their friends wrestled underneath her feet. Thia, Ivy knew, was in the hate-snow-days-camp. She said they made her want to impale herself on a butter knife.

It was days like this that Ivy questioned her decision to leave her career, and it made her feel like a bad person. The prior year, in an effort to strike some kind of balance, Ivy took on pro bono work. She completed two cases, each of which were far more emotionally consuming than her job had been, both of which left her in the same position of having to scramble for rides for her boys, find coverage while she had to be in court when her youngest son had a terrible flu, and left her drained and depressed when they were over.

The first was a sexual harassment case. Amanda Knowles was an associate at a large white-shoe law firm, which was a competitor of Ivy's former firm. Amanda worked directly for a highly regarded colleague of Ivy's, a man named Kevin Chilton. Ivy admired Kevin; he was professional, courteous, and known for eloquent arguments in court. His mind was a steel trap, and Ivy, who was a quick thinker with a near photographic memory, was at times in awe of his ability to reason and recall obscure precedents. Ivy knew the precedents were well researched, but there was a genius to having known to research it. *That* as it turns out was thanks to the supreme talent and preparedness of Amanda Knowles.

In determining a sexual harassment suit, the physical attractiveness of either party should be inconsequential. Yet as in every other facet of society it was of utmost consequence. Amanda Knowles did not fit the mainstream ideal of attractiveness. It wasn't that she was unattractive in any way she was just completely non-descript. Five foot three, 128 pounds, medium brown hair, medium brown eyes, a snub nose, thin lips, tiny almost baby sized teeth (which were probably her most distinguishing feature). She was completely unadorned, no make-up (Ivy didn't even think she wore moisturizer or lip balm), no jewelry, and she favored well-cut A-Line skirt suits in navy or charcoal, and crisp white button downs. She wore conservative work shoes and despite her somewhat short stature, had a stride as long and as fluid as any man including her boss Kevin. Kevin however, looked like an Adonis. Six feet four, well built, (Ivy envied his discipline — he hit the gym every morning at 5:00 AM, true he lived in Manhattan so his commute was a three-block walk, and he was unmarried and childless — but still), had bright green eyes that when they landed on you made you feel like you were the only person in the room, a wide gregarious smile, and the propensity to call everyone Pal, so it made you like him. The problem Ivy had from the very beginning of the case was one of perception. Why would Kevin Chilton sexually harass a plain-Jane like Amanda Knowles? Kevin was a serial monogamist. He dated super models, actresses, and socialites. And anyway, everyone knew Amanda was a lesbian (she wasn't, not that it had an ounce of relevance or any bearing on *anything,* but this was the stupidity Ivy was dealing with).

In addition, the harassment charges seemed nebulous to many. Amanda and Kevin worked long late hours together. They often wound up eating at the conference table; sometimes Amanda (who lived far out in Sheepshead Bay Brooklyn) even wound up napping on the hard leather couch in the conference room before ubering home at 2:00 AM. They had a professional relationship, and no one had ever seen a flirtatious moment between them. These were all facts that Amanda herself couldn't deny. They were true. And had as much bearing on what happened as the way she looked or what her sexual orientation was. Because, as it turns out, sexual harassment isn't logical and it has nothing to do with anyone else's perception. And because it was a he said/she said, it did come down to which person you believed, and it seemed Ivy was the only one who believed Amanda, which is why she took the case pro bono.

Amanda stated that for most of their working relationship Kevin had been nothing but professional. There were however, two incidents that occurred in the past month that changed their working relationship forever and rendered the work environment a tenuous one for Amanda.

The first incident occurred one night when Kevin and Amanda split a taxi from Tavern on the Green where they had been entertaining an out of town client. The plan was to drop Kevin at home and then Amanda would go directly to Brooklyn. The clients also happened to be good friends of Kevin's and therefore he was more at ease and quite liberal in serving himself wine. In fact, it was the first time Amanda had ever seen Kevin inebriated at all, whether with a client or just with colleagues from the firm. She'd never seen him drink more than two glasses of wine.

Part of the reason Amanda wanted to share a cab with Kevin was to make certain he arrived safely at home. When they pulled up in front of his building, Amanda thought she would just hand him off to the doorman, who dutifully came out as soon as they pulled up. Kevin however, wasn't ready to leave the cab he leaned over Amanda and kissed her on her mouth. Startled and uncomfortable she froze. Which he may have mistaken for permission and suddenly his hands were all over her, on her breast, behind her neck pulling her closer, at her hip, and then an attempt to reach under her skirt. It was so quick, she barely had time to register what was happening. When she was able to move, she pushed him off and said, "You need to go. Now."

Kevin grinned his lopsided grin that made so many women swoon and said, "Come with me."

"You're drunk. You need to go."

Kevin stuck his lower lip out in what some may have found to be an endearing little boy pout and said. "Manda's no fun."

"Go. Now." She pushed him, not gently but not aggressively. He laughed and tried to kiss her again. This time she got out of the other side of the cab, into traffic, nearly got sideswiped, and left him to pay the driver and deal with doorman.

Amanda had no problem finding another taxi and went home telling herself he was drunk, it was a fuck-up, nobody's perfect, and to get over it. The next morning, she showed up at work and acted as though nothing had happened. Kevin was his usual good humored, professional, and courteous self. He made no mention of it, and Amanda wavered between wondering if he really didn't remember, or if she had in fact imagined the whole thing. Amanda had a tremendous amount of shame around the incident, not because of anything she had done, for the most part she thought she'd handled things okay, but for the thoughts she'd had at one time. Because the truth was, when she'd first started working for Kevin, she had found him attractive. Sometimes, when they were working, she even caught herself wondering what it would be like to kiss him, if his lips were as soft as they looked. She imagined him leaning across the table and doing exactly that, kissing her. She imagined him to be gentle, yet commanding, the stuff of romance novels and soap operas. But it was a short period and after working with him for a while, the crush began to dissipate and soon she couldn't muster a romantic thought about him. And even if she had, the drunken lunge and grope in the back of the cab with the driver and doorman watching was the stuff of nightmares, not daydreams. As practical and logical as Amanda was, she couldn't help wondering if somehow Kevin had intuited those long-ago fantasies of hers and had decided to carry one out because of something she had said, done, or thought.

Two weeks went by and while Amanda hadn't been able to forget about the incident, she kept it in a locked corner of her mind. So much so that during their next extended day-to-late-night work sessions, Amanda had forgotten to have her guard up or feel awkward. Consequently, when she looked up to find Kevin staring at her with an intent gaze and a lopsided smile, she automatically smiled back. This time, Kevin did exactly what she'd longed for him to do all those years ago when she'd first started working with him, he leaned over, slid his hand behind her head, cupped the nape of her neck and leaned in. Although surprised, she maintained her composure and pulled away while pushing him. He looked hurt.

"Don't be like that, Manda."

"Don't you be like that."

He grinned, "Okay, a little hard-to-get. I can get behind that."

"Those were his exact words." Amanda said when she recounted the story for Ivy, "And he had the nerve to waggle his eyebrows at me."

Amanda said she told him to knock it off, made an excuse that she had an appointment (it was 9:30 at night and implausible but she didn't know what else to say), and left. Kevin's account was that they were hard at work when Amanda suddenly remembered an appointment she was late for and left promptly. Kevin said she was a diligent hard worker and although it was uncharacteristic of her to leave in the middle of a project, he understood and said he'd see her the next day. He was baffled and confused by her accusations, said that neither incident ever occurred, and quite frankly couldn't even think of anything inappropriate between them. Ivy saw all the "tells" of a lie. The way he looked her straight in the eye during the deposition for a full three seconds but then bounced his gaze to the corner of the room, and the overly sincere tone he used when expressing his concern for Amanda. He remonstrated shock and disbelief that Amanda, his trusted colleague, could make such allegations and questioned her mental stability. The idea that she would just blatantly lie for financial gain or attention seemed so out of character for her, that the only thing he could imagine is that she'd had some sort of delusional episode.

Everyone, including the support staff and all of the women Amanda worked with believed Kevin. The one time she bumped into him during the case (on the street no less) he looked at her kindly and said with what seemed real sincerity but what she now read as complete bullshit), "How are you feeling, Amanda?" As though the entire thing was an episode of illness on her part.

Every time Amanda thought of that she'd get a churning in her stomach and a flush of heat culminating in sweaty palms and a rapid heartbeat. She'd wish for the thousandth time that she'd had some sort of pointed response, something to jar him or put him in his place. But she'd merely glared at him and kept walking.

Ivy and Amanda never went to trial. The firm offered a settlement, which Amanda rejected. Instead, she collected the severance she deserved, received a stellar review without mention of the charges, and went to work for Ivy's old boss. Amanda worried that the scandal and story would follow her (which it did), but she was good at her job and was on a partner track. Amanda learned to ignore the side-eyes and nudges, the whispered "as ifs." Ivy had been an attorney long enough to know that the truth did not always prevail. That blind justice meant that he said/she said cases were nearly impossible to win for the she, so while Ivy couldn't really say the outcome surprised her, she wasn't sorry she'd taken the case. If only to show Amanda that she believed her and that her story mattered, even if the resolution was that it didn't.

Ivy still had lunch with Amanda on a semi-regular basis (once every two or three months). They rarely even talked about the case anymore — there was always something else to catch up on or discuss. But it was always there between them. Ivy hoped it made Amanda feel less alone, but she wasn't sure it did.

The other pro bono case Ivy took was an environmental suit by a local Hudson River protection agency. One of the river towns was beginning a water development project with severe environmental impact. Ivy was successful in getting the town to adhere to the recommendations of the agency and was instrumental in building a relationship with the village board and the agency. Ivy insisted it was largely due to the fact that the village board was a newly elected (and receptive one), but she received much of the credit and was asked to join the agency as a board member. Ivy, in fact, had a tremendous amount of reading to do that day for an upcoming project they were working on and wondered if she could just take all the food in the house, leave it on the counter, and lock herself away in the study. She knew she'd have an unholy mess to clean up later, but the tradeoff seemed worth it. She felt her spirits lighten at the thought of her study, a full floor away from the noise and mess and mindless demands of a snow day. With new resolve, Ivy made a fruit salad, a thermos filled with (powdered) hot chocolate, a host of sandwiches, and took out paper hot-cups, napkins, and little plates (all left over from a summer BBQ at the beach which assuaged her environmental guilt). Surveying her efforts, she shouted above the wrestling and grunting of the six boys, pointed to the counter, admonished them to clean up after themselves, then pointed upstairs before backing out of the room and escaping to the relative peace of her office and the documents waiting for her there.

Ivy's earlier ruminations about the snow day at Alecia's house were not far off. There was snow globe perfection to the scene. The bank of floor to ceiling windows on one wall coupled with the French doors on the adjoining wall and the large picture window across the room did have a snow globe effect. The fact that Alecia's house was at the top of a hill with only the bare reaching branches of the tree tops visible behind a flurry of snow added to the effect. Everywhere else the storm seemed a fury of wet driving slush against the windows and ground, but here in the seeming stillness of the room the storm seemed slower, the flakes articulated, the wind silent.

Alecia and Hannah were indeed sitting in front of a roaring fire (albeit gas powered) in a pool of golden lamplight to brighten the stark morning. Alecia was indeed reading *Cutting for Stone,* but Hannah was not rereading *Harry Potter.* She was in fact sitting at the base of the plush sofa, the white flokati rug soft beneath her, her left elbow leaning on the coffee table, a mason jar of colored pencils at the ready as she worked on an intricate design from the "sophisticated adult coloring book" her mother had given to her for Christmas. The theme was woodland fairies, and Hannah seemed immersed in the vibrant colors of the world she had created.

Alecia did not, in fact, move with the precision and robotic rhythm of a wind-up toy to make Belgian hot chocolate. She had already made a tray and placed it a few inches from Hannah's colored pencils, like a composite from a still life. The tray was replete with a chocolate pot, mugs, and a plate of tiny almond croissants. Alecia was the most relaxed she'd been in weeks. She sighed contentedly and said to Hannah, "Sometimes I marvel at how perfect life can be."

If Ivy had been watching the tableau inside a snow globe, it is unlikely she would have seen the look in Hannah's eyes when her mother said that. The laser focus that if it manifested itself into a physical object would have been as sharp as a surgeon's scalpel, with a gleam as bright and menacing as any sharp instrument reflected in the powerful light of an operating room.

If Ivy had been watching the snow globe scene unfold, she would have seen Hannah lay her pencil gently on the pages, a woodland fairy's hair only partially colored the softest lavender, a compliment to the pale green of gossamer wings. She would have seen Hannah rise gracefully from the flokati rug, her athleticism and youth making it unnecessary for her to use her arms or the table as a means to propel herself upright. She merely stood, appearing almost to glide vertically. It only took her two strides, to cross the short distance to her mother's seat. From outside the globe, Ivy may have thought Hannah was tenderly reaching down to kiss her mother's cheek, or give her a spontaneous hug. Not typical behavior for Hannah but possibly brought on by the warmth and happiness of a well enjoyed snow day, or the dopamine flush of hot chocolate and sweet buttery almond croissant. What was visible was the way Hannah bent over her mother, her hands gently on her mother's shoulders, not needed so much for balance on Hannah's part, but a way to make sure her mother didn't pull away. It appeared to be an embrace, possibly a kiss. It wasn't. It was a whisper, a whisper that would change everything.

***

Ivy knew that Thia usually detested snow days. This time however, she was relieved. She welcomed the idea that she wouldn't have to leave the house and see anyone. Even trapped with the Rugrats was preferable to facing the world. Lila was in full on "Angelica Rugrat" mode, and Thia wasn't convinced they would both make it out alive by the end of the day. So she decided to give in to her maternal instinct of keeping her child alive and herself out of jail by announcing to all of them that any fighting by anyone no matter who started it would result in an entire day's punishment of cleaning out their closets and giving their excess of toys to children who deserved them (Thia had once actually implemented this brand of punishment and had been able to threaten it effectively ever since).

She promised them a frozen pizza at noon if they left her alone to read her book club selection for the next hour and a half. She relegated them to the playroom and said they could watch anything with a G rating and could leave the room only to use the bathroom or get a drink of water — and only if they were on the verge of dehydration or pants wetting.

Thia settled herself in the living room with a mug of overly sweetened Lipton tea and began to read, losing herself immediately in the world of *Cutting for Stone*.

During the night, Fiona woke up on the couch with a sore neck and a dull headache from drinking three quarters of the bottle of wine. Her book had slipped onto the floor and she saw with regret that the corner was mangled. The storm was still raging, the wind howled, and Fiona wasn't sure if the window glass rattled from the constant onslaught of weather, or if the 2:00 AM train had just passed.

She carried the remnants of dinner (an empty soup bowl and spoon, and the wine glass with dregs clogging the bottom) into the kitchen and placed them into the sink without bothering to even rinse them. Going back into the living room, she compulsively straightened the couch cushions, retrieved her book (doing the best she could to smooth the damaged corner), and shuffled into her bedroom. She brushed her teeth and splashed water on her face, then decided to take a quick shower hoping it would loosen her stiff muscles and warm her up. By the time she got into bed she was wide-awake, so she opened *Cutting for Stone* and immersed herself in the world of the novel while the storm raged around her.

Hours passed and day broke without Fiona noticing. At 6:00 AM, Fiona's eyes grew heavy, she turned over to her side and placed the book face down in the center of the bed, thinking she'd just close her eyes for a few minutes. She saw the earthy colors she associated with Ethiopia behind her lids, muted reds, deep yellows the color of a sunflower petal, bright blues, and dark greens, before she fell into a deep and dreamless sleep.

She woke hours later, momentarily disoriented but not at all tired. She was tiny bit dismayed to see that it was a quarter past ten in the morning but also realized that she had the luxury of no schedule to keep. She sent a quick text to Chloe. *Morning, Sunshine. How's your snow day?* She watched for a few moments hoping to see the return bubbles, but it sat delivered and unread. Deciding to make the most of her freedom, Fiona went into the kitchen, brewed coffee, pulled a raisin bagel from the freezer, toasted it, and lathered on cream cheese. Then taking her breakfast back to her room, she piled her pillows against the headboard and climbed back into her bed to read, easing away her loneliness with the lilt of language and someone else's story.

Thia did indeed have a full hour and a half of uninterrupted reading time before the children came clamoring in saying that the storm had slowed and they wanted to go sledding.

Reluctantly, she marked her place in the book and told them to dress and she'd take them to Rockwood. Before getting up to supervise the bundling of the kids, she sent a quick group text to the book club. *Loving this book, good pick, A.*

Ivy texted back quickly, *Glad to hear, haven't gotten into it yet.*

Fiona was right behind her *right? Loving it! Can't wait to discuss.*

Thia waited expectantly for Alecia's reply and found herself disappointed when nothing came.

Fiona also noted that there was no text from Alecia. How unlike her, Fiona thought. Maybe she was reading far from her phone or baking something elaborate with Hannah. Fiona felt a physical pain beneath her left breast, right where her heart beat. Perhaps it was Abraham Verghese's vivid description of the human body and how it functioned, causing her to imagine a rending of her own rubbery heart muscle. She checked her text history with Chloe only to see her last text still hovering there unread and shimmering with need. She wished she could delete it and settled instead for opening her book and picking up where she left off.

CHAPTER SIXTEEN
THE AFTERMATH

The storm left Westchester County with a foot of snow, some of which began to melt then refreeze, leaving hazardous conditions everywhere. By Monday, the magic had worn off, and neighbors were no longer waving cheerily to one another. Instead, they were bundled up with their heads down, busy digging out. The snow collected into mountains of filth along the curbs, and morning drop-off at the school was a mess. Fiona saw one of the PTA moms hold her middle finger out of her window for a cool thirty seconds while another PTA mom tailed her, blaring the car horn.

Chloe dragged herself through the halls wondering how she would make it through the day. The pretense of acting normal was wearing on her. It was a form of constant vigilance, and she wasn't sure she could keep it up another second let alone an entire school day. The storm had created a four-day break that allowed her to hibernate, and rather than it being a reprieve that infused her with new energy the way it may have been before, it had debilitated her. All she wanted was to go home to the emptiness of her father's house and lie in her bed, in what had once been an unfamiliar room, and now felt like the only safe place in the world.

Chloe knew she was lucky. She had friends who slept on pullout couches because a family of four crammed into a one-bedroom apartment. One of Chloe's best friends, Kamila, only had one set of sheets for her bed, and there were times she slept on a bare mattress if her parents weren't able to get to the Laundromat. Both parents worked two jobs with a combination of day and night shifts, and finances were always tight. Kamila's mom was the housekeeper for two grades above them and her mother would come home with bags full of hand-me-downs for Kamila. One day Chloe and Kamila were walking through the halls, and they passed the girl standing with her friends at a locker.

"Hey! Hi," the girl said as they passed. She reached out and touched Kamila's arm. "That looks good on you."

Kamila blushed, smiled, and said thank you.

"Your mom's so nice," the girl continued. "My mom said she's the best housekeeper we've ever had."

Kamila nodded and smiled again. Managed to say thank you but the words came out as a croak, as if the muscles in her throat had petrified, holding her words back.

Chloe and Kamila walked in silence to their next class. Chloe wanted to ask Kamila about it but didn't know what to say. On one hand, she was pissed that the older girl didn't get that she had outed Kamila for wearing hand-me-downs. It wasn't as if they were sisters or close friends sharing clothes. On the other hand, Chloe could tell the girl thought she was just being nice by paying a compliment to a younger kid. In the hierarchy of high school, a junior even noticing a freshman was a big deal. Chloe looked at Kamila and tried to gauge how she felt about it, but Kamila's head was down and she wouldn't make eye contact.

Kamila was the only friend Chloe was really keeping in touch with these days. Primarily because Kamila hadn't given up on her the way the other girls had seemed to. Not that Chloe blamed them. Chloe hadn't heard from Hannah since Thursday night when Hannah had texted her a picture of a spoon in the freezer and inside-out pajamas, a reference to long ago snow day rituals. But then she sent a picture of a half smoked joint hidden under a flowerpot in her bedroom. Chloe laughed — surprised that Hannah was taking a risk by having that in her room. Alecia was not big on privacy and was very big on going through Hannah's things in order to "organize them."

Chloe spent the first snow day of her life without her mother. She had woken up to a few texts from Fiona and sent the minimal response she could get away with. It hurt too much to think about Fiona and their house together, so Chloe did everything she could to block it out. Her father and his wife were able to get to work, and Chloe was happy to be alone. She texted Hannah a picture of them driving out into the storm then a pic of McCauley Culkin clasping his face and screaming. Another reference to their childhood, but Hannah didn't text back, and Chloe was relieved that she could let go of any pretense at caring about this snow day as anything other than an excuse to lock herself away from everyone and everything.

Later in the day Hannah posted on finsta, pretending to have oral sex with a cucumber. Kids did stuff like that all the time on finsta, but there was something about the way Hannah was looking at the camera, the knowledge in her eyes, that frightened Chloe and made her think it was more than Hannah just trying to shock people. After that, Chloe turned her phone off and reread *Harry Potter and the Goblet of Fire*, her favorite in the series. She checked her text messages late at night and was relieved to see nothing from Hannah. There was a long chain of group texts from her friends, which Chloe ignored. She texted Kamila away from the group chat, and they arranged to meet third period. Chloe wondered if she'd even be able to last that long.

Thia found herself playing catch up for the entire week following the snowstorm. She wasn't alone in that feeling. Exams had to be made up, commuters seemed to be packing onto earlier and earlier trains, traffic was more congested and volatile than ever, the weather was unseasonably warm one day with nasty raging winds the next, leaving people in a loop of hope and frustration. Thia was slammed at work because of all the rescheduling, and one patient had actually bitten her that morning as she was removing the bite block. The skin didn't break, but her finger was black and blue and throbbing. Thia cleaned the affected area, swallowed two ibuprofens, and gave thanks that at least it was Friday.

She'd been so irritable last night that Eric looked at her like she was a she-devil from his nightmares and said, "I'm taking you out to dinner tomorrow night. I'll get the babysitter and make the reservation."

Thia hadn't even been able to muster the grace to say thank you, or agree, or just accept it. Instead she said, "I'll believe it when I see it."

It wasn't even one of her smart-ass comments that would make him laugh. Instead he'd looked hurt, and Thia hated herself for being mean. Then she hated him for making her feel mean.

She knew she was unreasonable and on edge and couldn't find a way to shake herself out of it. And while she was looking forward to getting away from the house and kids for a night, she was nervous about being alone with Eric. Having to make conversation. Even the idea of putting on make-up and dressing in something other than scrubs seemed like too much effort.

By the time her last patient left and she'd cleaned up, it was time to pick the kids up from school. She was about to leave when a text came in. It was Eric.

Picking up kids and driving them to my folks for a sleepover. Will pick you up at 6:00 for our date. xx

Thia smiled for the first time in days and texted back. *Wow u must really be worried. This lunatic thing is working out well for me.*

Eric picked her up as promised. Thia made an effort and wore a pair of black jeans and an emerald green sweater that Eric had bought her for Christmas. They went to Mint on Main Street in Tarrytown, which was her favorite restaurant. Even on a drab winter evening, she walked in and felt transported to summertime in another country, maybe Southern Spain or Morocco. She'd never traveled anywhere outside of the Unites States, didn't even own a passport, but she could imagine. The thought of the Moroccan chicken and a full-bodied, glass of spicy red wine was enough to lift Thia out of the spiral of anger she'd been in for days.

Two glasses and several appetizers into the dinner, Thia found herself telling Eric about the guy at the gym. She told him about the rounds of drinks at book club, about the way she'd invited them over and pushed him on Fiona even though Fiona clearly wasn't interested. About Alecia's stink eye and Ivy's detachment. How it was all her, and that she found the attention exhilarating, how flattered she was, how harmless it seemed, until it wasn't.

Thia checked in on Eric as she spoke. The wine had loosened her tongue, but her brain seemed hyper focused. She saw his pupils contract, the blue of his eyes deepened, his gaze narrowed as she recounted the moment in the gym.

"I'm sorry. I don't want to make you angry — I'm telling you this because I felt I had to."

Eric was silent. His hands had stilled. His wine was untouched. The waiter brought their plates over. Possibly sensing the tension in Eric, he set them down gently and melted away without his usual explanation of the food.

"What's his name?"

"Doug something."

"You don't know his name?"

"I don't actually. I could find out. But what's the point?"

"Did he put his hands on you?"

"No." She thought of his hand on her hip, the way his lips brushed her cheek and ear when he leaned in. She watched to see if Eric relaxed with that information, if he believed her. She couldn't tell.

"Are you mad at me?"

He shook his head. "I don't like it, but I'm glad you told me. I knew something was bothering you."

"I've been such a bitch."

"You haven't seemed yourself."

"I shouldn't have let those guys come over to the table. I know better."

"If a guy sends a woman he doesn't know a drink, he's trying to get over on her."

"Have you ever sent a woman a drink?"

"Nah. Not my style."

Thia laughed because it was true. But Eric grew serious, "Thia, is that what attracted you to those guys? That they're different from me?"

She thought about it. "Maybe. But to be clear, I didn't find either of them attractive. I think — I just liked the flirtation. And yes, maybe it was appealing because I saw a glimpse of another way of life."

"A different life than the one we have?"

"It doesn't mean I want a different one. It just intrigued me."

"The money?"

Thia hesitated. It wasn't something she wanted to be true. "Yes."

And there it was. Out on the table. She had a family she loved, a job she liked (aside from the occasional human bite), and a house she could only have dreamed of as a little girl. Yet she felt overworked, overwhelmed, exhausted, and angry. She compared herself to her book club friends and felt her house was shabby next to theirs, her wardrobe lacking, her financial concerns constricting. She thought of that old Sesame Street song she'd sang along to as a child, *one of these things is not like the others.* She felt ugly and greedy and ungrateful.

Eric was looking at her intently. "I feel like that too. Like rats on a wheel trying to keep our heads above water."

"Why didn't you ever say anything?"

He shrugged. "I didn't want to rock the boat. I like our friends and our neighborhood and the fact that our kids can run around outside. I don't want to move back to Queens, I don't want a longer commute, my business is here, so...."

"Do women hit on you?"

"I don't know. Maybe. I just ignore it. It's easier for guys. Women aren't usually as aggressive."

"Ha. You haven't seen the moms gone wild then."

"Only when they're in a pack, and I can usually avoid that."

Thia laughed. "You don't think I'm an ungrateful whore?"

"Don't even say that."

Thia looked down at her glass of wine. She believed Eric. He didn't think she was a whore. Intellectually, she didn't even believe in the concept of a whore. But she also knew that her mother's spell had worn off. The magic didn't hold. And deep down she felt as broken, sullied, and damaged as a girl could feel.

Ivy forgot to lock the kitchen door after James took the boys to basketball. Which is why, just as she was about to take her first sip of her second cup of coffee and go onto her deck for her daily cigarette, Sally-Ann came bursting through the kitchen. The deck was at the back of the house and off her bedroom. Sally-Ann wouldn't have seen her. There were many mornings Ivy sat looking at the river behind her house, listening to the flap of Sally-Ann's flip-flops at the side door, the incessant ringing of the bell. But today Ivy was late, or Sally-Ann was early, and she barged into the kitchen before Ivy could make her escape.

Ivy knew her former colleagues would find it hilarious that she was so powerless against her neighbor. Ivy, who could command a courtroom, a conference of 1,000 listeners, or the most brutal deposition, cowed in the face of such poor manners and a strong will.

"HA!" Sally-Ann barked as she let herself in, "Finally! This is the time I gotta come over if I want to catch you."

Ivy put her coffee cup down and looked directly at Sally-Ann. "No, it isn't. It's too early. You can't come over this early."

Sally-Ann didn't miss a beat, "Well, I need to catch you before you leave, and I go to Zumba at 9:00 — so I can't wait much longer."

"What do you need Sally-Ann?"

"I need you to file a restraining order on the old lady who ruined my life by letting her dog run underneath my car."

"I'm not doing that."

"She gives me dirty looks every time I pass her house!"

"It's been a while since I've practiced, Sally-Ann, but I'm pretty sure they don't issue restraining orders for dirty looks."

"But she's ruining my life!"

"How?"

"By making me feel guilty when it was her fault."

"Oh, for heaven's sake, come here." Ivy led Sally-Ann to the kitchen table and sat her down.

"Wait! Let me pour a cup of coffee."

"No coffee. Just listen." Ivy watched as Sally-Ann's mouth rounded and her eyebrows shot up. Ivy waited until Sally-Ann's features settled and their eyes met. "What happened was a terrible accident. It's called an accident because it wasn't purposeful. She did not purposefully try to ruin your life and you did not purposely try to kill her dog. It happened and it's terrible. It's upsetting for you and heartbreaking for her."

Sally-Ann nodded.

"You need to stop trying to fix this by making yourself right and her wrong. Right and wrong don't apply here. Got it?"

Sally-Ann nodded again. And whispered, "So what do I do?"

"You write her a letter. You tell her how terribly sorry you are about her dog. You tell her you know how much her dog meant to her and you're sorry, you don't make excuses, don't blame her. You just say you're sorry because that's the truth. You are sorry."

Sally-Ann began to cry. "I really am."

"I know."

"What if she won't forgive me?"

"That's up to her."

"What will I do if she won't?"

"You'll have to live with that."

"But..."

"That's the way it works. You are sorry. You tell her that. If she forgives you or doesn't forgive you, your work is done. You find a way to move on."

Sally-Ann gulped and sniffed and cried harder. Ivy got up, poured a glass of water, and tore off a paper towel and placed them in front of Sally-Ann.

Sally-Ann drank and blotted her face. "It's that easy?"

"There's nothing easy about it. But it is that simple."

"I don't know if I can."

Ivy got up again and rummaged around in her kitchen desk drawer. She found the folder of cards and handed it to Sally-Ann. "Pick one."

Sally-Ann began to sift through the pile placing the wedding, birthday, and baby shower cards aside until she found two sympathy cards. She hovered over them, her eyes darting back and forth. She selected the white one with a yellow bird that said *with deepest sympathy*. Ivy handed her a pen.

With a shaky hand Sally-Ann wrote, *Dear Mrs. Henderson, I am so sorry I killed your dog. Muffin was a really sweet dog and I know you loved him. I will regret it every day of my life. Sincerely, Sally-Ann.*

She showed it to Ivy who nodded. Sally-Ann sealed the card. "Should I drop it off now?"

"Yes."

"Will you come with me?"

"No. But I'll watch from my window and if anything happens I'll come out."

"Ok."

Ivy hugged her. "Go. And have a good Zumba class."

"Thanks."

Ivy walked her to the kitchen door. Sally-Ann turned around before leaving and said, "Ivy?"

"Yes?"

"Can I still come over sometimes?"

"Sure — but after eight."

"Thanks, hon."

Ivy watched Sally-Ann cross the street, stride across to Mrs. Henderson's mailbox, and turn toward the window. Ivy waved and watched Sally-Ann open the box and slide the letter in before pouring her cold coffee down the drain and collecting her Kretek from her hiding place. She shrugged into her heaviest coat, picked up her copy of *Cutting for Stone*, and went upstairs to the deck so she could watch the frozen river and read the final chapter in preparation for book club that night.

Fiona was excited about book club. She welcomed the discussion of the book (there was so much in it!), and she welcomed the company of her friends, the disruption of her loneliness, and the distraction from worrying about her daughter. Her worries about Chloe had become part of the fabric of her day. Woven into the way she saw color, heard notes, the taste of food, the scent of the air. Worry, Fiona discovered, was a sense in and of itself. A seventh sense permeating and overwhelming all the others, any possibility of the sixth sense eradicated, and if there was such a thing as premonition, worry had dulled it leaving only knowledge that there was something ominous and impossible to prevent. Book Club, Fiona hoped, would be an antidote to worry.

Once Fiona tried yoga. It wasn't something Fiona wanted to do, but there was a required staff training called 'Yoga and Mindfulness.' Putting on her game face, Fiona changed into workout clothes and attempted to bend her body into positions named after animals that resulted in all of her colleagues sticking their butts in the air. Fiona, unsurprisingly given her attitude about it, did not take to yoga. Yet there was something the teacher said that stayed with her. During an unfortunate 30 seconds of red-faced sweating while she balanced on the balls of her feet and forearms in a hideous torturous thing called "plank," gulping air and blowing it out through her nose in an inexact approximation of the teacher's instruction, she heard the teacher's voice as if from a distance, slow and calming, like ocean waves from the other side of a window pane: "It's just sensation."

The teacher's words didn't resonate with Fiona at the time because she was too busy thinking 30 seconds was a long fucking time. But later she heard the words again, as if time and space were mere illusions and the teacher's words were hovering in the air waiting for Fiona to hear them. It is just sensation.

Fiona understood the words as knowledge that the pain would pass. It wasn't permanent, and she could transcend it. Simply by focusing on something else, she could choose not to suffer in that moment.

Fiona understood that the defense mechanisms of denial, or disassociation, were useful unless you over-applied them.

Denial and disassociation had their purpose, giving your brain a chance to withstand shock. To find a way to adapt, to switch from the flight/fight part of your brain to the creative part of your brain, to unfreeze your muscles so that you could run or climb or dodge or do whatever you had to in order to survive. She wondered, while she laid out cheese and crackers and grapes and almonds for book club, while she set out wine glasses and water glasses and cocktail napkins and little plates, if that was what had happened to Chloe. If her daughter was in a state of shock, frozen in a moment of time. Fiona just didn't know what moment. Neither she nor Dr. Schaeffer had been able to pinpoint the moment, but she knew there *was* a moment. Not a phenomenon, such as the divorce, or the remarriage, but a moment and an aftermath undiscovered. Fiona hadn't known to look for something until the morning Chloe hadn't gotten out of bed, and Fiona had seen the cuts on her thighs. The problem was she had no idea where the moment occurred, and Chloe wouldn't tell. She insisted that it didn't exist, that there was no precipitating event. It was as if she and Chloe were in a holding pattern and they needed to find a way to land without crashing and burning.

The doorbell rang, startling Fiona, causing her to drop a glass, which shattered on the ground. Fiona scooped up the cat to stop her from sniffing the broken glass and ran to answer the door.

Ivy and Thia came in together bringing the cold with them. Thia handed Fiona a bottle of Cabernet, and Fiona put the struggling cat down to take it. Ivy hung her jacket up and waved a bottle of Prosecco around.

"Let's get this party started."

"Careful, I broke a glass."

Thia laughed. "Off to a rowdy start!"

155

By the time Fiona swept up the remnants of the glass and everyone had drinks in their hands, it was a quarter past the hour.

Thia looked at her watch. "This may be the first time in the history of the world that Alecia is actually late."

Ivy pulled out her phone, "I'll text her."

"Maybe she's driving." Fiona said.

"I'm dying to talk about the book — but we should wait, right?" Ivy asked.

"Yeah," Thia said, "but did you like it?"

"Loved it!" Ivy hugged her book.

"I did too." Fiona said.

"Hmm." Thia said, "The writing was beautiful in some places, and the story was compelling, but…"

"But?" Fiona asked.

"I lost patience with it."

"I'm surprised," Ivy said, "I thought out of all of us you would find it the most interesting."

"I just — I've been in a foul mood, maybe nothing would have held my interest. Or maybe I needed to read something powerful in a different way."

"Like?" Fiona asked.

"Like *The Handmaid's Tale*. Not that it's fair to compare."

"Huh," Ivy said. "I loved it, the language, the story, the use of medicine as metaphor."

Fiona looked at her phone. Alecia was now 30 minutes late. In all the years she'd known Alecia, since the girls were in pre-school, the many play-date drop offs, after school pick-ups, coffee dates, and book club meetings, Alecia had never even been five minutes late. Punctuality was practically an illness with her. Fiona knew because she lived in constant fear of being late, and Alecia was the one person she was rarely late for. Fiona punched Alecia's number into her phone while

Thia began pouring more wine into the now empty glasses. Ivy placed her hand over her glass, the unlucky designated driver. Fiona checked her phone again, and when she still hadn't received a text from Alecia, searched her contacts, pushed Alecia's number, and listened to it ring. Although they'd decided not to keep discussing the book until Alecia arrived, Ivy was now reading a passage aloud.

"Hey," Fiona said. "I think something's wrong."

Ivy placed the book down. Thia took a sip of her wine.

"Does anyone have Everett's number?"

"No," Ivy said, "but I think James does. I'll text him."

The minutes ticked by while Ivy obtained Everett's number and sent him a text, Thia kept sipping her wine, and Ivy began running down possibilities. A flat tire, a fender bender, no cell service. When Everett didn't reply, Fiona texted Hannah.

Is your mom on her way to book club?

Another fifteen minutes went by without a word from Alecia, Everett, or Hannah. Thia drained her wine glass and reached for the bottle.

"Do you think we should drive over there?" Fiona asked.

"I don't know." Ivy said. "It seems intrusive. She's a grown woman. Maybe they're having a family situation."

Thia snorted, "Like what? Some curtains clashing with a couch?"

Ivy laughed, "You're drunk. Alecia would never make a mistake like that."

"What? Hannah got a B on an exam?" Thia knew her tone was taking an ugly turn but she was annoyed. She'd been looking forward to this discussion, especially because she'd disliked the book. Sometimes it was boring when they all loved a book and gushed over it. Thia glared at them, "Seriously, we're all losing our minds because Miss Perfect blew off a book club?"

"It's just..." Fiona gripped her phone, "It's so unlike her."

"I know what you mean." Ivy said, "But I think we just need to give her some space. If God forbid she's hurt, or there was an accident, bad news travels fast." She looked at her watch. "She's an hour late, we would have heard by now. I think there must be a personal situation, and I don't want to go barging in on her."

"What if we just take a ride over there?" Fiona attempted to keep her voice modulated. She felt an inexplicable hysteria that embarrassed her. "If her car is in the driveway we'll just turn around and leave."

"Seriously?" Thia said. "She blows us off and we're gonna give up book club and chase around after her?"

"Please? I'm worried."

Thia softened at the pleading in Fiona's voice. "Fine. But I am so paid back for last month's debacle after this."

Ivy laughed. "Yeah. Alecia owes you for sure. I'll drive."

The moon was full and bright when the women stepped into the night. The cold air felt good to Thia, whose cheeks were hot from the red wine. Before they even pulled onto the road, Thia switched the radio on. Ivy had it tuned to a 70's funk station and Superstition by Stevie Wonder was playing. Thia sang along at the top of her lungs. Stevie was right, she thought, when you believe in things you don't understand, you do suffer; but Thia believed you also suffered when you tried to understand. Maybe blotting everything out was the only true way to happiness, or if not happiness, a lessening of unhappiness. Superstition she knew was a futile attempt to control the chaos.

Fiona let the music wash over her. The three of them driving up the moonlit road, the wine, worry, and companionship created an almost desperate feeling, reminiscent of the way she'd often felt when she was young, a few years older than Chloe and Hannah, when she and her friends had finally been able to drive and spent half their night in a car. The thrill of uncertainty, the beginning of a Saturday night when anything was possible, and you didn't know if it would be beautiful or terrible.

Ivy wished the car ride was longer. The edge of worry about Alecia dulled by the near certainty that they were over- reacting, and Thia singing Superstition was Carpool Karaoke worthy, but before the song even ended, she'd pulled into the driveway.

"Huh," Fiona said. "No cars. Maybe they're both out? The house is dark."

"Or, the cars could be in the garage. And you wouldn't see lights on in the back of the house from here." Ivy said.

Fiona jumped out, ran to the garage door, and punched in the code Alecia had given her years ago, Hannah's birthday, so easy to remember. She tried the numbers twice more, but the door didn't budge. "Strange…I guess she changed it."

Thia walked up to the door, "This is stupid. I'm ringing the bell."

The three of them stood on the wide front step and listened to the chiming of the bell. The porch light was on a sensor and had come on automatically when they walked up to the porch, making it difficult to see through the panes of glass on either side of the door. Thia pressed the bell and listened to the chimes a second time. Thia pressed it once more and Ivy said, "This is weird."

Fiona ran down the front steps, along the side of the house, and onto the back patio. Ivy and Thia followed her. Moonlight poured over them and into the back of Alecia's house where the locked French doors barred them from the kitchen and family room. What was apparent when they pressed their faces to the doors, hands cupped against the glass, was the gleam of the stainless-steel appliances, a white sheen glowing from the marble counter top, and the emptiness of the space all around it.

Fiona turned and stared at Ivy and Thia. "They're gone."

The air was sultry but fresh this early in the season. The no-see-ums weren't biting yet, although the sun sank into the water hours ago. Alecia watched the texts roll in. Her iPad powered up and all it took was a well-timed touch of her manicured fingertip to keep the screen refreshed and trained on the house in Westchester.

Ten minutes past the time Alecia predicted (she blamed an argument among the women about whether they should drive over or not with Fiona pressing for it, Ivy thinking it was unseemly, and Thia protesting that it would distract them from drinking wine and discussing the book) for the delay. The women wouldn't have been surprised by how accurately Alecia had gauged their conversation and motivations or been offended by her summation. They would love how well they knew one another, which would make the fact that Alecia had moved away under cover of darkness and secrecy an even more bitter pill to swallow.

Alecia's lip lifted in a half smile when Ivy's SUV pulled into the Westchester driveway and Fiona tumbled inelegantly out of the car. She watched the frantic pushing of her alarm code, the second, then third attempt, and wondered if Fiona would have the presence of mind to attempt a different code. Alecia had made it easy for her replacing Hannah's birthday with her own. But Fiona had given up on the garage door and joined Thia on the porch. She watched Thia ring the bell, her impatience telegraphed by the set of her shoulders. Ivy was peering through the glass into the dark empty hall. Then Fiona hightailed it to the back. Alecia pushed a few buttons and went to camera number 3. She watched the shadowy figures of her friends and wondered if she would be able to tell the moment they knew. The answer was yes. She saw it in the slump of Fiona's shoulders, the way she turned her head to Ivy. The surprised way Thia dropped her arms from the glass, the stillness in Ivy. They knew. Alecia looked down and waited for the flurry of texts.

Fiona wanted to speak with Chloe. At 10:00 on a Friday night she was reasonably sure that was possible. Instead of texting Chloe or Bryce, she texted Val. Which under the circumstances, struck all of the women as the appropriate thing to do.

Can we talk?

Val texted back almost immediately, *everything ok?*

Not sure.

They pulled into Fiona's driveway and the phone rang in her hand. Fiona just gave Val the facts. No editorializing, no questions, simply repeated what happened. Then reported a fact that had been in the back of her mind. "Chloe slept there the week before I found the cuts."

Before the women even made it out of the car, Val said, "I think you need to come over, and we need to speak with Chloe."

Val met them at the door. There hadn't even been a discussion whether Thia and Val would accompany Fiona.

They just did. Val led Thia and Ivy to the back of her expansive newly constructed home (not unlike Alecia's, same builder and price point) into the kitchen (similar layout but vastly different design style). They sat at a glossy counter while Fiona went up, knocked on Chloe's door, and forced herself to wait for an answer before opening it.

"Mom!"

Fiona searched Chloe's face surprised to see that her smile seemed genuine. "Hey, Clo. Love what you did with the place."

"Thanks! What are you doing here?"

Fiona sat on the end of the bed where Chloe sprawled surrounded by schoolbooks and scattered papers. "We need to talk."

"What's up?"

"Have you heard from Hannah recently?" Fiona saw the discomfort register on Chloe's face.

"Not since the snow day."

"That was a week ago. Do you typically go a week without texting each other?"

"Not really, but — why do you care?"

"Have you texted her and she's ignored you?"

"Since when do you care about kid drama?"

"I'm not asking if you're fighting — I literally need to know if you've heard from her."

"What's going on?"

"Alecia never came to book club, so we drove over there, and…"

"Mom, tell me!"

"They're gone."

"What do you mean?"

"They've moved — they aren't there."

"Maybe they're on vacation."

"Chloe, the house is empty. They've disappeared."

"That's crazy."

"Did Hannah say anything to you?"

Chloe thought about that day on the roof parking lot at the mall. How Hannah had said she wanted to disappear to someplace beautiful. "No."

"Can I see her last text to you?"

Chloe thought about the picture Hannah had texted of the joint under the flowerpot. Chloe had erased it immediately. She reached for her phone and flipped through her texts until she'd found the one from Hannah. The Home Alone picture, and right above it the backward-pajamas-selfie Hannah had sent, looking like an excited little kid anticipating a snow day. Above it was a picture of the spoon in Alecia's meticulous freezer drawer, nestled between carefully labeled packages of frozen meat.

Fiona flipped through them, "Nothing else, you're sure?"

"See for yourself."

"Chloe. I'm worried. Something isn't right."

Chloe stared at Fiona. Her mother could be hyper focused on her. She and Hannah lamented the plight of only children. But Chloe knew her mother was not overly dramatic; she had common sense and trusted Chloe, more than most moms did. Even taking her to see the therapist, her mother hadn't pried, and she'd let her move in with her dad, even though Chloe knew how much it had hurt. The fact that her mom sounded scared was scaring Chloe.

"Clo, did something happen the night you stayed at Hannah's? Something to do with Everett?"

Chloe felt the sensation again. Of zooming far away, almost as if she'd flown up and against the corner of the ceiling and was watching herself talk to her mother. Her vision was growing blurry and there was a pounding in her head that was quickly becoming a roar. Soon she couldn't hear or see anything. Not even blackness, as if she'd simply stopped being.

"Clo, baby, it's ok."

When Chloe came back into herself it was her hand she felt first. Ice cold between her mother's palms, she felt the warmth, the rush of blood that almost hurt. She left it there, needing the softness of her mother's skin, the pressure of her mother's hands against her own. She realized that tears were pouring down her face. That her body was convulsing with the effort of holding back sobs. She hadn't been out of her body after all. She hadn't gone anywhere. She'd been sitting right there trying not to cry and trying even harder not to remember.

"It's my fault." The words hissed out between her flattened lips, her throat constricting with the effort to hold them back.

"Chloe. Listen to me. Nothing that happened is your fault. No matter what you think. But you need to tell me about it. For Hannah's sake."

Chloe looked up at Fiona. The thought that maybe Hannah needed her help had never occurred to her. Caught in a cyclone of shame, Fiona's plea was an escape from the eye of the storm.

"It was my fault. She was jealous and trying to get back at me."

Of all the things Fiona had prepared herself to hear, this wasn't remotely what she'd expected. Could a middle school crush have been the problem all along? Was Alecia's disappearance nothing more than a move away and their friendship so inconsequential that she'd forgotten to tell them?

Fiona took a deep breath. "Okay. Tell me about it. From the beginning."

Chloe surprised herself by the steadiness of her voice and the calm that spread through her as she began to talk. Once again, she felt that odd distancing feeling. Yet this time, she was far away, watching events take place, rolling through her mind, and simply reporting them, as if they were happening to some other girl in some other place and time.

She'd been excited to stay at Hannah's. There was something comforting about being somewhere she'd been when her parents were still married. All her other friendships made in middle school happened after her parents divorced. Ivy and Thia's homes were also familiar in the same way, but she and Bobby were different with each other since middle school. She felt shy with him in a way she never had when they were children. All her friends at school thought he was cute and teased Chloe about him. It made her see him differently and made herself conscious in a way that confused her. Hannah's home felt familiar, and when she walked in that night, she'd had the sensation that everything was back to being as it was when they were small, except they got to be 8th graders. After the divorce, Chloe did her best to stick with the program her parents had laid out for her. "We're still a family, we always will be. Dad and I will always love you, and we'll always love each other, but instead of being husband and wife, we're going to be co-parents." Chloe told herself that two homes were better than one and she was lucky her parents' divorce was so friendly, unlike Caitlin Jacob's parents who were fighting in court and Caitlin had to speak to her own lawyer to say who she'd rather live with. Chloe had shuddered at the idea of having to take a side against one of her parents, and until her dad remarried, she didn't think she would have to, and then, all the platitudes about them still being a family, and how she'd always be his number one — went right out the window. Her mother could smile that bright fake smile all she wanted. Her new stepmother could act like the cool kid, and her father could profess his love all day, but Chloe wasn't stupid and she'd felt the seismic shift. She also felt like a spoiled brat for wanting her father's attention all to herself. She felt ungrateful for thinking spiteful thoughts about Val and how she reminded her of her English teacher — who always tried to act like one of the kids using the wrong words and quoting stupid song lyrics that no one in her grade listened to. And she felt guilty for thinking her mom was somehow diminished by pretending to be okay with something she clearly wasn't.

That night at Hannah's, Chloe found herself seeking out Everett's attention. He spoke to the girls as if they were adults, unlike Alecia who still treated them like babies. He asked Chloe's opinion about things and seemed to consider her ideas even if they differed from his own. When Alecia excused herself and said she was going to her room to read, all three of them knew from years of experience that she was in for the night. She'd given them the requisite homemade pizza, followed by hand-popped buttered popcorn and hot cocoa and whipped cream Alecia made from scratch. She'd made sure they had access to age appropriate movies, and she'd made up the trundle bed in Hannah's room with new linens, soft pink with blue forget-me-nots scattered everywhere. By nine o'clock, too early to have the girls go to bed at this age, Alecia was relieved to turn them over to Everett and go upstairs to her tangerine walls and sky-blue ceiling, to rest in a bed fit for a princess without a pea. Chloe wondered if she would be able to have a bedroom as magnificent as Alecia's when she grew up — but without having to be as crazy about everything.

When Alecia went upstairs, her steaming mug of chamomile tea in one hand and her copy of *Daisy Miller* in the other, Everett shared a conspiratorial wink with the girls. After enough time had gone by to make sure Alecia wasn't coming back down for anything, he laughed and said, "How about a tea party — but with wine!"

Chloe was shocked, but feigned nonchalance. The tiny sherry glasses he took out seemed harmless and adorable, and it was clear this wasn't the first time Hannah and he had done this. He poured a thick syrupy white wine into each of their glasses and poured himself a normal sized glass of red for himself. Hannah gave Chloe a knowing look, and they all clinked glasses. Everett said, "Santé!" which he told the girls was cheers in French. He had them take a sip. It was sweet and tasted like honey but a little bit sour. He said it was dessert wine and was practically all sugar and no alcohol, which is why they were allowed to have it, but to make it their little secret so "mom wouldn't have a bird." He had them practice the toast again with a French accent, and when they finished their tiny fairy sized glasses, he refilled them, again and again. Soon, although Chloe knew she couldn't be drunk because it was dessert wine, she did feel a strange buzzing in her ears and the world looked wobbly. She wondered if this is what everyone meant when they said buzzed. She giggled at the thought and caught Hannah's sly glance at her. Everett walked over and put his hands on her shoulders. He leaned down and smelled her hair. "Mmm." He murmured and she felt his lips moving against her scalp. "Your hair smells so good. Like apples in sunshine." Chloe was embarrassed. And his hands felt heavy on her shoulders. He moved his thumbs up and down against the column of her throat, gently, making slow circular motions against her skin. It tickled and his hands were

167

warm and dry. It made Chloe feel weird, and she wanted to move, but she didn't want to hurt his feelings. Hannah was watching them with narrowed eyes, the way she did when Chloe talked for a long time and Everett paid attention to her as if she were an adult with interesting ideas. Finally, Hannah got up and pulled Chloe by the arm, "Come on let's go watch that movie."

"The dog movie?" Chloe was excited. Alecia always let them choose a pay-per-view, even the expensive ones she felt too embarrassed to ask for.

"Yep." Hannah pulled Chloe to her feet not at all gently, and Chloe found herself falling. Everett pulled her against him and held her closely to steady her. Chloe straightened up quickly and tried to pull away. She'd felt something stir against her lower back, and froze, too stunned and nauseated to move. Could she have imagined it?

"Come on!" Hannah said, and seemed mad at her.

"Night night, Hannahbanana," Everett said. He was still standing behind Chloe, his hands still resting on her arms, but she'd managed to pull far enough away so their bodies were no longer touching. Chloe tried to go to Hannah, but Everett tightened his grip, "Night night, Chloebalogna." He said, and leaned weirdly around her to kiss her cheek. His lips were dry and hard and almost touched her own. Chloe froze in a moment of panic and disgust. She didn't want to make Hannah mad or hurt Everett's feelings so she told herself it was only a night time kiss like her own dad would give her. As Everett let go of her, she wobbled slightly, then caught her balance and followed Hannah upstairs to her room, which had its own TV.

Hannah smiled at Chloe when they got to her room and Chloe wondered if she'd imagined that she'd been mad at her.

"Got a little buzz on Chloebalogna?"

"I guess. But your dad said it was mostly sugar. Like dessert."

"Yeah. You're a lightweight."

Chloe laughed, "Yeah." But she felt stupid. She busied herself changing into her pajamas while Hannah queued up the movie. "Oh. I thought we were watching the dog one."

"This is better."

"It's R."

Hannah gave her a look. "Don't be a baby."

Chloe had seen the coming attractions for the movie about a guy who kidnapped two young girls and held them captive. He had a bunch of different personalities, and it was the scariest thing she'd ever seen. Her mother would die if she knew they were watching it. But other kids in school had seen it and talked about it all the time. At least now she'd be able to join in on the conversation. "Okay." Chloe said. "Let's watch."

Hannah smiled that sly smile that Chloe loved to be on the receiving end of and pressed play.

The movie was every bit as terrifying as Chloe thought it would be. But Hannah seemed unfazed. "It isn't real, Clo. He's just a good actor."

Chloe nodded and tried to relax her shoulders, tried to appear as nonchalant as Hannah. Then just as the creepy kid transformed into a terrifying adult, Hannah climbed out of her side of the bed. "Be right back."

"Wait!" Chloe almost shouted, "Don't leave!"

Hannah laughed, "Don't be scared Clo, I'll be right back."

"Pause the movie."

"No, it's okay, you can catch me up." Quick as a cat, Hannah was out the door and into the darkness of the hall.

Chloe scrambled for the remote and hit pause, but the scary face froze on the screen and Chloe had the horrible sensation that he would be the one to appear in the doorway. Her whole body was trembling. She squeezed her eyes shut and pulled the covers over her, which was even worse. Her eyes flew open, and she stared at empty space, averting her eyes from the image on the screen. Her breath was coming in shallow gasps. Too afraid to stay where she was but too terrified to move, she willed Hannah to come back. Where could she have gone? Finally, a spasm of fear propelled her out of bed and into the hall away from the menace on the screen. *Breathe*, she told herself, *stop being a baby. It's just a movie. Where the hell did Hannah go? I'm going to kill her when I find her.*

Afraid to call out and wake Alecia, Chloe crept around the third floor. Everett's office was down the hall. It was dark, but Chloe thought she saw the blue light of a computer monitor glowing from the crack where the door was slightly ajar. More terrified of what was behind her than the dark hallway or bothering Everett, Chloe moved toward the door. What she saw made her wish with all her might that she'd stayed and watched the stupid scary movie by herself. Chloe realized with a pulse of horror and shame, when she peered through the crack in the door to Everett's office, that it may very well have been jealousy Hannah had felt toward Chloe. That Chloe's playacting at being an adult, an equal of Everett's, had resulted in Hannah wanting to one up her. Chloe shut her eyes against the memory. She couldn't see it again. And she didn't know how she would ever describe it, but the one thing she could remember was the look of triumph Hannah had on her face, as if she'd won something. Everett's back was to Chloe, she remembered that. Maybe she hadn't seen what she thought she saw, maybe she'd imagined the glow of Hannah's skin in the blue light, the white hand of a ghoul as Everett reached up and drew Hannah's head down to press her lips against his. Yet Chloe knew that was wishful thinking. She'd seen what she saw, and she needed to be brave and tell her mother.

"It's okay, Clo. Whatever it is, you aren't in trouble, and neither is Hannah."

"She was naked." Chloe whispered. "On his lap. And they were kissing."

Chloe lifted her eyes to Fiona's face in time to see her pale, but she also saw her mother steady herself.

"Did he touch you?"

Chloe shook her head. "Not like that — but—"

"But?"

"I could tell he wanted to. And Hannah knew it too. That's why she did that. To stop me from doing it."

"Clo. Listen to me." Fiona waited until Chloe met her eyes. "What you're describing is sexual abuse. And it isn't something that happened the first time you saw it. Abusers work by manipulating and tricking their victims over a period of time. We need to find Hannah. We need to help her."

The day of the snowstorm when Hannah whispered the truth into Alecia's ear, it never occurred to Alecia to doubt her daughter. Nor did she have a sudden realization, as if she'd known or suspected all along. She'd been completely blindsided. Gut punched. She couldn't understand how she'd missed it. How she'd failed to protect her little girl. How she hadn't known about Everett. Looking back, Alecia failed to see the signs even with the 20/20 vision of hindsight. All Alecia could think of was how furiously she'd fought to protect her daughter from the outside world, when all along, the danger was within their own home. Her strife for perfection had been nothing more than a resting place for evil.

Hannah had whispered the truth into Alecia's ear and pulled back to see her reaction. She'd watched her mother's face and body freeze in knowledge. Watched her squeeze her eyes shut against it. Watched her lips part when her mother whispered back, "How? They're so different. I thought he was different."

The words confused Hannah. She didn't know what they meant. She also realized that there were no words her mother could have said that would have made things right. The next words out of her mother's mouth clinched that knowledge for Hannah. "I know now. He won't be able to get near you again. I promise. You'll be safe. But you have to listen to me and do exactly what I tell you."

Hannah wanted to scream. She wanted to throw things. But she wanted protection too. So, she just nodded and resolved at once to do it, to stop her silent war against Alecia, to stop protecting her father, and to let her mother sort things out.

That night after dinner, Everett didn't come in to say good night to Hannah. Alecia came in and pointed to the lock she'd installed on Hannah's bedroom door while Everett had been at work. "Keep it locked. I have a key in case of an emergency, but he'll never find it."

Hannah cringed when Alecia walked over but Alecia stood far enough away; there was no worry that she'd reach out to touch her. Alecia dropped down to her knees so they were eye level, as if about to offer a prayer. "Hannah, I'm sorry I didn't protect you, that he hurt you. He never will again. But I need you to know — to understand — this isn't your fault — none of it. It's his fault. All of it, mine too for not protecting you. It's important you understand that. You may not believe it, but it's true."

And with that, Hannah began to cry.

CHAPTER SEVENTEEN
TAKING PRISONERS

Once Hannah was safely at school, Alecia began the first of her preparations. If Hannah had disclosed to her what had been happening, it was a possibility she had disclosed it to someone else, which meant it was only a matter of time before the authorities would intervene. Therefore, she worked intently to execute things as quickly as possible.

There was one thing Alecia needed to do for herself. It would require time Alecia didn't have, but she was a woman who knew her strengths as well as her limitations. And if she was going to have the strength required of her in the coming weeks to do what needed doing, this particular step, though purely personal, was a vital one. It solidified, Alecia believed, an eternal resolution. One she had to complete.

The nursing home was a mere 15 minutes away in Dobbs Ferry. Yet aside from the one time she'd been there to complete the admissions procedure a year and a half ago, she'd never been back. She paid the bills from her personal checking account so Everett was not aware of them. The only number the home had was her cell, and it was under simple initials in her contacts, impossible to detect if Everett ever became nosy or inadvertently saw a call come in. It was her secret.

Hannah and Everett believed both of Alecia's parents were dead. For all Alecia knew, her mother may very well be dead. She hadn't seen or heard from her since her third birthday and had zero memories of her. Not even a photograph. She had only her father's word that her mother had actually existed. She didn't know any of her mother's relatives, although she was fairly certain she could have tracked them down at some point had she cared to. Here is what Alecia knew about her mother based on her own birth certificate: Her maiden name was Cynthia Rodgers, and she was 18 years old when Alecia was born. She'd given birth at a now defunct hospital in lower Manhattan. Her father, Richard A. Dixon was 41 at the time. Any other knowledge of her mother came from the following statements her father made over the years.

Your mother thought she was better than me, but she was nothing but a whore.
Your mother was very beautiful. That's what lured me in.
That was your mother's favorite song; she loved all the filthy hippie songs (referring to Lady Madonna by the Beatles.)
She left you behind so I could raise you right.

Alecia wondered if her mother was dead, or if she'd simply run away. She had no grandparents, aunts, uncles, or cousins that she knew of. She found it nearly impossible to converse with her father and found herself mainly letting him begin and finish his long diatribes, afraid that interrupting or speaking would just prolong them.

Alecia's life revolved around her father, their squalid one bedroom apartment, and taking care of him. Cooking his meals. Doing what she could to clean the layers of grime in the apartment. Bringing their bed-sheets, towels, and meager bundle of clothes to the Laundromat, and the job he'd taught her of servicing him. Which required no skin-to-skin contact because as he told her many times, 'he wasn't no perv.' Only in the dark of night, the blanket between them, and his movement against her until she'd feel him shudder, hear his moan, and wait until he'd turn his back to her before allowing herself to dive into the darkness of sleep, where mercifully, she never dreamed.

In 1988, the song Fast Car by Tracy Chapman was popular. Alecia listened to it as frequently as she could whenever her father wasn't around. She recognized the story as their own, the strange protectiveness she felt over a man who should have protected her and didn't. The destitution. And maybe the hint of something else that no one ever spoke of, the bedtime secret that was hers to keep.

School was the only place she felt safe. The breakfast and lunch programs were her main meals. Her homework and her studies the bright spot in her mind, a respite from the gray of her every day existence.

When Alecia graduated from high school she became emancipated, went to college in Connecticut on a full ride, worked as an RA, and took out small student loans each semester to make ends meet. She never looked back. When she married Everett, she put her past behind her and became a new person. Until a year and a half ago when someone from the old neighborhood who'd recognized her on Facebook through a friend of a friend of a friend messaged her to tell her that her father still lived in the same apartment and was declining. Shocked to find he was still alive, Alecia wanted to ignore the message but was afraid the woman would persist. Alecia never went back. She couldn't face the neighborhood, the apartment, or him. She hired an attorney to handle the nursing home contracts and finances and a social worker named Betty, who had a private practice and specialized in geriatric care. Betty was the one who contacted her father and helped move him into a nursing home. She told Alecia that her father, although in his late 70's, presented as if he were in his 90's. He was mentally competent but confused. He had a series of health problems, none of which precluded him from the nursing home. Alecia learned to her surprise that he was neither belligerent, nor resistant to help. In fact, Betty described him as compliant and a bit of a charmer. Alecia paid her to visit him once a week and give her updates. Part of it was to ascertain that he would receive proper care from the staff, and part of it was to make sure Alecia saw him once before he died or before he lost his mental faculties, whichever came first.

At the time, Alecia's gratitude toward Everett was all encompassing. She couldn't tell him why she was grateful so she showed him in a myriad of ways, preparing his favorite dinners, making sure his dry cleaning was organized in his closet, picking up small gifts such as his favorite brand of cashmere socks in navy, camel, black, brown, and even an argyle. She washed them personally, not trusting her maid service to lose one from a pair or worse, accidentally toss them in the dryer and shrink them. Alecia had been grateful to her husband because his wealth had enabled her to sanitize the filth of the past, covering any sense of responsibility she had to her father as effectively as a hose and a bucket of bleach on blood soaked concrete.

It was a sunny morning when Alecia drove to see her father. Her world had collapsed, but she wouldn't show it. She needed, for Hannah's sake, to hold it together for a while longer. She'd dressed carefully in navy slacks, an ivory silk blouse, gold hoops in her ears, and that season's Gucci Dionysus handbag.

The smell of the nursing home hit her as soon as she walked in the door. Alecia instinctively buried her nose into her scarf and breathed the scent of her own perfume, which calmed her sufficiently to keep going. A few inquiries, an elevator ride, and a long walk down a beige corridor, her heels clipping on the linoleum, and she was there. The door to his room was open and she stepped in. He sat in a chair fully dressed. She drew in her breath, a sharp cut inside her chest. She was unprepared for his visage despite the reports of how old and frail he was.

Alecia pulled a visitor's chair over, her coat fastened, scarf wrapped tight, she clutched her bag in her lap, sat opposite him, and leaned forward waiting for his eyes to focus on hers. There were cataracts over his irises, his eyes which had once been a bright blue, were now a cloudy gray, Alecia looked for the meanness that had always been there, a hard glint of warning, but all she could see was the confused gaze of a very old man.

"Dad. It's me, Alecia. Do you remember me?"

He nodded slowly.

"I've been gone a long time."

"Yes."

"How are you?"

He was slow to respond and his voice, though weak, still had the timbre and tenor she remembered. "They take good care of me here."

Alecia nodded. "I've come to ask you — have you heard from my mother?"

He didn't respond and Alecia watched him closely. Was

he unaware or thinking? She watched him make up his mind. "She died in '92. Cancer."

"How do you know?"

"Her sister wrote me. She went back to Indiana to live with her."

"My mother was from Indiana?"

"Yeah. Her people are still there."

"What type of cancer?"

"Lung. Smoked two packs a day. That stuff'll kill ya." He laughed.

"I need to ask you something."

She saw the wariness come into his eyes. "Don't like dwelling on the past. No good comes of it."

"I did everything I could to leave it behind."

"I forgive you."

Alecia drew back, "You. Forgive me?"

"For leaving me. Like your mother did."

Alecia knew then that she'd never get the answers she'd come for. She would never know how she missed the signs in Everett. What made her father the way he was? It was simply a fact. Like the sky being blue. She attracted men who preyed on girls. Like the magnetic pull of the earth, she was their gravity, and it would *have* to end with her.

Val, Fiona, Thia, and Ivy sat in Val's living room gripping coffee mugs, incapable of making small talk. They were waiting while Bryce cajoled Chloe into taking a late run to Rocky's, an all-night deli a few towns over, for her favorite fried shrimp sandwich. It wasn't difficult to persuade her. Bryce was a better actor than he'd ever given himself credit for. He spoke to Chloe as if nothing had changed, as if it were a normal Friday night escapade. The two of them bundled up, and he was relieved to see Chloe's eyes shine and cheeks pink up, the physical manifestation of happiness she'd exhibited since babyhood. It wasn't until they jumped into the car and Bryce said, "Buckle up" the way he always did and Chloe complied, that he allowed his features to settle in the dark. Chloe saw it then. The rage. It frightened her, so she turned to the window and watched the darkness speed by, wondering if her dad was mad at her after all. Bryce took 117 at 80 miles an hour without realizing it, thinking about the ways he was going to harm Everett Caulding before the man ended up in a cage.

"We have to go to the police." Val said the moment the door closed behind Chloe and Bryce.

Thia put her mug carefully on the glass coffee table, "What will happen to Hannah?"

Ivy looked at her, "Most likely she'll be removed from the home."

"Why can't she stay with Alecia?" Fiona asked.

"Because," Ivy said, "her mother knew what happened and didn't remove her from Everett's care."

"We don't know that!" Fiona sounded desperate. "She could have kicked him out of the house. We don't even know if this has anything to do with them moving."

Ivy looked at her, "It's likely. And it's likely Everett's still with them. If that's the case they're going to pull Hannah. You know it, Fiona."

Val nodded. "Agreed. But none of this speculation changes the fact that we need to go to the police right away."

"Where will Hannah go?" Thia asked. "Alecia has no

family, and Everett's parents are old and he's estranged from his sister. Last I heard, she was in an ashram somewhere."

"Really?" Ivy asked, "I didn't know that."

"He told me that once," Thia answered, and she felt a bite of shame at how proud she'd felt when he'd relayed what appeared to be a confidence to her at the time. "What's Hannah supposed to do? Go live with an aunt she's never met? Go to grandparents she barely knows? Foster care?"

Val looked at her, "You're way ahead of yourself. The first step is finding her and we can't do it. We need to report this."

"I'll take her if it comes to that." Fiona said.

Val looked at her. "You can't. Not after what Chloe's been through. She needs to be your priority right now."

Ivy looked at her, "It's true, Fi. It wouldn't be good for Chloe, and it wouldn't be the answer for Hannah. Val's right, we're way ahead of ourselves. We need to find her first and we can't even do that. We have to go to the police. Fiona, you're a mandated reporter."

Fiona began to cry. "They'll want to interview Chloe."

Val looked at her, "She's already been through the worst. She's a strong kid, and she'll have you by her side."

"She'll have all of us." Ivy said.

Thia nodded, but she knew how alone Chloe would feel through all of it.

Alecia calculated that she would have at most 24 hours before the women went to the authorities. She imagined them gathering somewhere (Fiona's or Ivy's, ironically she never considered Val's) and weighing their options. She knew Ivy would push hard for reporting, while Fiona would want to wait and speak with Chloe and her therapist first. Alecia wondered if they'd had the discussion about Hannah yet, if it occurred to them that Hannah might be taken from her. As soon as Alecia made her decision to move the three of them away together, she knew she had sacrificed any chance she had of keeping Hannah.

She hadn't had long to make those plans. It wasn't the move (money can pretty much smooth any path), it wasn't convincing Everett (it was almost insulting how easily he accepted the fact that she wasn't going to turn him in, instead just *watch* him from then on. Keep them *separated*. As if she would move forward as though he'd never harmed her daughter. Alecia wasn't wrong that her father and Everett were very different. She realized that now. Her father would never have allowed someone else to call the shots. Would never have shown remorse or admitted he'd done anything wrong. Everett sobbed. He acknowledged that he was weak. That he'd loved Hannah so much that it had become a romantic love. That she was an extension of Alecia, that it hadn't been intentional, that he'd never liked young girls before, but that their relationship was so special. He was sorry. He'd stop. They would become like a normal father and daughter. He had never hurt her. He'd been gentle. It was something that was going to happen anyway one day; why let it be with some rough callous boy when he could care for her so much better? He was doing it to protect her. All of those words had come out of his mouth. Spewed forth like vomit. His eyes red and watery, his nose streaming mucus as he'd cried. He was pathetic, but Alecia didn't have even a moment of compassion for him, and it surprised her. She'd gone from loving him to despising him in the same amount of time it took to flip a switch and the room went from shadowed darkness to blinding light. The worst part was stomaching his gratitude and empty promises when she told him she wasn't turning him in or breaking up their family. He mewled like a kitten and tried to come over to her, but she stopped him with a look. He accepted everything she told him to do. He took a leave of absence from work. He went along with the furtive move to another state and allowed her to put everything in her maiden name which none of the women knew. Just to give them more time, she left the D out of Rodgers and added a false middle name becoming Alecia Marie Rogers. It would give the authorities a little more of a run for their money when they began searching. She didn't need much time, but Everett didn't know that.

The hardest part for Alecia was determining what would become of Hannah. She was too young to emancipate, and there was no way in hell she would allow her to live with Everett's decrepit parents or his weird sister, whom Alecia now wondered about. Had he abused her too? He was six years older than her. It wasn't something she had time to worry about. Alecia needed to feel in control, needed a plan, and the undetermined missing piece made her unsettled. It was an answer she hoped would come to her before it was too late.

Right now, the one thing Alecia knew for certain is that Hannah would be without both of her parents. What Alecia hadn't determined yet was how long that separation would be. Alecia calculated that she had maybe two weeks from the time they moved until the authorities caught up with them to figure it out.

Hannah watched as Alecia paced the deck while glued to the iPad. The air was turning a purple/gray, almost the same color of the walls in her new bedroom. For the first time Hannah lived somewhere other than the house she had grown up in, and even though she had all of her own furniture, the paint colors were there when they moved in. "The lucky thing is," Alecia had pronounced standing in Hannah's new room, "...is that white furniture goes with everything, some new curtains and voila!"

Hannah turned from the window. The move had happened so quickly. She'd relinquished her phone to Alecia as requested. Her iCloud was wiped clean, a handful of photos saved to her computer, and the only numbers she had were those she'd memorized, none of which made it into her new phone because Alecia checked it every night. Hannah wondered if this was Alecia's great plan. Move to a different state, change their names, and pretend none of it ever happened. True to her mother's word, Everett hadn't come near her again. They were only together at dinnertime when her father turned Hannah's stomach by behaving like an obsequious ass. Obsequious had been a vocabulary word the week she'd left school, and Hannah decided that if she believed in God, she would have thought it was a sign since it perfectly described what her father had become.

Hannah couldn't believe that Alecia hadn't dragged her immediately to a shrink. She'd underestimated how much Alecia needed to keep up appearances. She'd thought this revelation might have been the thing to wake her mother from the perpetual state of perfectionism. Hannah had always thought that other families were just like hers — filled with secrets and alliances. Hannah couldn't know how masterfully she'd been groomed and manipulated. She could only know what life had prepared her for.

Hannah turned away from watching Alecia on the deck below. She picked up the cream-colored journal with the gold trim she'd received last Christmas. She searched through her pencil case until she found her favorite purple gel pen. Settling on her canopied bed, she turned the thick smooth pages until she found an empty one and wrote in perfect penmanship, *if everyone has a secret, I am his.*

Ivy returned home the evening of book club at 11:30 and found James reading in the family room off the kitchen. He lifted his eyebrows when she opened the kitchen door and said, "Wow that must've been some discussion."

When she stepped into the light, and he saw her face, he let his book fall on its spine and jumped up, "Babe, what's wrong?" She stepped into his arms and cried as though someone had died, which in a way they had. What Everett did to Hannah was a type of murder. He'd murdered her innocence, her sense of self, and her soul. Or maybe, Ivy thought, it wasn't murder but attempted murder. The act he'd committed against his child was an attempt to obliterate her very being and turn her into a vessel for his own selfish depravity. Yet Hannah was strong. With the right interventions and therapies, she would get past this. It would always affect her, but it wouldn't define her. Ivy had to believe that.

When James held her and asked her what was wrong, she didn't have the words to answer him and she didn't know how to find them.

"Hey," he said and pulled away enough to look at her. "Just start from the beginning."

So, she did.

James was a doctor. He'd heard many disclosures of sexual abuse, in the medical literature, from colleagues, patients, and when he thought back to his own childhood he remembered a donut shop where it was rumored kids could get free donuts if they just went behind the counter and showed their privates.

Yet every telling of the sexual assault of a child, James believed, stood on its own. There were common traits of the sexual offender and common ways survivors suffered, but there wasn't a profile, a single way of identifying when it happened, and each healing needed attention and care. There was no 'one size fits all' treatment or an injection that would heal the trauma of sexual abuse. Yet healing *was* possible for Hannah. James believed that. But first they had to find her.

James thought about Everett. Everything he knew about him. His financial net worth was probably close to 300 million, so he could be on the run for the rest of his life if he was careful. But it would be almost impossible to do that with Alecia and Hannah at his side, even if they were willing. James thought about how equable Everett was, how generous he could be without being ostentatious. He was a scratch golfer with a low handicap, but he practiced great humility on the golf course. Until that moment, James had firmly believed the golf course revealed a man's true character. It never occurred to James not to believe Chloe's version of events, although he was sure that many people would doubt her. But he couldn't reconcile the man he knew with the act he'd committed. And yet, James knew that most of the time when human beings committed monstrous acts, they'd been monsters all along.

One Halloween when the children were small, he and Everett had taken Benjamin, Bobby, and Hannah trick-or-treating, while Ivy and Alecia stayed home to hand out candy. James and Ivy's neighborhood was a favorite place to trick or treat, with wide quiet streets laid out in a perfect grid and houses separated by a mere driveway in a town called Sleepy Hollow. Alecia and Everett on the other hand lived in a newer development, which hadn't yet become a neighborhood; few children trick-or-treated there and no one gave out candy, so it became a ritual for them to bring Hannah to James and Ivy's, and it became a ritual for James and Everett to bring the children out. James remembered that first one, it must have been about 8 years ago, and the children had just started kindergarten. Hannah was taller than Bobby then, and a faster runner. She'd been the leader, and he'd been happy to follow. James couldn't remember their costumes, but he remembered a flash of pale blue as Hannah ran across the lawns and a red cape streaming behind Bobby as he tried to keep up. Some of the homeowners enjoyed living up to their village's name and went all out decorating. Bobby preferred the houses with friendly decorations, but Hannah liked all of them, even the big house on the corner that had spooky sounds and ghoulish figures sitting on the porch. James knew that Ivy was home wearing a sparkling purple witch hat and earrings shaped like black cats when she answered the door and gave the kids handfuls of candy, but some of the homeowners wore more elaborate costumes to answer the door. One of the homes (a family that waited at the same bus stop as their kids) did things opposite of James and Ivy; the mom took the kids trick-or-treating and the dad stayed home giving out candy. James knew him a bit. He was extremely tall, over 6'5 and very thin. And he'd chosen to dress as a clown. Not a horror movie clown. But still. When he appeared at the door in yellow onesie pajamas, a giant-sized tomato-red wig and garish makeup with a mouth that looked like smeared blood and a swollen red nose, Bobby jumped three feet in the air, let out a blood curdling scream and ran back toward James his red cape flying behind him. James scooped him up in his arms. "It's okay Buddy, it's just make-up. Look, it's your friend Ryan's dad from the bus stop wearing a costume."

While James tried to comfort Bobby, he also kept an eye on Hannah, who yelled "trick or treat" fiercely, bravely took candy for herself, and even got a lollipop for Bobby before yelling "THANK YOU, SCARY CLOWN!" in a loud voice and running happily back to them. "Look Bobby, I brought you a tootsie roll pop!"

James put Bobby down and watched his indecision as he alternated between looking at the candy and back at the house, where the clown had mercifully shut the front door and gone back into the depths of whatever hell he was waiting to reappear from.

"Take it Bobby, I got it for you."

Eventually Bobby swallowed his sobs and stretched his fingers for it. Hannah cheerfully handed it over and shouted, "NEXT HOUSE!" And off they ran with Bobby sticking to her like glue.

Nothing had scared Hannah that night. She was fast, brave, and kind. James prayed those traits would see her through what was to come.

James and Ivy sat facing one another in their family room. It was past midnight, and Ivy was exhausted. The mug of tea James had fixed her had grown cold in her hand and she placed it on the side table without ever having sipped it. "What will happen to Hannah? Where will she go?"

"You're assuming she won't be able to stay with Alecia."

"It just seems — like they're on the run."

"From Everett?"

Ivy shook her heard. "No. Everything's gone, all the furniture. And I emailed that realtor friend of Alecia's — she confirmed that the house is going on the market in April. She said the sellers wanted to wait until it was nice out. If Alecia took Hannah from Everett she never would have moved everything like that. She simply would have left. And I guess I could be wrong, but I really think she would have told me, just so we would know not to go to the authorities. I think they moved together, and she's covering for him."

James thought about it. As difficult as it was to imagine, he knew there were women who covered up for the offenders. He'd seen it first hand as a resident in the ER. Alecia was a perfectionist. Maybe the way things looked was more important than the safety of her daughter. It was frightening how easy it became to believe the worst about people, even your friends.

"The thing I can't stop thinking about — and it makes me sick…"

"What?"

Ivy picked the cold tea up and put it down. She placed her hand across her stomach and sat back in her chair, pulling her feet up in front of her. "The way Chloe described it…"

James waited.

"It sounds — I mean — the way she said it…"

"It's okay. Just say what you're thinking."

"It sounds like Hannah initiated it…" Ivy felt sick to her stomach. Disloyal to Hannah and sick at the thought of what she'd heard, albeit second hand from Fiona.

James considered Ivy before speaking, "How much do you know about the sexual abuse of children?"

Ivy shrugged, "I know it happens. I know I want to castrate any man who touches a child, but if you're asking what I know clinically? Very little, and it isn't as though I ever had cases where that came up."

James looked at her, "Most cases of incest…" Ivy cringed and James looked steadily at her, "…that's what this is. When a custodial parent sexually abuses a child, it's incest. Whether it's a biological father or a stepfather." Ivy nodded, and he continued, "It's rape. Straight up rape, but the method is coercive. And often takes place over years. The offender grooms the child for a long time, and it's often the only experience the child has, so she won't even know it's unusual. Children trust their parents, and when manipulated, they keep the 'secret.' People won't understand, but to her, the acts are special, *she's* special, and people will be jealous or will say it's wrong, but *they're* the ones who are wrong. The offender may scare the child, tell them that he'll be taken away, or their mother will be angry at them, or that daddy and mommy will go to jail because the world doesn't understand how special their relationship is."

"It's sick."

"If what Chloe described — that Hannah initiated that particular contact, it's because she was taught to do that from a very young age. Children love their parents. They trust them and believe them."

"But — she couldn't *like* it…"

James shook his head, "That isn't the point. It's harmful to her, but it's like being fed a poison that your body has built up a tolerance to. You know you don't feel well, you know something's off, but you don't know why, and you keep taking the poison thinking it's expected, you don't know how *not* to take it."

"Chloe thinks it's her fault. That Hannah became jealous of Chloe and that's why she went…"

James ran his hand over his face and dropped his head into his hands. "Look, he may have started grooming Chloe, or trying to see if there was a possibility to violate her. And

Hannah may have recognized that. Think about the tools of manipulation an offender uses, such as the sanctity of the parent child relationship. They use the love and trust a child has for them. If Hannah felt her father was going to remove his love, or transfer it somewhere else, it makes sense she felt jealous. Chloe's perceptive, and she may have picked up on that. Hannah going to her father may have been a well-established ritual."

"But Fiona said Chloe's slept at Hannah's countless times and nothing like that ever happened before."

James ran his hands over his head, "We don't know for sure what happened. But if Everett was moving onto Hannah's friends, that could have precipitated a crisis, maybe before that night when there were sleepovers that Everett kept his distance. Or maybe he was more covert. We don't know. I'm just saying none of what you've told me is inconsistent with the manipulations of a child rapist."

And with that James got up and went into the powder room where he allowed himself to cry. This wasn't a textbook case, or a patient a colleague was discussing. This was Hannah, brave, fierce, little Hannah who wasn't afraid of scary clowns and remembered to take candy for a friend.

When Alecia moved Hannah and Everett away, she and Hannah agreed that for the rest of the school year she would be home schooled. Everett was now 'retired' and forced to play golf six days a week, successfully turning his favorite activity into a chore. He wasn't to come home until dinnertime, after which, he went to the guest cottage where Hannah was never to step foot. The three of them ate breakfast together every morning and dinner together every evening where they fell easily into their regular pattern.

Hannah learned that things that remain unspoken felt remarkably like the secret she learned to hide years before. The anger she'd previously felt at Alecia and the bravado that came with it had mysteriously vanished, leaving her bereft in a way she didn't understand. Her father, diminished by the truth of what he had done, was absent from her life other than those two meal times, and Hannah hated herself for missing him. She wanted to explain but didn't have the words to articulate that although he'd destroyed a part of her, he'd also been interesting and engaging, listened to her ideas, and was a large part of her identity.

Everett had always had a quote on his desk by a German expressionist painter named Franz Marc. It read, "Blue is the male principle, stern and spiritual. Yellow the female principle, gentle, cheerful, and sensual. Red is matter, brutal and heavy and always the colour which must be fought and vanquished by the other two."

A print of *The Fate of the Animals* by Franz Marc hung on the wall opposite his desk. Hannah always thought it violent *and* beautiful. Like watching something terrible through a prism. She thought about the quote on her father's desk, wondering if he'd unpacked it. For Hannah, it seemed the male color blue, stern and spiritual, was Alecia. The female color yellow, gentle, cheerful, and sensual, was Everett, and she was red, brutal, and heavy — to be fought and vanquished by the other two. She was the violence behind the prism of light and color.

The day after Alecia watched the women discover her absence, she knew she had a short time to complete things. After a light breakfast of yogurt, fruit, and granola, Everett left for the golf course, and she and Hannah went on their planned outing to the art store. Alecia watched as Hannah walked up and down the aisles carefully selecting a case of pastels with the largest variety of shades, a sketchpad of textured paper, and several small to medium sized canvases to work with.

Alecia bought what seemed to be a year's supply of sketchpads and charcoal pencils. Hannah would be welcome to use as many as she wanted, but Alecia bought them for herself. She imagined many hours of blankness. Ugliness. And thought it would be a way to capture it.

Hannah placed her items carefully in the shopping cart, noting the sketchpads and pencils. She looked up at Alecia with a question in her eyes but seemed reluctant to ask. Alecia smiled in what she hoped was a reassuring way, but it felt tight even for her. Hannah had been remote, quiet, and docile in a way that broke Alecia's heart. Alecia knew that Hannah missed Everett, but didn't know how to explain to Hannah that she understood, so it remained unspoken. It was why Alecia allowed the dinner hour together; she recognized that while Everett and her own father were similar in the most horrible of ways, their methods varied greatly. While her father had used brutality and power to coerce her, Everett had used love and protection as his tools of manipulation. She found Everett's to be far worse, far more treacherous, and far more effective in keeping his daughter bonded to him. It was for this reason as much as any that Alecia planned to kill him.

While Alecia and Hannah placed their art supplies in the trunk of the car, Fiona and Val were at the village police station sitting at the desk of Detective Vern Matthews. The room was cramped and smelled like burned coffee, but sunlight filtered through the windows on beams of dust motes.

Detective Matthews listened carefully, his face registering nothing, his eyes moving intently to whichever woman was speaking at the moment. It was a difficult story for Fiona to tell, and she let Val do most of the talking. It was equally difficult to listen to, and all she could feel was a desperate need to protect Chloe coupled with an urgency bubbling in her chest to find Hannah. Fiona gave in to following the thought pattern that had been wheeling around in her mind all night. *Did Alecia know? Is that why they'd moved? Was Hannah safe? Was she still with Everett? How would they find her?* Her final thought pulled her back to Detective Matthews. *Would he help them?*

He hadn't spoken and had taken a few notes whenever Val mentioned times or places, but other than that he was just listening and watching. Finally, when Val stopped speaking and leaned back in her chair, he leaned forward and said, "I'd like to speak with Chloe."

"Why is that necessary?" Val asked. Fiona was grateful, because she was afraid if she spoke she would start to cry again, and she didn't want to distract the detective, but she didn't want him to speak with Chloe.

Detective Matthews looked at Fiona. His gaze was probing, not unkind, but not kind either, and it made Fiona sit up straighter and lose any desire to cry. "It would help to speak with your daughter." He held his hand up when Val began to argue, "I know. And I believe that you are reporting back accurately what she said to you. But if you're serious about finding Hannah it would help."

What could they say to that? Fiona nodded and let Val make the arrangements.

Thia called in sick to work for the first time in the history of her job. She thought about ways to accomplish what she needed to do without calling in sick but decided she wouldn't be as effective, and it was imperative she utilized every resource available. She needed God's speed not for revenge but for justice and protection. Archangel Cassiel, the protector of orphan children and the enslaved, Thia believed, came to her because Hannah had in her own way been enslaved and was about to become orphaned. Thia was patently aware of the awful irony that justice and the need to protect Hannah might in effect orphan her. Thia was going to the woods on Saturday, the day of Saturn and Cassiel, wearing brown clothing and a pewter amulet, carrying obsidian in her breast pocket. She knew the exact hilltop where a Yew tree reached its branches in two directions at once, the earth and the sky. She had 30 minutes to get there by noon when the concentration of energy would be highest for absent healing.

The morning had gone by in a blur for Thia; she'd barely been able to go through the motions of everyday life with the children, but Eric had picked up her slack. He was able to give his full attention to them without displaying the effects of the lack of sleep and heightened emotions from the night before. When Thia came home and told him what Chloe had relayed, his fury and desire to physically harm Everett was gratifying to Thia in some ways, giving voice to the same thoughts she herself entertained, but it didn't begin to address the reality of what life had been for Hannah and what was still to come. She was grateful that he was able to hold onto those feelings and still behave normally for their kids, because he had a long day ahead with them. She suspected her distraction was a hindrance rather than help and felt his relief when she kissed him goodbye at 11:30 and set off into the trails of the Pocantico reserve.

The carpet of frost-covered-leaves crunched beneath her feet while the sound of a woodpecker drummed high above breaking the stillness of the air. She walked swiftly, anxious that she may have misjudged the time it was going to take to walk along the river and up into the hills.

When she cleared the top of the crest right before the Yew tree, she took a moment to pause and breathe deeply, planting her feet against the ground and stretching toward the clear blue sky. The air shimmered in the noon sunlight, although it did little to banish the chill seeping into her bones. It was a few minutes before noon, and it took only moments before she'd found the right sized stick to draw her circle. Thia was angry and scared. She'd learned over the years that the energy she carried into the rituals she performed informed the outcome. Anger and fear had their rightful place. But they wouldn't serve her now. The protection she was looking for was strength. Attraction. Love. Magic had a way of resolving this conundrum. It consisted of allowing her mind to empty, her body to soften, her breath to regulate. She replaced fear with faith, anger with patience, and began to pray.

Thia hadn't been praying for an action or a result. So, when her phone chirped in a dead zone it startled and irritated her. She fumbled for it, breaking her concentration and registering with a sense of loss the evaporation of warmth, which had only moments before been filling the joints of her neck, spine, and shoulders.

Finally, she retrieved the intrusive vibrating rectangle of technology with clumsy fingers and turned it over to reveal the letters in large font declaring the name of the caller. Alecia.

CHAPTER EIGHTEEN
FLIGHT

Hannah woke up to the sound of Vesper Sparrows singing. It was Sunday and Hannah wasn't sure what that meant for her anymore. Without the structure of school days or friends, Saturday was no different from Monday. She noted the lemon-yellow light streaming in through the chink in her blinds and listened to the bird song. She wondered, not for the first time, if today would be the day she summoned the courage to take her own life. Each morning she woke up disappointed that her dream of slipping into death hadn't happened when she'd surrendered to sleep. She wasn't interested in the act of suicide or even in the imaginings of what her funeral would be like. She just wanted everything to stop. She wanted off the carousel of confusion she lived in. She thought back to the before, when Alecia didn't know, how her only desire had been to escape and be someplace else. Well here she was, but Hannah felt more trapped than ever, even though her dad couldn't touch her anymore.

Hannah turned away from the light. She placed the pillow over her head to block out the birdsong. She breathed slowly and deeply, in and out, longing for the escape of a dreamless sleep. She focused on the colors behind her eyelids. At first, they were pale yellows and greens, gentle swirls of color and movement. After a while the colors deepened to emerald and orange. The shapes shifted to geometric patterns of squares and rectangles. She thought about the canvases she and Alecia bought the day before, and she visualized the charcoal pencils and pastels lined up in their respective cases. The image enabled her to get out of bed. She would wait one more day before figuring out a way to stop being alive.

Alecia worried when Hannah didn't come down for breakfast. The table was set and Everett was halfway through his newspaper, finished with his first cup of coffee. All of the bacon had been cooked and Alecia needed to serve it or it would be cold. She washed her hands carefully with geranium scented soap, dried them on a soft linen cloth, and went upstairs to check on Hannah. She needed to get this breakfast over and done with and get Everett out of the house. She had exactly three hours to get Hannah ready for the next step, and Alecia felt considerable anxiety about whether or not Hannah was going to comply.

Alecia didn't know what to think when she went upstairs and found Hannah engrossed in the pastel she was doing on canvas. Alecia could see the careful charcoal lines forming a variety of geometric shapes layered upon one another until you couldn't tell the original shape from the ones that came later. Some of the pattern filled by blurred combinations of pastels, softening the hard edges and making it impossible to see the charcoal lines beneath. It reminded Alecia vaguely of the print Everett had above his desk back in New York and it disturbed her.

"Breakfast is getting cold, Hannah. Come eat."

"I'll be down later."

Alecia watched as Hannah carefully blended the edges of color until they bled into one another. "Your father will be leaving soon."

"I'm busy."

Alecia found herself biting the inside of her bottom lip. An ancient habit from childhood she thought she'd left behind, with remnants of her fear and shame. She needed Hannah to come downstairs. She needed her to see Everett one last time, yet she didn't want to push Hannah and have her come down resentful and distracted. She bit her lip harder and did something so uncharacteristic, that Hannah jerked her head around. Alecia backed out of the room without saying another word.

Hannah, uncomfortable with the "win" as she now perceived it, and irritated by the distraction, found herself letting the colors bleed too far over, rendering her yellow square the color of a clementine along the whole right side. In order to rectify it, Hannah had to turn the square into a rectangle, throwing off her carefully constructed pattern. Irritated, she put the pastels carefully into their rightful places in the tin and stood up to see for herself what was going on downstairs. She thought spitefully for a moment of leaving her hands stained with color and trailing whorls of color along the walls — how upset Alecia would be — and wondered if she would act like her old self and have a conniption or if she would continue to be this silent creature trying to keep Hannah happy. Or maybe, maybe it wasn't happiness she was seeking, but silence. And just like that, Hannah's anger was back. She ruthlessly wiped her hands on the soft cream-colored carpet. It would be much more difficult to clean than the walls. Then she headed downstairs to see what Alecia was up to.

Thia arrived in Savannah, Georgia, dressed like a New Yorker. What had seemed perfectly appropriate in the gray corridors of JFK (dark jeans, black peacoat, Doc Martens, and a purple leather backpack the size of a small handbag) seemed conspicuous in the small bright airport. She made her way to the rental car booth and imagined detectives pouring over video footage (one of them looking exactly like Vincent D'Onofrio from Law & Order: Criminal Intent) pointing at her grainy image, yelling, "Gotcha!" Thia told herself to stop being ridiculous, this wasn't a criminal act, she was simply renting a car. After she acquired the car, she stowed her peacoat in the trunk and made her way to town, where she eventually found parking at the far end of Ogelthorpe Street. Thia registered the loveliness of the Square lush with greenery and tried to calm her speeding heart rate. She sought to match the honeyed gait of the people wandering through the small park. She took deep breaths and concentrated on the sun warming her bare arms — how good it felt after the long winter. She needed to calm down and appear normal. She had exactly an hour to kill and didn't want to draw unnecessary attention to herself.

She wandered the small square stopping to read the plaques displayed strategically along the charming walkways. One told the story of an Italian artisan, who had been among the first of the Europeans to settle in Georgia in 1732. She read the words without comprehending them, her mind flashing ahead to the trip home. She forced herself to reread the plaque and began again from the top, this time registering the Latin words, *Non sibi sed aliis.* She skimmed quickly over the rest of the plaque until she found the English translation at the end, *not for ourselves, but for others.* In that simple phrase, Thia found the courage she'd been lacking since the moment she'd agreed to come here and turned to find the appointed spot where the meeting would take place.

Everett and Hannah ate the breakfast of peach waffles with warm syrup and crispy bacon Alecia had carefully prepared. Alecia tried hard not to give away the knowledge that this was the last meal the three of them would ever have together. Everett seemed completely at ease, asking Hannah what she was working on so intently. He could tell, he said, from the traces of pastel on her cheek, throat, and forearms. He mentioned that the smudges of deep green and bright yellow looked like war paint. Alecia, standing at the stove, saw how casually he spoke, but how hungrily he looked at their daughter, and she had to force herself to stand in one spot. She imagined turning around and hitting him with the hot skillet — blood and brain matter like war paint all over the kitchen walls.

Everett wasn't giving up. "So, Hannahbanana, what is it you're working on up there?"

Hannah looked at him impassively and said, "Nothing."

"Well," he smiled, "it surely is something. All those bright colors."

Hannah shrugged and went back to eating her waffles no longer looking at her father. Everett, seeing that he had gotten as much conversation as he could get from her, turned back to the book he was reading, a title with the words 'killing,' 'England,' 'brutal,' and 'struggle' in it by Bill O'Reilly. *Enjoy it,* Alecia thought. She wondered if he would have chosen that book if he'd known it was the last thing he would ever read.

* * *

One of Ivy's favorite book club choices had been *The Language of Flowers* by Vanessa Diffenbaugh. She'd loved everything about it — the story, the writing, the characters, the biology, and symbolism of flowers woven throughout, the way the novel had made her sob so hard she burst a capillary, a tiny bloom of red appearing in the white of her left eye. That book had changed forever the way she saw flowers, and it changed the way Ivy thought about love.

Ivy had always known love. Love had come at Ivy both gently and fiercely, unabated from each parent, two sets of grandparents, and a host of aunts, uncles, and cousins. Love was in and of itself a protective force for Ivy, yet she'd been born and raised in New York City in the East Village in the 1970's, making it impossible for her to have been completely sheltered or immune to the harsh realities of the streets or the world in general. Confident but streetwise, Ivy knew how to handle herself, which served her well from childhood through the minefields of adolescence and into adulthood.

The one thing love had never prepared Ivy for was the way it changed with motherhood. For while love had come in many forms to Ivy — heartbreak, first love, true love, all potent, intoxicating, and at times enough to make her both euphoric and ill — Ivy had never really found a way to reconcile the great joy of loving her boys with the seemingly irrational fear that something catastrophic would happen to one of them. She tried relaxation techniques, self-help books, therapy, and prayer. None of it worked, so Ivy began to carry her fear like a shameful secret that she hid from the rest of the world. Ivy exuded confidence and an air of exceptional competence her entire life, and she knew how to project it without even trying.

Ivy thought Victoria, the protagonist of *The Language of Flowers*, was represented by the symbolic meaning of the white rose *unacquainted with love.* Ivy knew 'unacquainted with love' referred to purity, innocence, the absence of romantic love, or lust. Yet Victoria, having grown up in foster care, never knew any form of love at all. *The Language of Flowers* was a book about becoming acquainted with love for the first time, a simple miracle that shredded Ivy's heart along with thousands of other readers and made the secret Ivy carried with her all the more shameful: a desire to love less, to feel an absence of love for even one minute, to return to her life before motherhood, and to meet life head on — without fear.

Ivy believed the fear made her less than she had once been. At no time had she felt it more than the last 15 hours, which is precisely how long it had been since she learned about what happened to Hannah, and by bearing witness, Chloe. Ivy felt this way because as devastated as she was, she had a keen desire to distance herself from all of it, all of *them.* That's how she was thinking about women she'd known for years, children she'd watched grow up, *them.* She didn't want the knowledge of what happened to touch her boys. She wanted to insulate herself and James and their sons from it. She wanted to go back to that original book club meeting at the local coffee shop and unravel the thread of time that led them to this place that had allowed her friendship with the women to form and deepen. She wished that her boys, Chloe, and Hannah had never been friends. She wished she'd never loved Alecia or Fiona or Hannah or Chloe, and by association Thia, Eric, and their children. She wished them all away, a desire and an accompanying shame she would have to carry. Unlike the characters in *The Language of Flowers*, love had not transformed her for the better but instead had made her selfish, callous. Even if she didn't behave in an unkind way, how would her thoughts and feelings not seep out into her behavior, making her unkind as well? She wished that at least she could have repressed them — claimed not to have been conscious of them, but she was, and the only way to mask them was with pretense, which would require vigilance she wasn't certain she was capable of. Yet, in spite of her yearning for a clean break, an absence of knowledge, Ivy was obsessively wondering where Hannah was and if she was safe. If Alecia hadn't moved them away to protect Everett, how was she protecting Hannah? Where was Everett? Ivy wondered if Fiona and Val had made any progress with the local police department. She kept checking her texts to see if she'd missed an update, but the last comment in the chain was her lone question mark hanging in a dull blue against the white screen of her phone, delivered but unanswered. Thia wasn't responding to any of Ivy's texts either and Ivy worried, torn between relief that she wasn't required to do anything and a desperate need to know that Hannah was ok. After her eleventh attempt to refresh her text messages, Ivy shoved her phone into her purse and headed out to the car. There were groceries to buy, errands to run, and the world was still clipping along at its usual pace, even though her heart felt frozen and her breath short in her chest.

* * *

Fiona asked Val if they could park down at Kingsland Point Park and walk along the water, hoping it would cleanse the fear and uncertainty muddying her thoughts. Val agreed, and the women found themselves facing the rough water and harsh wind coming off the river.

Fiona shivered and pulled her jacket tighter. "Do you think they'll find her?"

"Yeah. They will."

"And then what?"

Val sighed, "I'm not sure."

"And Clo? Do you think she'll recover from this?"

"She's strong. And therapy…."

"It will never be the same though."

Val looked at Fiona who looked paler than usual in the harsh winter light, her freckles more pronounced, the creases deepened around her eyes, the tip of her nose reddened from the wind.

"Fi, it can't be undone. So no, she won't ever be the same."

"I need to pull it together."

"You will."

"How's Bryce taking it?"

"He wants to kill Everett."

"I wish he would." Fiona looked at the white caps rolling in, the spray from the rocks misting their face, leaving a film of salt and grit. "We should get back."

Val nodded, then put her gloved hand over Fiona's, which looked red and chapped, her grip tight against the railing. "We'll get Chloe through this."

Fiona nodded, removed her hand, and turned toward the car, away from the river spray.

On the way home, stopped at a red light, Fiona saw Ivy drive by, squinting out at the winter glare. She seemed so far away, impossible to reach. Fiona wondered where Thia was, then forgot about it as the car lurched forward and they drove toward Chloe.

* * *

Thia watched as Alecia and Hannah walked toward them, struck by how young Hannah looked. As if somehow, all that had happened had aged her in her mind. Hannah was wearing a pair of jeans and one of those cold-shoulder tops. She looked like a little girl on the way to becoming a teenager with her hair in a French braid and wheeling a pink weekender suitcase. Thia wondered why she'd expected something different.

Alecia smiled and waved, but as they drew closer, Thia saw the change in Alecia — she looked thin and haggard, anguish in her eyes.

Thia stood up and hugged Alecia, who reflexively stiffened then allowed herself to settle into Thia's fierce embrace. When Thia let go, Alecia stepped back and Hannah's eyes moved vigilantly back and forth between her mother and Thia.

"Hey, Hannah," Thia said, reaching her hand out then instinctively pulling it back when Hannah flinched.

"Hi, Thia," Hannah smiled, and for a moment Thia thought she'd imagined it all. Hannah's voice sounded so normal, so friendly.

"You ready for a visit?"

Hannah nodded, "Mom said you would take me to visit Mino. Is that ok?"

Thia nodded, "Absolutely."

Hannah sighed with what may have been relief, or possibly happiness. Thia couldn't tell.

Mino was the horse Hannah rode at the country club stables her parents belonged to. More than her school, or her friends, or the familiarity of the only home Hannah had every known, he was what she missed most about her old life. When Hannah came to Savannah, she'd had a numb feeling in her fingers and toes, heaviness in her legs and shoulders.

She'd spent the first night in her new room feeling simultaneously claustrophobic and exposed. She'd desperately wanted to escape, but sleep wouldn't come. She'd been afraid she was going crazy. That she'd start screaming and never stop, or worse, be locked in a nightmare moment of trying to scream but unable to. It was Mino who'd saved her. His image appeared in her mind. The softness of his nose nuzzling her hand, his pale gold coat glinting in what Hannah recognized as the light at the end of a day in late summer. It was her favorite time of year, and favorite time of day, and it was as if Mino had taken her there. She felt herself connecting to him as if they were one and were riding through the hills of Pocantico, up the rise past her favorite tree, the one with prickly branches that reached up to the sky and down to the ground at the same time. She didn't know the name of the tree, but she knew exactly where it was, and was happy Mino was bringing her there. They rode higher and higher until they were in the sky, galloping through the clouds, she could feel cool air on her skin, and the world was streaking by in color and shape with no form. Hannah felt free and happy and safe and must have fallen asleep, because the next thing she could remember was waking up in her new room to bright sunshine that felt odd and stifling and far too hot in the middle of January. Hannah tried every night to conjure Mino again, to recreate that sensation of riding up into the sky. A few times, she was able to recapture a moment, a glimpse, a sensation, but never the sustained experience of that first time. She longed to see him in real time again and began to make elaborate plans for getting back to him.

Then suddenly, after that morning's breakfast of peach waffles, her mother told her Thia was coming to bring her for a visit. Hannah had been suspicious and wondered what her mother was planning. Yet the idea of leaving, of going to Thia's house, that messy happy home with noise and children and a big slobbering dog, was irresistible to Hannah. Hannah knew that Thia was the least favorite of her mother's book club friends, but she also realized that it was the perfect place to go, because there would be less attention on her and more distractions. She asked if she could visit Mino, and Alecia gave her a real smile. "Sure, as often as you want."

Which is why Hannah had packed her weekend bag and let Alecia hustle her to town without trying in tiny ways to thwart her, a game she'd been engaging in for so long she couldn't remember when it had begun.

CHAPTER NINETEEN
PURSUIT

Detective Matthews made the rounds on Alecia's block trying to determine who had been home to see a moving truck. Apparently, nobody. One woman had been walking her dog and had passed the truck but hadn't taken note of the company, and in fact seemed to remember it simply as a large white truck with no logo or any kind of advertising on it. Detective Matthews made a mental note scoring one for Alecia, because no moving company in the world did that. Their primary marketing opportunity was on the sides of their trucks. That meant she hired movers and a truck separately. She'd preempted his first move, which worried Detective Matthews, because he couldn't figure out her end game.

From her iPad, Alecia watched the detective walk around her property. She also watched (courtesy of Camera D angled specifically for this reason) as he crossed her yard to knock on her neighbor's door. They were actively investigating, which meant Fiona had gone to the police. Now that Hannah was safely with Thia and on her way home, Alecia needed to move quickly.

She set the car up.

She placed the letter in her pocket.

She had a Glock 43 9mm loaded and ready.

Throughout her marriage to Everett, Alecia had been diligent about organizing couple activities for them. Golf was Everett's thing, used for business and leisure and personal time. Spin class was Alecia's thing, keeping her strong and svelte, and giving her an opportunity to clear her mind for an hour. Alecia had tried several couple's activities soon after Hannah was born in an effort to retain the husband and wife bond.

Hiking (Everett didn't like), museums (relegated to a family activity), couple's massage (Everett's idea that made her skin crawl), swimming (ruined her hair-color), and bird watching (boring). When Everett suggested the shooting range, Alecia bristled at the idea as it wasn't anything she'd ever done or thought of doing. However, she'd promised herself she'd consider anything Everett came up with, and so in her indomitable way she researched extensively, then executed. No one was more surprised than she to discover how good she was at it and how much she enjoyed it. It became their primary couple activity. They both agreed that Hannah would learn to shoot as well, but not until she was 16. They agreed never to purchase a gun and only used the guns at the range. Alecia, it turns out, was — as in most things she worked hard at — an excellent shot.

In Savannah, Georgia you can buy a gun and store it without a permit. A license to carry is required, but Alecia didn't need to carry it anywhere.

Detective Matthews looked at his watch and realized he'd be late for his appointment with Chloe Payne and her family if he didn't head over right away. The drive was a short one, and he pulled into the massive driveway and walked up to the front door, noting, not for the first time, that wealth didn't insulate people from the worst things human beings could do to one another. The stepmother opened the door and ushered him in, not in a hostile way, but she wasn't happy to see him. He followed her through a foyer (with roughly the same square footage as his apartment). The parents were sitting on either side of Chloe, who looked small against the oversized couch. The stepmother gestured to the chair across from Chloe, and she took the one next to the mother. Detective Matthews eyed the three adults trying to get a sense of them. They seemed united and pretty comfortable for exes and a remarriage. He wondered if uniting against him was the reason for it, or if the relationships were as natural as they appeared. Chloe wasn't looking at him. She had one of those fidget spinners in her hand and was staring down at it, not moving. The chair he was in, although directly across from the couch, seemed far away with a coffee table the size of a car between them. A huge glass bowl reminiscent of an octopus in color and form sat in the center of the table, an enormous book of European art flanked the octopus bowl on one side and a modern bronze sculpture rose up on the other. He noticed the absence of dust and thought how nice it must be to have staff to keep the filth at bay; he also thought it was a shame that none of it had isolated Chloe or Hannah from the filth of a human being.

He knew it was going to be difficult to build a rapport with the kid while all three of parents were hovering. He hoped for the requisite offer of coffee so that at least one of them would leave the room, but they weren't giving into social niceties. They were standing guard, so he would just have to do his best.

"Chloe, thank you for agreeing to speak with me."

She looked up briefly, met his gaze, and nodded while letting her eyes slide back to the motionless fidget wheel in her lap.

He tried again, "I'm here because I want to help Hannah, and I think you may be able assist me with that."

It did the trick because now she was listening — he could see it in the stillness of her head and shoulders, even though her eyes were down.

"Chloe?" At the question in his voice she lifted her face to his, meeting his gaze head on. "Has Hannah tried to contact you?"

"No."

"Have you tried contacting her?"

Chloe nodded, "She won't answer my texts, and when I call her it goes straight to voice mail."

"Any activity on social media sites?"

Chloe shook her head.

"Chloe," Detective Matthews spoke in a soft voice so she had to strain forward a little to hear him, "Do you understand why I want to find Hannah?"

"I think so."

"What do you think?"

"To save her."

Chloe took note of the way the detective leaned forward, the way his eyes sharpened. It was almost imperceptible but she saw it.

"Chloe, do you think Hannah needs saving?"

She nodded.

"Because of what you saw the night you slept over?"

She nodded again. Swiftly. A short head bob.

"Can you tell me what you saw?"

Chloe told him. It was almost word for word what Fiona had reported at the station. Hearing it from Chloe made his blood run cold in a way it hadn't from her mother. Not because the facts themselves had changed. But because he could see the horror in Chloe's eyes when she spoke. Her words were steadier, more matter of fact than he would have expected, but her eyes reflected the truth of it.

"Chloe, did Hannah ever mention anything, a place they may have gone?" He saw Chloe about to speak, and then a hesitation, a question in her eyes. "Anything, no matter how irrelevant it may seem."

"She said she wanted to disappear. And go someplace beautiful. I didn't understand at the time."

"And now you do?"

"Someplace beautiful, but not here."

"Like a different town? Or different state?"

"No. Someplace else. Not this world."

"Do you think she wanted to harm herself?"

Chloe thought about the cuts she'd made on her own thighs. The need she'd had to feel something other than her own existence. Had Hannah wanted to hurt herself? Chloe didn't think so. She believed Hannah just wanted to be some place where her father wouldn't be a part of her. And there was no place on this earth where that could happen.

* * *

Alecia placed the letter in her pocket. She hadn't decided yet if she would need it. If she used the letter, then she had chosen the easiest path for herself, which she didn't believe she deserved. The question pecking at her brain like a vulture on road-kill was whether or not Hannah would be better off without her. She was hoping the answer would come to her after she killed Everett. But she needed to prepare for both. And so, she had. If she didn't need the letter, she would undo the car, destroy the letter, and get ready for prison. She'd prepared for that as much as she could. Cigarettes, Tampax and sanitary pads to trade, charcoals and paper to sketch with. Copies of *Moby Dick, Ulysses, Vanity Fair, Don Quixote, A Fine Balance, Middlesex, Rumi's Little Book of Life,* and Ralph Waldo Emerson's *Essays: First Series.* Alecia didn't believe she deserved such luxuries. But, if she decided Hannah needed her to live, then she also knew Hannah needed her to survive in prison, and feeding her mind was the only way she would. If she decided Hannah was better off without either parent, the note was ready. The one thing she had complete clarity about,was that she needed to kill Everett as swiftly as possible. She pulled her phone out and hit speed dial. She knew that no matter where he was on the course, or whomever he was with, he would answer her call.

"Alecia?"

"There's an emergency, I'm in the garage." She spoke softly, without urgency. She knew he'd come.

"What is it? Is Hannah okay?"

"Hurry. Please hurry." Before he could answer, she pressed end and waited.

Alecia heard Everett's car pull up. She counted the seconds as she imagined him frantically pushing the button for the garage door. She'd disabled the automatic door opener. In four heartbeats, he was opening the side door, and she was waiting for him. The Glock pointed between his eyes.

"Close the door Everett."

"What's happening? Where's Hannah?"

"Close the door."

He listened to her out of habit as if he hadn't yet registered the gun, and his gaze sought Hannah. When he realized she wasn't there, he turned to Alecia. She watched comprehension seep into his features and her heart sped up. She thought of Shakespeare's *Measure for Measure.* Of Isabelle saying "truth is truth until the end of reckoning." She remembered their book club discussion many years ago, and how she'd thought then that she knew what it meant, how well she understood Isabelle's conflict and perhaps her intent, and how differently she understood it now. Alecia knew some truths to be too terrible for mercy and that reckoning would not lead to revenge or even justice. Nor would it lead to redemption or deliverance. Alecia believed in the soul. Yet she could no longer worry about the fate of her soul, or Everett's. Revenge, justice, forgiveness, mercy, and deliverance — none of these were Alecia's jobs. She'd leave those jobs to the law and God. Reckoning for Alecia meant only one thing. Clarity. She needed to know what to do and knew that the next five minutes with Everett would guide her.

"Sit down," Alecia said and nodded to the chair she'd placed near the door, far enough away that he couldn't lunge for her, but close enough that she could put the bullet neatly through his head.

She needed to kill him, but she also needed to talk to him in a way she couldn't when she'd first put this plan into motion, when she'd still needed him to believe she would protect him.

"Where's Hannah?" He sat gingerly in the chair, his face chalk-white, and she wondered if he was in shock. That wouldn't do. She needed him to feel everything.

"I sent her to live with Thia."

He jumped up. "What?"

"Sit down or I'll blow your head off."

"Easy! What's wrong with you?"

"Well Everett, what's wrong with me is that you raped our daughter."

He sunk into his chair, his eyes squeezing shut, his jaw clenching. "Don't call it that."

"What would you call it?"

"I told you already — it wasn't like that! I love her. I would never hurt her."

"You did hurt her. "

"I was gentle. She — it wasn't like that — it was…"

She watched his face soften, and it took everything in her not to squeeze the trigger.

"What was it Everett? What was the rape of our daughter?"

"Don't call it that!" He leaned forward in his chair and roared, his mouth wide and cavernous, the glint of his teeth sharp, the soft pulp of his throat exposed. She watched as he caught his breath, closed his mouth. As his eyes took in the gun and her steady hand. He leaned back, his breath short. "Are you going to shoot me?"

"That depends." *Yes,* she thought. *I am going to shoot you, but not yet. Not until I understand.*

"What do you want from me? I said I was sorry! I know it was wrong! I can't undo it — I can just — not do it again."

"I don't think you believe it was wrong Everett. I think you believe it was okay. More than okay. What were you going to say — how were you going to describe it?"

He shut his eyes and whispered, "Kill me for it if you want to."

"How would you describe what you did?"

He shook his head. "You won't understand."

"Of course I won't because it's depraved. But I want to hear what you told yourself. It's your only chance to live. Your only chance to see Hannah again."

He swallowed. She noticed that he couldn't look at her directly. That worked for her, because she didn't want his gaze to touch her.

"Tell me, Everett, or I'll pull this trigger right now."

He shook his head and closed his eyes, "It was beautiful."

"Do you think Hannah found it beautiful?"

"Yes! She did! She knew it was pure. It was love!"

"She said she doesn't remember a time when it wasn't happening. That it was just touching at first. When you read her books or gave her baths."

"It was so natural. It just — it just happened. I never planned it."

"It isn't natural, Everett. And you did plan it. You planned not to get caught."

"Not at first!"

"Explain it to me." Alecia's voice was conversational. Not so different from the moments when they were discussing an article in the Wall Street Journal, when Everett would opine, and she would ask questions, a true desire to understand.

He spoke so softly, that Alecia had to lean forward to hear him. "It was as if we were meant to be together. That way. It was an extension of how much I loved her, a way to express it. I never thought about it or planned it. I was never attracted to children — never! I would have recommended castrating anyone who even — it wasn't like that."

"Was it something about me? Something that led you…."

"No! It had nothing — no. It was just…I loved her and… touching her, making her feel good…making me feel good… it just seemed right. It seemed natural. It seemed…"

"What?"

"You won't believe me."

"Try me."

"It seemed…Godly."

"You're right. I don't believe you."

"Not in a religious way…but a spiritual way."

"You think God moved you to abuse our daughter."

"Don't call it that!"

"That's what it was. You abused her. And you think God made you do it?"

"No! He didn't make me. It just seemed so right. So natural."

"It isn't."

He looked angry. "How do you know that?"

"Because she told me."

"Told you what?"

"That it made her feel dirty."

"You're lying."

"Why would I lie about that?"

"Because you want her to feel that way!"

"No, Everett. I don't want my daughter to feel dirty. I want her to feel safe."

"You don't understand! You put those thoughts in her head. She did feel safe with me. What we have is special! You're the one who sullied it! Turned it into something it wasn't."

"You're wrong. I had no idea. She came to me. She told me. She wanted it to stop."

He shook his head. "I don't believe you."

"You're going to jail. You'll never see her again. The police know. They're coming for you. We're both going to jail and Hannah will live with Thia and Eric.

"You can't do that to Hannah. She needs us. Both of us!"

"The police will be here soon. It's done."

"Please Alecia, don't do this to her. I'll never touch her again, even if she wants me to. I won't, I promise."

Alecia moved her finger away from the trigger. There was no safety and if he kept talking like that she was going to pull the trigger and that would be the end of it. *Maybe she should just get it over with*, she thought. There wasn't anything left for her to learn. There was no mystery to unravel, no secret truth. Men like Everett did what they did because they wanted to. She wasn't going to unlock his mind, there wasn't anything to unlock. He felt a physical urge, and he acted on it. He manipulated and coerced and lied and raped. There wasn't anything more complicated than that. What had she hoped to uncover? What had she thought she would learn that would make one bit of difference?

"Alecia…think of Hannah, she needs us."

"She's better off without us. And you're better off like this. You don't deserve to die. You deserve to spend the next 20 years being raped in prison."

He began to sob. Alecia checked in with herself to see if she felt sorry for him. She didn't. She wondered if it meant that she'd lost her humanity or confirmed it.

"Stop crying, Everett. The police are on their way. If you go into prison weak, they'll smell it. You'll be raped that much sooner. That much more brutally."

"Alecia…please."

"It's out of my hands. They're on their way. I told them. I took Hannah to her doctor and filed a report. She told him, and they gathered physical evidence. It's happening, I couldn't stop it if I wanted to. And I don't want to."

"Alecia, please!"

"Shhh. Do you hear that? The sirens? They're on their way."

"No! Alecia!"

"I'll try to stall them, give you a minute to collect yourself."

Alecia placed the gun on the floor and slipped quietly out the side door of the garage, away from Everett. She walked toward the front of the house where she hoped someone would

219

see her, a neighbor, a dog walker, the postman, anyone — and waited. She counted, it took thirty-five seconds, and she was already at the mailbox checking her mail. Mrs. McCalister right on schedule, strolled by with her dog Twinkles on their afternoon walk. Alecia waved and smiled and Mrs. McCalister was about to wave back when the shot rang out. It could have been a truck backfiring. Or someone target practicing. But there was something about that single shot tearing through the quiet of the street. And even though Alecia had been hoping for it, waiting for it, it still caught her by surprise and made her jump. It made Mrs. McCalister jump too. It made Twinkles bark. Alecia and Mrs. McCalister's eyes locked.

Mrs. McCalister told her husband that night, over a beef stew and a dark ale, how shocked Alecia had looked, how her eyes had widened and her face had crumpled before she dropped her mail on the ground and ran, the pile of gloss coated catalogues skittering into the street. She described Alecia running toward the sound (like a bat out of hell) and how she didn't know if she should follow or not, so she bent down and picked up Alecia's mail and was putting it back in the box when she heard Alecia scream. It was a long and terrible scream, and that's when Mrs. McCalister pulled out her phone and called 911.

Hannah couldn't remember the first time she'd ridden in a plane. Her parents took at least two vacations a year with her, somewhere tropical in the winter and somewhere European in the summer. She was an adept traveler, a doted-on child, and because she asked for it, she always got the window seat. Today was no different — buckled in with her backpack neatly stowed in front of her. By habit, she'd taken a wet-wipe out first and wiped down the buckle, tray-table, screen, and the armrests, remembering the little button used to recline the seat. Then, when she realized Thia wasn't doing the same, she diligently wiped Thia's down as well (there were many ways Hannah wanted to rebel against Alecia, but contracting disgusting people-germs from filthy disease-ridden airplane seats was not one of them). Thia smiled uneasily when Hannah finished, and Hannah primly placed the used wipe in the seat pocket in front of her then used a fresh wipe to clean her hands before carefully stuffing that one on top of it. "Don't worry," she said to Thia. "I'll throw them out later when they collect the garbage."

"Oh, I wasn't worried."

Hannah smiled at her, put headphones on, and leaned back in her seat, turning her gaze to the window just as the plane began to taxi. Soon they were soaring at a right angle, and Hannah felt that familiar flattening of her insides as the world tilted backwards and they climbed into the sky. Once the plane righted and settled into the atmosphere, Hannah could no longer decipher whether or not they were even moving. She pressed her fingertip to the window, oblivious of germs, and wished she could stay up there forever.

Hannah fell asleep instantly. One minute Thia was watching her wipe things down like she was about to perform surgery and the next she was asleep with her head against the window. The poor kid looked exhausted, and even in profile Thia could see the purple crescents under Hannah's eyes. Thia felt anxiety threaten, the same feeling she'd been warding off since Chloe disclosed what had happened. It felt ancient and familiar, and Thia had years of practice tamping it back down.

She took a deep breath in and visualized two lines from a chant that moved like tickertape through her mind. *I am always safe from harm, Goddess holds me in her arms.* She applied the same prayer for Hannah and comforted herself with the knowledge that for the moment anyway, Hannah was no longer in harm's way.

For the next 90 minutes, Thia read *Little Fires Everywhere* by Celeste Ng. It was her turn to choose this month's book, and she'd planned on recommending it, but of course she'd never had a chance.

Thia read and reread the words on the page in front of her. *"Like after a prairie fire. I saw one, years ago, when we were in Nebraska. It seems like the end of the world. The earth is all scorched and black and everything green is gone. But after the burning the soil is richer, and new things can grow. People are like that, too you know, they start over. They find a way."*

Thia wondered if that was always true, or if there were some fires too terrible for new growth. She thought of the Yew tree in Pocantico, the way it stretched from earth to sky and how the Druids believed the Yew is the sacred tree of transformation and rebirth.

Thia watched Hannah sleep, noticed how her brow wrinkled and her eyelids shuddered, the fine blue veins an almost imperceptible pattern like decorations on a moth wing. She closed her book and closed her eyes and imagined Hannah in a circle of light with an outer circle of Yew trees protecting her and a third circle of red hot fire burning everything outside of the circle until there was nothing left but possibility.

Hannah was dreaming. First, she was riding alongside the plane. It was quiet, and all she felt was stillness. She wasn't afraid, because it didn't feel like she was doing anything. Just sitting alongside the plane in the sky. In the transitory way of dreaming she was suddenly in a tunnel, breathing was laborious, and although she could make out shapes of people, she didn't know who they were. Frightened, she began searching the shapes looking for her parents. Once, she saw Alecia in silhouette, but when Hannah drew closer and touched her, she was nothing more than cardboard. There were lots of men, but none of them was Everett. Still searching, she caught a glimpse of him smiling and beckoning her, but when she ran toward him she realized he wasn't smiling, but grimacing. His face seized in torment, his eyes hollowed, mouth a cavernous oval like Edvard Munch's *The Scream.* Hannah tried to stop, tried to turn around, but she couldn't; her body wasn't moving of her own volition. Some force was propelling her toward that horrible twisted version of her father.

She woke with a start. Her heart thudding and her mouth dry. Thia placed a gentle hand on her arm. "Hey there, chica," she said with a smile. "I got you a soda and some chips."

Hannah closed her mouth, expelled the dream from her mind, sat up straighter, and focused on Thia. "Gracias amiga."

Thia smiled, "De nada."

Hannah drank her soda and ate her chips, telling herself it was just a dream and that everything would be all right.

Alecia spoke to several police officers, a soft-spoken medical investigator, and a host of other people. She was interviewed in her driveway, in her home, and at the Fulton County Police station.

The same questions were asked in a variety of different ways with a variety of different tones, by many different people, and although it was now 8:00 PM and she had not yet been able to make contact with Thia or Hannah, she was the calmest and most relieved she'd been since Hannah whispered the truth in her ear. They had come through the eye of the storm — and survived. All that remained was the debris of their emotions and the need to heal her child.

Fiona drove up Bedford Road toward The Church of the Magdalene. It was rare for Fiona to visit during a weekday. Although for the last couple of years she'd become an infrequent participant on Sundays as well. When they'd first moved here from the city as a family and discovered the beauty and charm of the church, they had attended enthusiastically. The community had been warm and welcoming, and both Bryce and Fiona had marveled at the bucolic setting, the English cottage feel of the building, the color, and light from the multitude of stained glass windows. The fact that this church was the only one dedicated to The Magdalene in the entire New York Archdiocese fostered in Fiona a desire to join. Fiona found the Sunday sermons to carry a consistent message of compassion, which sustained both her faith and her person.

Before her decision to divorce, Fiona had ramped up her attendance at church, listening carefully for signs that she should remain in the marriage. It went against her faith to leave, it went against the best interests of her family, and it wasn't something Bryce wanted. Yet she knew that if she stayed, the good will she had for Bryce, Chloe's knowledge of their love and respect for one another, and any possibility for her own sense of purpose would erode until nothing remained. There was no abuse in their marriage — there hadn't even been much unpleasantness. All attempts at conversations with her priest led her to a path of staying in a lackluster marriage, of finding the good, of working harder. Divorce was a sin and although the language of her priest was compassionate, gentle, (there was no talk of ex-communication), she knew that if they divorced without an annulment, she would never again be able to receive communion — but how could she request an annulment without in some way denying Chloe's existence? Fiona felt no criticism in any of her priest's counsel. All of it was fair and nuanced and at times profound and true.

As it turned out, when Bryce realized Fiona needed to work that hard to muster any feelings for him, his interest in her began to wane. He grew resentful of her, became withdrawn, sullen, and punitive, and their hard work to stay together began to feel like the unraveling of their marriage. In the end, it was Bryce who wanted out. Fiona changed her mind and decided she wanted to plow through; she missed the optimism and sunny disposition of the man she'd married and wanted to regain it. But Bryce couldn't forget how she'd felt, and more importantly he couldn't forgive her for it. Fiona never blamed the church for the failure of her marriage. She was grateful for the solace she found there both during and after the divorce, but for Fiona, the church became emblematic of everything she'd lost when her marriage ended; it was as though without one she could no longer have the other. Bryce continued to go, Val accompanied him on major holidays and rare Sundays when he pushed her hard enough, and Chloe went with her father most Sundays, eager to see her friends and make her confirmation with the same children she'd received communion with. In the divorce, Bryce got The Church of the Magdalene. Fiona viewed it as part of her penance for her desire to be on her own.

As Fiona drove the few minutes from work to The Magdalene, she felt a gnawing behind her breast bone, similar to the way she'd felt when she'd been pregnant and nursing, a need to feed herself or perish. Another church wouldn't do. Simply reading scripture wouldn't do. Even a meeting with her priest, which she knew she could arrange with a phone call, wouldn't do. She needed to be in the physical building, her gaze at the altar, surrounded by winter light through stained glass. She needed a healing.

At 4:00 on a weekday, the church was remarkably quiet, and Fiona sent up a prayer of gratitude for it. She walked purposefully toward the pew closest to her favorite stained glass, a depiction of the woman washing the feet of Jesus with her tears. Bent over at work, a cloth in one hand and a small vial of perfume in the other, her hair flanking her face, she wore a robe of gold with a prominent section of deep purple. Fiona often wondered if the choice of royal colors for the woman thought to be a sinner was a statement by the artist? Was this an acknowledgment that she was as worthy as any who wore the colors of royalty. Fiona knew it was her art history background that led her to search for such things, and perhaps it was mere wishful thinking that the artist even cared to make such a point, but Fiona's conviction gave her the extra impetus she needed to find a like-mindedness in a world which seemed to polarize more definitively every day.

In the stained-glass depiction, Jesus watched the woman work at his feet, and Fiona searched his face for the gratitude he must certainly have felt in that moment, the sense of relief, his hand outstretched above her head in what may have been a blessing or a simple thank you. The artist captured the disdain and condemnation in the face of Simon the Pharisee as he looked down on the woman he considered to be a sinner. The artist rendered strong emotion in Simon's face. Fiona recognized Simon's countenance, and the derisive sneer she'd felt turned on her again and again when she'd stepped outside of the bounds of what someone else thought a woman should be. It was hate. And in that moment Simon's face, before Jesus taught him the lesson of forgiveness, became synonymous for Fiona with the subjugation of women around the globe.

Rage filled the space around her. She let it burn. She needed the cleansing more than the salve of forgiveness. The story depicted before her was one of forgiveness. Jesus would forgive the woman's sins and teach Simon that those granted forgiveness will in turn love the most. What Fiona couldn't forgive was the condemnation of the woman in the first place.

She thought about Everett and what he'd done to their daughters. Fiona would leave any form of forgiveness for Everett up to Jesus; she had nothing but rage in her heart for him, and she would allow it to burn until it was pure white ash, she would take that ash inside of herself until it was part of the cellular structure of her body, and she would use it to distil any residue of Everett's attempt to contaminate their daughters with his depravity. Fiona looked up at the picture of Magdalene at the feet of Jesus and thought of all the terrible things human beings do to one another. Of God's forgiveness and the white heat of rage and decided that for her forgiveness would be her acceptance of her rage.

Feeling a sense of peace wash over her, she stood up and walked out; it was time to pick Chloe up and bring her home.

Chloe stood at the top of the hill of the middle school, waiting for her mother to pick her up. From her vantage point she could see a wide slice of the Hudson River, a sparkle of silver against the pale sky, the almost imperceptible ridge of the

Palisade mountain range visible if you knew where to look. Fiona and Chloe had plans to cross the bridge and go to Woodbury Commons, where she was going to pick out new sheets and a comforter at The Ralph Lauren outlet. Afterwards they were going to have dinner at The Shake Shack. It was an unusual outing in general and even more unusual for a weeknight. Chloe could tell Fiona was trying to get her to spend more time at home. She didn't know how to explain to her mother that her old sheets and comforter weren't the problem. It was only compounding her guilt that her mother was spending money trying to fix something that wasn't an issue in the first place. On the other hand, having a destination and an errand that would allow them to spend time together was exactly what Chloe longed for — time with her mother but a distraction from their usual routine together. For the first time in a long while, Chloe found herself looking forward to something.

The sun was going down rapidly and the temperature was dropping. Chloe took a deep breath and became aware of her anxiety. Her mother's car appeared on the road below and made the turn onto school grounds. At that precise moment Chloe's phone pinged; she knew her mom would never text while driving. She looked down and saw Hannah's picture on her phone and the accompanying text, *I'm baaaaaaaack bitch.*

***

Thia and Fiona sat on the screened porch on the side of Thia's house. It was the only place they were reasonably sure the children wouldn't find them. Bundled in their winter coats, they sat on two rickety wicker chairs, each holding a mug of spiced mulled wine, their words disintegrating in puffs of frosted air.

"Alecia called me yesterday and asked me to take Hannah. She was planning to turn Everett into the local authorities and didn't want Hannah there when they picked him up. She said she left town because she didn't want the news to break in Hannah's home town."

"It just seems so — elaborate."

"I know — but — I guess she was really thinking long term. For Hannah."

"I guess I'm not that imaginative. I would have gone straight to the authorities here."

"You think you would have. But who knows? You didn't want to report it right away. It was Ivy and Val who pushed us."

Fiona nodded slowly, "So what happened? Was Everett arrested?"

Thia looked at her, "I don't know. I haven't heard from her, and her phone just goes straight to voice mail."

"I think we should go see Detective Matthews."

"And say what?"

"The truth! That Alecia is in Savannah, Georgia, reporting Everett to the authorities and you have Hannah."

"What if they pull Hannah from me? Put her in foster care? I can't risk it."

"Why would they do that?"

"I just don't see the point in going to him. Alecia asked me to take care of her and that's what I'm doing."

"There's been a serious crime committed. We can't just ignore that."

"We aren't! Alecia is reporting it. We already did that on this end."

"But they think Hannah's missing! We can't just not tell the detective."

"Well if he's any good at his job he'll investigate and find her here."

"Let's just ask Val and Ivy what they think."

"They'll say to go to the local authorities."

"Thia — we've gotta do it."

Thia looked out at the night. She took a sip of the mulled wine and felt acid at the back of her throat. "I can't help feeling like it's a betrayal of Alecia."

"It isn't."

Fiona watched as Thia's face became a swirl of light and color, just as they heard the crunch of tires at the curb and the sound of a car door slamming. Apparently, Detective Matthews was better at his job than either of them gave him credit for, because he'd found them on his own.

Shortly after the pizza arrived, while Eric was knee deep in small children demanding pizza cut into "boxes not triangles" and the moms ensconced on the porch with their mugs of wine, Hannah and Chloe made their exodus by shouting loud enough so everyone *could* hear (but into the general din so that no one actually *did*) that that they were going for a walk.

The temperature had dropped to near bitterness and Hannah declared it the eternal winter from a special kind of frozen hell. In tacit agreement, the girls made their way down to Devries playground, a few blocks from Thia's house, and the place where they had played often as children.

On the way over, without looking at Chloe, Hannah said, "I'm not mad at you for telling. Just so you know."

"I didn't tell. Not at first."

"I figured. Because nobody came."

"Did you want someone to?"

"Maybe. I don't know."

Chloe was quiet. "So, I should have told?"

"You didn't do anything wrong, Clo."

They made their way into the deserted playground and walked straight to the swings where they sat side by side, Hannah lifting higher into the air by pumping her legs ever so slightly while Chloe twisted as far as the chain allowed, then releasing into a dizzying spin.

"I told my mom." Hannah spoke the words from high up and Chloe felt them sitting in the air above her.

"Is that why you moved?" She asked when her swing was still and she could see straight again.

Hannah didn't answer just pumped her legs and swung higher.

"It's okay if you don't want to talk about it."

"Yeah. That's why we moved. Everett's in the guesthouse, and I'm only allowed to see him for breakfast and dinner. He doesn't even have a key to our house. My mom gave me my old phone back when Thia picked me up, but his number is blocked. Her idea not mine."

"Do you miss him?"

Hannah was quiet again and her swinging grew slower until she'd almost stopped next to Chloe. "I don't miss *that.* But sometimes I miss him."

"Yeah."

"Alecia thinks I should just hate him."

"She said that?"

"No, but I can tell. She hates him now."

"Yeah. Well, he isn't her dad so it's not the same thing at all."

"Exactly."

Chloe looked at Hannah, "I'm sorry. About that night."

"Why are *you* sorry?"

"I think — whatever I did — the way your dad was with me — I guess — is that why you and he...?"

"No."

"Then why?"

"I can't explain it."

"Just try."

"You'll never understand. Your family is so normal."

Chloe felt an ache inside her take root and bloom. All this time Hannah thought Chloe had the normal family. She'd wanted Chloe to tell. And Chloe had let her down. Flashes of that night often intruded into Chloe's brain, breaking her concentration, waking her from a sound sleep. One of the things she kept seeing was the look on Hannah's face; it had seemed to Chloe a look of triumph, the kind girls gave one another on the soccer field when their team scored, or when someone received the highest grade in class and they shot a look at the student who got the second highest grade. Chloe remembered how irritated Hannah had seemed when Everett was pouring Chloe the sherry glasses filled to the brim with wine. Chloe recognized jealousy. It wasn't that different from feelings she'd had when she was on the U6 soccer team and her dad was coaching. She remembered how jealous she would get when her dad handed all the other kids on the team their ice cream first before handing Chloe hers. As she'd grown older, Chloe realized he was just being polite, while teaching Chloe to be polite as well. But at the time envy dominated her thinking that her dad liked the more talented soccer players better than her. It had been childish, and the memory embarrassed Chloe whenever she thought of it, but it was the truth — she had felt jealous. What if Hannah's jealousy was no different? Everett was Hannah's dad. She loved him even if he did terrible things.

All of these thoughts became tangled in Chloe's mind: her desire for Everett's attention on that last sleepover, the horror at what she'd felt from him when he'd stood behind her and rubbed her shoulders, what she'd seen him do to Hannah. How Hannah might have normal feelings for her dad even if he did disgusting things to her. How those things were indelibly burned onto Chloe's brain as if she'd done them too. She felt a pervasive sense of shame sticking to her, reminiscent of images in a news article she'd seen after the Exxon oil spill — baby ducks smeared in thick sludge, suffocating to death because they couldn't clean themselves.

Hannah jumped off the swing and gave Chloe a sideways look and a slow smile. "Had to get rid of my entire stash when we blew out of town. Time to replenish!"

"Wait! Where are you going?"

Hannah ignored Chloe, leaving her no choice but to follow her through the playground and into the woods.

"Hannah, we should get back. My mom's going to be looking for me."

"Come on Chloebologna, it's my first night back and I haven't gotten high in two weeks — after all of Alecia's *drama* I deserve it."

"Who are you meeting?"

"That's for me to know and you to find out."

Chloe heard the sound of leaves crunching a low whistle, and then two older kids appeared out of the weeds. One of them was Josh Wells, a sophomore who lived a few blocks away. Considered the hottest boy in his grade he had solidified his reputation with upper classmen by selling weed brownies out of his locker at school. The other kid was Philip Rowland, and Chloe literally felt her heart skip a beat. He helped her dad with odd jobs now and then. Last summer, when her dad moved into the new house with Val, Philip had come to Fiona and Chloe's house to help her dad empty their garage.

Chloe had spent the entire day stealing glances at Philip as he'd carried things from the garage to the curb, finding excuses to go out there, bringing lemonade and cookies once, relaying messages from Fiona about what to toss and what to keep. He'd been nice to Chloe even if he did talk to her like she was five years old instead of a mere three grades behind him. As dark as it was and difficult to see, Chloe thought she detected a moment of surprise and maybe even fear when he recognized her, but a heartbeat later his eyes flattened and his body slouched in the universal cool of cute guys everywhere, and she thought she must have imagined it. They only exchanged a few words, and despite Hannah's flirtatious looks and invitation for them to stay and party, they took off pretty quickly, much to Chloe's relief and Hannah's disappointment.

"Well that was subtle, Clo. You may as well have worn a sign that said *first time copping.*"

"You should have warned me. I know him. He works for my dad sometimes."

Hannah laughed. "Well, he's not gonna tell, he looked nervous as fuck."

Chloe followed Hannah back to the swing set, and Hannah fired up a one hit. She took a deep breath and held it in, a small happy smile curling the ends of her lips.

When she passed it, Chloe shook her head. Hannah shrugged and winked, "More for me."

Chloe watched as Hannah leaned back on the swing, her body perpendicular to the sky. When Chloe craned her own head toward the sky it was an inky dark with few stars visible. Her eyes began to water from the cold air.

"Hannah, are you happy you're back?"

It was awhile before she answered, "I think it's just a visit."

"Yeah, but — is it good to visit?"

"I missed you, Clo."

"I was afraid you wouldn't want to be friends anymore."

"I never wanted you to know — and then when you did — I thought maybe it would stop. And when it didn't, I thought maybe if I tell Alecia…."

"Did Alecia make it stop?"

"I thought she'd be mad at me. Hate me."

"Hannah!"

"Everett always said she would…but she didn't. She said it wasn't my fault."

"Well, it wasn't!"

Hannah was quiet for a while. "Yeah well, two to tango and all that."

Chloe tried as hard as she could to hold still, afraid that any inflection in her voice, or barely perceptible movement in her body would reflect the waves of revulsion washing through her at the mental image Hannah's seemingly cavalier statement conjured. She also knew Hannah well enough to know she was watching Chloe closely. And that whatever she said or did next would be a definitive moment.

"I think I get it — if you had nothing to do with it then you just feel stupid, like you were taken advantage of." Hannah was holding still now. "But, I think what your mom meant when she said it wasn't your fault is that your dad taught you, and he's the responsible one, and kids only know what parents teach them."

Disappointment washed over Hannah's face and Chloe knew she'd failed her. "Look, Clo. We're going to have to face that my dad's a perv and he made me a perv. So, whether it's my fault or not, it's the truth."

And with that Chloe began to cry.

Hannah looked at her sadly, "Clo, you need to move on. This didn't happen to you. It isn't your fault, you just had the bad luck of choosing me as your best friend, and I needed you, so I let you be my best friend. But girl, you need to find some nice basic bitches at your own school and move on. This right here is gonna be too much. I'm giving you permission."

Chloe felt the thickness of mucus running into her mouth, her tears escaping down her cheeks. "I don't want to."

"Bitch, pull yourself together."

Chloe cried harder.

Hannah sighed. "I'll let you come horseback riding with me tomorrow." She whipped some tissues out of her purse. "Here, fix yourself up, you're a hot mess."

Chloe took the tissues and mopped at her face.

"Come on, Chloebologna. Let's go home." Hannah jumped gracefully off the swing and began the walk toward Thia's house, Chloe beside her. "Geez, Clo. You are *such* a buzz kill."

Chloe turned to her looking so stricken that Hannah laughed, "Nah, I'm kidding. That kid's shit was weak as fuck. Last time I cop off him."

Chloe felt relief throb through her. Maybe things could get back to normal now. Hannah was home and tonight Chloe would be sleeping back in her old room. She felt profoundly grateful that they hadn't bought new sheets and a comforter. She didn't want any more changes. Maybe she could just start to forget instead.

Hannah and Chloe saw the cherry top swirling on Thia's block before they'd turned the corner.

"Maybe it's nothing." Chloe said.

Hannah tried to gauge what part of the block the lights

were coming from but couldn't be sure. "Fuck it. That shit was weak." She took the rest of the weed she'd copped, dug a hole with the heel of her boot in the icy dirt near a telephone pole on the side of the road, tossed the one hits into it, and covered it back up with her boot.

Fiona watched as she slid a stick of gum into her mouth, "Look into my eyes, Clo. Any red?"

Chloe peered into Hannah's eyes. They were wide and clear, without a trace of redness. Or fear.

"Nope. All good."

Hannah straightened up, tossed her hair back, and walked toward the flashing lights with Chloe right next to her.

When Detective Matthews got out of the squad car, the women greeted him from the screened porch on the side of the road. The fact that they were together didn't surprise him, and it would give him an opportunity to watch both of them closely. He wanted to gauge their reaction to the news and their interaction with one another.

Thia Daniels ushered him into the porch, "Sorry for the cold, Detective, but the kids are running around in there."

"No problem, this is fine."

"Can I get you anything? A warm drink?"

"No, thanks."

"So how can I help you?"

"I understand Hannah Calding is here with you."

Thia nodded, "Alecia called me yesterday and asked me to come and get her. She was planning on reporting Everett Calding to the authorities in Savannah, and she didn't want Hannah there to witness it."

Fiona leaned toward the detective, "Do you know if she did?"

Detective Matthews watched them both closely. "Everett Calding died by apparent suicide at 3:00 PM this afternoon."

Shock. That was what registered on both women's faces and bodies. He waited for the moment that they made eye contact with one another. If there was any real kind of collusion there, it wasn't showing. Whatever suspicion he had about what Alecia may or may not have orchestrated, these women were not in on it. Either that or they were consummate actors, and the odds of both of them being that good weren't high.

"I don't understand," Thia was asking. "Did Alecia report him?"

Detective Matthews gave her a hard glance. "The first time the Savannah authorities heard from Mrs. Calding was when her neighbor reported hearing a gun shot."

Fiona's face paled, "Did she...? Was it definitely a suicide?"

"The neighbor and Mrs. Calding were out front when the shot was fired. Mrs. Calding ran to the garage and when she screamed, the neighbor..." He stopped to check his notes, "...a Mrs. McCallister, called it in." Thia looked confused. "But she said she was reporting him. That's why I went to pick up Hannah. She said they were going to pick him up, and she didn't want Hannah there."

"Did Mrs. Calding give you a specific time frame?"

"No. But I assumed it was all set. She was so definitive about what time to meet and how we had to make that plane. I just assumed that it was all set up."

Fiona placed her hand over Thia's, which was visibly shaking. "Well, that's how Alecia is. Every second accounted for. And she needs things to run like clockwork."

Thia nodded. "But why did Everett...? I mean why now?"

"Mrs. Calding told the investigating officer in Savannah that Everett knew she was going to turn him in. She said she didn't want the arrest to happen here in Hannah's community. She was hoping to keep it out of the local papers."

Fiona swallowed. Her throat was so dry it hurt. "Is Alecia in trouble?"

Detective Matthews sighed, "That's up to the DA. She failed to report a criminal act, and a case could be made for aiding and abetting when she moved her family under the cover of night to Savannah."

"Do you think the DA will press charges?" Fiona's hands pressed firmly together in what Detective Matthews thought looked like prayer.

"I don't know."

"But if Alecia is arrested, Hannah will effectively be orphaned! It wasn't like she knew what was happening to Hannah...."

Detective Matthews leaned forward. "We don't know what she knew or didn't know." He turned then to Thia. "Mrs. Daniels, where is Hannah Calding?"

"Inside somewhere. They had pizza and...."

"I need to talk with her."

"Are you going to tell her?"

"Yes. And we need to question her."

Thia sat up straighter. "I'm afraid that will have to wait. She's going to be upset."

"That isn't your call, Mrs. Daniels."

"Her mother asked me to take her. I'm responsible for her."

Fiona broke in before Thia could do what she looked like she wanted to do — eviscerate the detective with the swipe of a claw. "Where is Alecia now? Is she under arrest?"

"Not at this time."

"Then why hasn't she called?" Thia demanded.

He shrugged. "She's probably still being questioned."

Thia's shoulders slumped.

Detective Michaels leaned toward her. "Look, I'm not the bad guy here. We want the same thing, which is to protect Hannah. I'm not going to interrogate her. But I need to ask her some questions."

Fiona looked at him. "We'd like to be there when you do that."

"I'm not sure that's wise. I don't think she'll talk in front of you."

Thia sat up, "I'm her guardian until she's back with her mother. I need to be in the room when she's questioned."

"We have a child advocate standing by. She will be in the room when we question her. This is out of your hands, Mrs. Daniels."

"Well you can't bring her anywhere tonight. She's sleeping here."

"Actually, we can. You knew there was an active investigation and you had Hannah in your custody and you failed to report that. We could remove her from your care right now."

Thia stood up.

"I'm not saying we will." Detective Matthews made a conciliatory gesture with his hands and waited for Thia to sit back down. "My intention is to have Hannah spend the night here. You can bring her tomorrow to the child advocate's office, and we can talk to her there."

Thia visibly relaxed.

"When are you going to tell Hannah what happened?" Fiona asked.

"Tell me what?"

Detective Matthews looked up to find Hannah and Chloe standing on the other side of the screened porch, their cheeks pink with cold. The women had told him the girls were inside, but clearly, they'd been outdoors for a while. Struck by how terribly young they both looked, his face registered shock momentarily. He wondered briefly why that surprised him — he knew they were not yet 13, that one of them attended the local middle school. He had the disturbing thought that perhaps he'd expected something different, that because of what had happened to them, they would have at least appeared older than their age, as if the way they looked had any bearing on what had happened to them.

And now he had to tell Hannah Calding what her father had done to himself. He knew that as a detective he would be measuring her response, trying to read her reactions, it was as instinctual for him as blinking. He felt something building in his chest, a rising tidal wave of dread.

Hannah heard the words. She saw the concern in Detective Matthews face and sensed Thia and Fiona hovering. She couldn't see Chloe, because for some reason her peripheral vision had vanished and she was seeing the world as if through a distorted peephole. Whatever was in front of her loomed disproportionately large. A moment later she was receding backwards away from them, she put her hand out to touch Chloe, thinking maybe she could hold her in place, but she was moving too quickly. Soon she was somewhere up above, looking down at herself standing next to Chloe her arm outstretched. Chloe reached for her and took her hand. The three adults were moving toward them, rushing as one, through the door in the porch, but by the time they reached her, she was gone, watching the scene as though it were a video on rewind. And then, the world went as black as a starless sky.

Chloe watched Hannah disappear. That was how she'd remember it even years later. The vacant look in Hannah's eyes, the slackness of her jaw, the way her body went from vigilant to listless. Hannah's face paled until it glowed in the weak light emanating from the porch; she was still standing there in front of them, but it was as if she was a shell of herself and the real Hannah had gone somewhere else. Chloe took Hannah's hand, which was icy and limp. Her mother and Thia and the policeman all rushed forward. Thia got through the door first.

"Mrs. Daniels, we need to get her sitting down." Chloe noted that the detective's voice was low and calm. He didn't push Thia out of the way exactly, but he moved her surely and gently so that he could reach Hannah. He braced himself against Hannah and guided her through the porch and into the living room, getting her onto the couch. He covered her with a throw and spoke gently. Chloe caught her breath when Hannah began to tremble. The detective looked at Chloe. "She's going to be okay. Can you get her a glass of water?" He waited for her to nod then looked over at Fiona who followed Chloe into the kitchen.

"Hannah?" He spoke softly and looked into her eyes. He noted the dilated pupils and the rapid breathing. "Hannah, can you hear me?"

After a few beats Hannah blinked then dipped her head, slightly, but responsively. "Ok good. Hannah, I want you to take a deep breath in. Can you do that?"

She tried, but her breath was shallow.

"Ok, Hannah, look at me." He waited for her eyes to find his face. "Another breath ok? Deeper this time."

He breathed with her and this time she was able to do it. "Good. Now exhale." He exhaled, and Hannah followed him. Soon the trembling subsided. Thia, who hadn't left his side, felt herself breathing along with them. After a while, Hannah's pupils returned to their normal size and the trembling stilled. Chloe brought the water in, and Hannah was able to drink some. Fiona checked with Eric, who had somehow managed to get the kids into their beds and asleep without them ever seeing the swirl of police lights or the 6-foot-2 detective out on their porch. Fiona decided Eric Daniels was a wizard and made a mental note to drop off a pound of her homemade fudge and then chastised herself for thinking about inane things.

Detective Matthews looked up at Chloe and Fiona. "Hannah is going to be fine. She just needs some rest."

Fiona nodded. "Thia will take good care of her, Clo."

"I want to stay with her."

"We'll check in tomorrow. First thing. I promise."

Thia put her arm around Chloe. "I'll stay with her. She won't be alone."

Chloe nodded and followed her mother to the door. She turned to look back at Hannah, but her friend's eyes remained closed. She was still terribly pale, and she looked so small tucked into the corner of Thia's couch.

Fiona touched Chloe's arm, "Come on, Clo. We'll see her in the morning. She needs to rest."

When the house quieted Thia put her hand on Hannah's forehead. It felt clammy and cold, and she looked worriedly at the detective. "Shock?"

He nodded. "She'll be okay. She needs to rest." Hannah opened her eyes and looked in the direction of the detective, but he could see she was having difficulty focusing.

"Hannah? Can you hear me?"

She nodded.

"How are you feeling?"

"Tired."

Thia was relieved at how normal Hannah sounded. "Hey, Amiga. Do you want to change into your pajamas? Your bed is all made up and ready. Lila's bunking in the boys' room, and you get her room all to yourself."

Hannah nodded. "My pajamas are in my bag."

Thia smiled at her, "Your bag's in Lila's room. Come on I'll take you up."

"Is my mom ok?"

Thia looked at Detective Matthew. He spoke softly to Hannah. "Your mom is fine."

"Can I call her?"

"Of course," Thia answered. She had no idea if Alecia had access to her phone, so she looked at Detective Matthews. He nodded, but he looked uncertain. "Why don't we get you into your pajamas and then we'll call your mom. Ok?"

Hannah nodded. Then looked over at the detective. "Good night."

He looked at Hannah, "I'll check in tomorrow and see how you're doing. Ok?"

"Ok."

Then he looked at Thia. "I'll see myself out. You take care."

Thia nodded at him, conflicted over whether to feel grateful or throat punch him for bringing the news in the first place. She saw the corner of his lip lift and his eyes crinkle slightly, and she wondered if he'd read her thoughts. Then he was gone, and she was walking Hannah up the stairs.

Thia waited while Hannah changed into her pajamas and brushed her teeth, moving robotically. Thia felt a deep anxiety pierce the space beneath her breastbone and wondered what it would be like for Hannah when she woke the next morning, that moment when she surfaced from sleep to the shores of reality and had to remember all over again that her father had killed himself. How would she cope? Then Thia thought about Hannah getting on the plane, how determined she'd been when she'd wiped down the entire plane area for both of them. How she'd fallen into an exhausted sleep, and despite how frightened she must have been, she'd smiled and said "gracias Amiga" with true gratitude for something as simple as chips and a soda. Thia thought how exceptionally brave Hannah was, and that as difficult as things had been, and as difficult as they were going to be, that her bravery would serve her well.

Hannah climbed into Lila's twin bed. And looked expectantly at Thia. "Is it okay if I call my mom now?"

"Of course."

Hannah picked up the phone, and Thia went to leave the room.

"Oh!" Hannah exclaimed, and Thia looked over at her. "Are you leaving?"

"I thought you might want some privacy."

"Can you — can you stay — please?"

"Of course."

Hannah nodded and Thia perched on Lila's tiny chair a few feet from Hannah. She could hear the phone ringing. It only rang twice before Alecia picked up. "Hannah?"

"Mom?" And she began to cry. Wracking sobs, her entire body shaking. Thia moved toward her, but she saw Hannah's body stiffen, so she stayed where she was.

"Hannah, I'm here." Alecia said. "I'm so sorry."

"Are you ok, Mom?"

"I'm fine. You don't need to worry about me."

"Can you come home?"

"Yes. I'm coming home. I need to help with a few things down here but as soon as I can, I'm coming home."

"Ok."

"Are you with Thia?"

"Yes. She's right here."

"She'll take good care of you until I get there."

"I know."

"She's taking you to the stable tomorrow."

"Chloe's coming too."

"That's good."

"I'm tired now."

"Go to sleep then baby."

"Ok, Mom."

"I love you very much."

"Me too. I love you too."

Thia felt her cheeks flush. She thought about how many times a day she and Eric and the kids said I love you to one another. How natural it was for them. She had the traitorous thought that it sounded forced between Hannah and Alecia, that they weren't words they spoke often. She also knew that it had nothing to do with how much they loved one another, and *that,* Thia thought, was all that mattered.

"Hannah?"

"Mm?"

"Can you put Thia on?"

Hannah passed Thia the phone.

"Thank you, Thia. For everything."

"Oh, Alecia."

"I'll call you in the morning, ok?"

"Yes, and don't worry about Hannah. We'll take good care of her."

"I know."

"Goodnight."

Thia handed Hannah her phone and watched as she placed it carefully down before looking up at Thia. "Is it — could you — is it possible you can stay with me until I fall asleep?"

"I'll be right here."

Hannah nodded and sank her head back onto the pillow, then curled onto her side. Soon her breathing was even. Thia went back to her own room, changed quickly into a sweatshirt and flannel pajama pants, brushed her teeth, swiped off whatever makeup was still on, kissed Eric, grabbed her pillow and an extra blanket and went back to Lila's room. It wouldn't be the first time she'd spent the night next to a sleeping child's bed. She didn't want Hannah waking up alone.

Ivy was finding it difficult to focus. She'd misplaced her socks after carrying them around only to discover them made into the bed. She had no idea what went into the lunch bags, and she was pretty sure she'd put extra scoops of coffee into the pot because it was like drinking rocket fuel and her heart raced.

She checked her texts reflexively. The last missive she'd received was news that Hannah was safe and sound with Thia and her family, and no one had yet heard from Alecia. Her own texts to Alecia remained unanswered.

Ivy dumped her coffee down the sink, rinsed out her mug, and let the tap water run cold before filling her mug and drinking it. She needed to get a grip. As she sipped the water, she stared out at the gray morning. The Rhododendron leaves outside her window pointed straight down; icicles had formed at the ends of the tips, and it almost hurt to look at them.

Ivy was an analytical problem solver; she didn't like unanswered questions, and not knowing whether Alecia had really turned Everett in or not was haunting her. The fact that he might be out there playing golf and drinking exquisite bottles of red wine made her murderous. In fact, at 3:00 that morning while she was lying in bed, her eyes wide open and heart racing, she actually began to make plans about finding them and turning him in. She imagined showing up at their door with officers in tow, watching them handcuff Everett and shove him into the back of a squad car.

The other thing haunting her was her relationship with Alecia. Although their friendship was longstanding, it was not an intimate one. Ivy was self-aware enough to know she was as culpable as Alecia was. Ivy's female friendships were based on common interests or proximity, not shared confidences. Her friends were other women she'd see repeatedly on the sidelines of their son's sporting events; their conversations revolved mainly around whatever sport they were watching or booster they were raising funds for. Some shared her interests, and they would discuss books, politics, or music. There would be an occasional museum visit and dinner in the city. Ivy kept in touch with her college roommates, and they still met twice a year for a weekend away together. Yet, intimacy wasn't something Ivy was comfortable with. Her conversations were intellectual rather than emotional. She didn't like talking about her problems, and while she didn't think of herself as callous, it irritated her when friends would get together and talk about the same problem over and over again, complaining about their husbands, their mothers, or their mothers-in-law. Sometimes she'd just want to yell at them all to pull up their big girl panties and get over it. Consequently, her friendships were based on activities rather than emotions. She didn't call people to talk about her feelings, and if she did have a problem or a concern that was more emotional in nature, she tended to talk to her husband or her mother about it. Ivy liked her friendship with Alecia because she felt Alecia shared a similar sensibility. She didn't emote. Ivy didn't know anything about Alecia's past or where she even grew up other than it was somewhere in the boroughs. They had in-depth conversations about books and movies and similar interests in gallery exhibitions. So, while Ivy felt she knew Alecia well, she also realized she had no idea what her internal life was like. If Ivy had thought about Alecia's internal life at all before today (which she hadn't), she would have assumed it was a mixture of intellectual curiosity and perfectionism. If she thought about what motivated Alecia, she would have guessed aesthetics and status. Alecia leaving in the middle of the night seemed as though she was on the run, but then she called Thia, and it seemed she had a plan all along. One thing Ivy did know about Alecia, she was a master at planning and at execution. Nothing would be left to chance. So, asking Thia to come and get Hannah was not a change of heart. She must have planned all along to send her back. Ivy felt confused and unsettled, and neither of those feelings sat well with her.

Ivy took another look at the Rhododendrons curled against the cold and bundled up more than usual for her morning Kretek. She slid a cigarette from the pack and pocketed her lighter. Usually she left her phone behind so she could watch the river in peace, but at the last minute she slid it into the pocket of her coat and went up to her porch.

Ivy had just lit her Kretek and took the first drag when her cell phone vibrated in her pocket. It was from Fiona and said simply *call me.*

So, she did.

Alecia was not yet free to leave Savannah. She had paperwork to fill out, interviews with investigators to give, and it might be an entire week before she was free to return to New York. She had no idea what she'd be walking into there, if she'd be arrested for failure to report, or worse. These were all risks she'd been prepared for, and still was, but hearing Hannah cry last night was a physical blow — as if someone had walked over and round-housed her without warning. There was no way to prevent Hannah's grief. Nor could she unbind Everett's hold on their daughter. Killing himself, Alecia believed, was the only decent thing her husband had ever done. For a moment, Alecia pondered that. Did she believe it? Did Everett's depravity undo any good he'd done in the world? Alecia decided that if she had the final say, if she were judge and jury, his actions relegated every kindness and every good thing he ever did for anyone as suspect. Manipulative predators were just that. Anything they did was to get something for themselves at someone else's expense. Looking back, all of Everett's generosity was a way to ingratiate himself so that he could engineer things to go his way. Their entire life together had been a lie. The complexities weren't in whether Everett was good or bad or whether he was capable of — or deserving of — redemption, the complexities were in how Hannah felt about him. The fact that she loved him — that she would mourn him for the rest of her life or that his heinous acts weren't enough to diminish her unconditional love — was what made Everett beyond redemption, because he'd traded on that love and exploited it. Alecia was profoundly grateful he chose to end his life. And if anything she said or did helped him make that decision, she was ready for whatever that made her in the eyes of God. As a mother, she'd failed Hannah. She couldn't go back and do things differently. She could only go forward, whatever that looked like.

Chloe found it impossible to concentrate at school. She would begin each class with tunnel vision on her teacher. Yet within the first five words, scenes intruded into her mind as though someone had pinned her eyes open, tied her to a chair, and forced her to watch a movie on a screen in front of her.

In English (her first and favorite class), she watched as Thia's screened in porch came into view. She and Hannah were stealthily moving toward it, and she could hear Hannah's breath and feel the slight pressure of Hannah's arm when she brushed against her. That detective was there, perched ridiculously on a small wicker chair that looked as though it would collapse under his weight. He was leaning forward and looked angry. Light from a white globe in the middle of the ceiling cast a golden sheen on the tops of their heads and ominous shadow across their faces. Nightmarish, like the fever dreams Chloe had as a little girl. Then the adults were rushing toward them, all at once; Thia made it through the door first. Chloe turned to look at Hannah and saw the vacancy in her eyes.

In history, as her teacher began a new topic, Chloe determined not to miss a word. She had her pencil in hand and a freshly headed paper at the ready. Two sentences in, Chloe watched as Everett smiled at her, holding her gaze as he poured a liquid the consistency of syrup and the color of clarified butter into tiny wine glasses. Chloe felt herself holding his gaze, expecting to feel the glow of approval, sophisticated in the knowledge that a dad was treating them like equals. This time, when she looked into his eyes and took in the slow spread of his smile, she saw something unfamiliar, something she hadn't understood the first time. It was a look she would never forget. Even many years later when she was in college and later in bars with coworkers, when introduced to a man who smiled at her that way, her palms would grow clammy with sweat, her heart would accelerate, and she would have the instinct to either run or punch him in the throat. Chloe hadn't had the word to describe that look in Everett's kitchen that night. She didn't even have the word to describe it in the months following. As an adult though, she recognized it as lust.

In math class, as her teacher began a new unit, Chloe barely had the strength to listen. She repeated numbers and formulas in her head, and for a while that worked. She drowned out the teacher's voice, and solved equations that had nothing to do with the unit they were working on. Chloe knew that missing this unit would make it difficult for her to catch up, but she was powerless to do anything about it. Every time she actively tried to listen to the teacher, all she saw were flashes. Hannah's staring eyes, Hannah's boot heel digging a hole in the icy dirt, Hannah falling down as the policeman caught her, Hannah's tiny body in the corner of the couch tucked under an oatmeal colored blanket, her pale face pinched and scared.

By lunchtime Chloe was exhausted and listless. She couldn't face the cafeteria, so she took her bagged lunch and did something she'd never done in all the years of school. She went to the library to find her mom.

Hannah slept until 8:00 the next morning. When she opened her eyes, she was looking at a ceiling with stars stuck to it. They were the snot-green putty-tinted color of glow-in-the-dark-plastic without luminescence. Hannah felt inexplicable anger course through her. There were toys everywhere, piled on top of the dresser, and the dresser drawers had clothes sticking out of them. The bookshelf in haphazard order, sideways, some books with bindings facing in and random toys were shoved alongside.

Irritated, Hannah sat up. That's when she saw Thia, asleep on the floor next to her bed. She had a pillow but was lying on a braided rug in pastel colors with a giant purple stain. The blanket Thia had been using in a tangle beneath her. Thia's black hair fanned across her face. She looked so tired. Hannah had to use the bathroom but was afraid to wake her.

Hannah thought about how kind Thia had been to her yesterday; she didn't make a lot of stupid adult small talk. She'd smiled at her with sparkling mischievous eyes when she offered her soda and chips. What Hannah couldn't figure out was Thia's angle. Why she was being so nice, going out of her way like this? They had never been particularly close. What did Thia want from Hannah? Hannah realized she had no real home anymore. She could never go back to the house she'd grown up in. She couldn't bring herself to step through those doors, and she didn't even want to pass her block. She couldn't imagine going back to Savannah. That house had been a prison. And her father had killed himself there. Hannah tried that thought out. Everett was dead. She would never again hear his voice or see him. All the questions she wanted to ask him. Last night, she thought she would die from the loss of it. Now in the gray light of the morning in this horrible room that smelled vaguely like urine and grape juice, she just felt empty, and she wondered if this what she would feel like for the rest of her life, and was it better or worse than the grief she felt last night?

All those years of her life with Everett, Hannah alternated between two states: the power of sharing secrets with her father, the knowledge that she was special, the certainty that he was the center of her universe and that Alecia was in their orbit; the other state was a pervasive feeling of dread.

Without the first state, which she could never return to, now that she recognized the lie of it, she only had the second. She would have to learn to live with it.

Then Thia opened her eyes and looked straight into Hannah's. Hannah was surprised by how clear Thia's eyes were. Her face no longer held any trace of fatigue. It was as if she woke fully conscious.

"Hey, there," Thia said.

"Buenos Dias."

"Hungry?"

Hannah realized that not only did she need to pee, she was also starving — it didn't matter that her father was dead, her mother was far away, and she technically had no home, she was still going to have to do everyday things. Like pee. And eat. Maybe, she thought, this is how to get through it. Just do the next thing.

"I could eat."

Thia laughed and stood up. "So could I."

Then she turned and left the room, her flannel pants hanging off her thin hips like a high school boy. Hannah felt a rush of affection — which surprised her as much as anything.

Then she went to find the bathroom.

Ivy made her third attempt at writing an email to her local congresswoman on behalf of the environmental agency she was doing pro bono work for. She couldn't seem to string a sentence together, and she was so irritable she was ready to throw her laptop across the room. Her mind kept wandering to Hannah and Alecia, crowding any coherent thoughts out of her brain. This was so unlike Ivy that she wondered if something else was wrong, like a brain tumor. Desperate for distraction, she would even welcome a visit from Sally-Ann. Realizing she wasn't going to accomplish anything at her computer this morning, she decided to switch up her routine and go for her run now instead of her usual time. Ordinarily she may have skipped it, the icy ground, high winds, and extreme cold sending her down to the treadmill in the basement, but she needed to get out of the house and away from her obsessive thoughts. Maybe the frigid air would cleanse her mind.

As she was lacing her running shoes on, she heard the chirp of her cell phone, the ring tone set to Pachelbel's Canon. Ivy lunged for it and slid the arrow to answer, "Alecia?"

"Hello, Ivy."

"Are you alright?"

"All things considered, yes."

"Can I help?"

"I think I need some legal advice."

"I have someone. I'll put you in touch with her."

"I was hoping I could hire you."

"Alecia, I'm a corporate lawyer. You need an expert."

"Criminal?"

"It's possible. My hope is that won't be necessary, but you want to be prepared. Or perhaps family law? What about Val?"

"I'd rather not."

"Ok. Let me get the ball rolling with Susan Goldstone then."

"I appreciate it...have you seen Hannah yet?"

Ivy closed her eyes against the raw pain in Alecia's voice, "Not yet. But I spoke with Fiona. She and Chloe were with her when she found out. Thia took good care of her."

"Will you stop by and check on her? Let me know how she seems?"

"Of course. I'll do anything you need."

"Chloe cutting herself — was it because of this? Did Everett hurt her too? He denied it, but...."

"From Chloe's description of that night, it sounds like he may have been attempting to, giving the girls wine, rubbing Chloe's shoulders, pressing against her, she found it confusing, but at one point Hannah was gone, and she went to find her and saw them."

"Saw them?"

"She didn't have a word for it but her description — she saw him raping her."

Alecia was quiet for a while. Ivy waited listening to the wind howl through the glass.

"Ivy, I had no idea. What Everett was doing, no idea."

"I know." Ivy felt a loosening in her body. She realized how badly she wanted to hear Alecia say that.

Alecia's voice was strong, but it sounded hoarse, as though she'd been crying. "How could this have been happening and I not have known?"

Ivy didn't have an answer for that. "Oh, Alecia. Maybe it was just so inconceivable to you. Your mind couldn't take it in."

Alecia thought about how it shouldn't have been inconceivable. She'd lived it, but because the men were so different, the circumstances so different, it did seem inconceivable. "There were signs, now that I look back. How could I not have seen them?"

"You know what to look for now, so it seems apparent."

"In retrospect, yes. I keep thinking — all that time they spent together — I was happy. That they had a good relationship…." Alecia's voice broke and Ivy could hear nearly silent sobbing on the other end of the phone.

"Alecia, she's safe now."

"But the damage that's been done can never be undone. I wanted them to have that bond…I never thought…and I was selfish because it meant I could be alone in my room and read…go to sleep early…." This time the sobs were choking. Ivy waited until she heard Alecia take a breath.

"You have to move forward Alecia."

"That's what I keep telling myself." Alecia's voice was barely a whisper.

"For Hannah."

"Yes. For Hannah."

"I'm sending you Susan Goldstone's contact info. And I'm calling her as soon as we hang up. I want her to handle this personally."

"Okay."

"I'll go see Hannah and call you afterwards."

"Thank you, Ivy."

"You don't have to thank me. I want to help."

"I don't know what I would have done without all of you."

"We're lucky to have each other." Ivy realized it wasn't just a reflexive polite thing to say. She meant it. They were lucky to have one another even if it made life messier.

Ivy hung up and walked to the living room window to look out at the storm. There were already tree limbs down on her street, and she heard the distant scream of sirens. She slipped her coat off and kicked her running shoes off. It was too dangerous to run outside, and besides, she had phone calls to make. She felt a loosening in her neck and shoulders, a release of tension she hadn't even realized she was carrying. She began to search her contacts for Susan and prayed she would be able to help Alecia.

CHAPTER TWENTY
Reconciliation

As it turned out, Chloe wasn't able to go visit the stables with Hannah because she had an appointment with Dr. Schaeffer, and Fiona wouldn't let her miss it.

Mel seemed a little less irritating to Chloe during their session. Chloe even found some things she said interesting. She was trying to explain the movies she kept seeing in her head and the feeling that she wasn't always in her own body. Mel explained that was common for people who experienced trauma, that the "outside her body" feeling was called dissociation, a defense mechanism. Chloe described what happened to Hannah the night before, and Mel said Hannah was probably in shock, that her reaction was common to people getting bad news. Mel said she knew several therapists at the children's advocacy center for the DA's office and that they were very good and would be able to help Hannah.

"The thing is, Mel," Chloe said without realizing she'd called Dr. Schaeffer Mel, and she also missed the amusement that sparked momentarily in Dr. Schaeffer's eyes, "I don't think I suffered trauma. I mean, Everett—Mr. Calding — never did anything to me — I just — you know — saw him — with Hannah."

"Witnessing sexual abuse is a trauma in and of itself."

Chloe nodded. Opened her mouth as if to speak, then closed it again.

"Chloe? It looked like you wanted to say something just now."

Chloe shook her head.

"You can ask me anything you know."

Chloe wondered if Mel could read her mind. She wanted to ask her something, but it felt disloyal to Hannah.

Mel leaned forward. "You know our conversations are confidential. I can't tell anyone anything unless...."

"I know, I know, unless I'm going to hurt myself or somebody else. That isn't it."

Dr. Schaeffer waited.

"It's just..." Chloe looked out the window so she wouldn't have to look at Mel. They were on the second floor so Chloe could see tree branches swaying violently in the wind. "It didn't look like abuse — it didn't look like he was hurting her. But it was — horrible."

"That's because it is horrible."

Chloe looked up, surprised at the anger in Mel's voice.

"The thing is," Mel continued. "Sexual abuse of children is often done by someone the child trusts. So, while it may not look like Hannah was being hurt, she was. And you were perceptive enough to have known that. Witnessing it was harmful to you as well."

"I don't know what to say to Hannah to make things better."

"Is there anything I could say to you to make it better?"

Chloe thought about it. "Just this — you know — talking to me straight up, it kind of helps. I felt like I was going crazy."

"Because of the dissociation and intrusive thoughts?"

Chloe nodded.

"Hannah may be experiencing the same things. And when she talks to her therapist, she'll have the chance to find out she's not crazy. It's the way our mind processes trauma. Do you remember the breathing exercises we did when we started our session?"

Chloe nodded.

"How did you feel after doing them?"

"At first they felt stupid."

Mel laughed, "I felt stupid the first time I did them too. How about after you did them?"

Chloe thought about it. "Not as weird."

"Not as weird because you felt less stupid or not as weird because you felt a difference in your body?"

"A difference in my body — less — nervous I guess."

"Right. It relaxes you. Do you know what fight-or-flight is?"

"Yeah, we learned about it in health. It's the autonomic nervous system response to danger."

"Whoa!" Mel looked surprised. "Health class has come a long way since I was in 8th grade."

Chloe shrugged.

"Think about it, Chloe, every time those thoughts intrude, you are back in fight-or-flight mode."

"Huh."

"Do you know what happens when your body is in fight-or-flight?"

"Yeah," Chloe said. "We had a test on it. The adrenal cortex releases cortisol for heightened alertness, which results in dilated pupils, dry mouth, fast breathing, rapid heartbeat, muscle tension, and sweaty palms. I got a hundred."

"So, you understand the constant stress your body is under whenever you have intrusive thoughts?"

Chloe nodded slowly, "I never thought about that." Dr. Schaeffer noticed Chloe's leg jiggling, her hands fisting.

Dr. Schaeffer took a deep breath in and watched as Chloe's breath came in shallow gulps.

"Chloe?"

"Yeah?"

"Take a deep breath in and out." Together they took a large inhale, held it for a heartbeat, then blew out slowly. "Good. Again. Excellent. Now I want you to try and relax your body, starting with your head, roll it a bit to the left, then the right, good. Now relax your shoulders. Good, now your hands." Dr. Schaeffer watched as Chloe slowly opened her palms and let them sink against her thighs. "Feeling more relaxed?"

Chloe nodded.

"Okay, this time, when we talk about what happened, we are going to try and stay in this relaxed state. And any time I see you going into fight-or-flight, we are going to take a breath and self-regulate ok?"

Chloe nodded and noticed she wasn't finding Mel's low calm voice irritating today. She actually found it soothing.

"Chloe, the reason we are going to continue to do this, is because it will keep us in a relaxed body. If we talk about the original trauma in a state of fight-or-flight, we are effectively retraumatizing ourselves. Does that make sense?"

"Yes."

"This time, when we talk about what happened, we will make sure we are in a relaxed state. Alright?"

"Deep breaths and relax my muscles."

"Exactly. And I'll remind you if I see you becoming dysregulated. OK?"

"Ok."

"Chloe, can you tell me about the intrusive thoughts you've been having at school?" Dr. Schaeffer saw the trapezius muscles around Chloe's neck and shoulders tighten. "But first, we are going to take a deep breath in, and out, good, now lift your shoulders to your ears with a deep breath in, good, now exhale and drop your shoulders, good."

Dr. Schaeffer watched for signs of tension and dysregulation as Chloe spoke, "I don't like talking about that night."

"I know you don't. And we can stop at any point. Maybe just focus on the intrusive thoughts you've been having at school."

"I keep seeing it."

Dr. Schaeffer nodded, "Like a film strip you said."

"Yeah. It just keeps playing these…like clips."

"Can you describe them for me."

"Sometimes it's his face when he was pouring us wine."

"What did his face look like?"

"Like we had a secret, which I liked at first. He wasn't treating me like a little kid."

"I understand."

"But then, he got weird."

"How was he weird?"

"He came up behind me and rubbed my shoulders, at first I just thought he was acting like a dad, but it was weird, and it seemed…."

"It seemed?"

"Like Hannah was getting mad. Jealous even."

"Okay. That makes sense. Many times, children feel jealous when their parents pay attention to other kids."

Chloe nodded. "Then, when he was rubbing my shoulders he kind of pulled me back against him and it was weird, and then I felt something, disgusting."

"Do you think it was an erection?"

Chloe tensed.

"Deep breath in Chloe, good, now exhale. Relax your hands. Good."

"I think that's what it was, moving against me, like twitching, against my back. I was sitting at the counter, and I didn't know what to do. I tried to move away but he…he kind of held me there, and Hannah looked mad, and I wasn't sure what was happening."

"Chloe?"

"Yeah?"

"What he did was wrong. It was sexual abuse. And your confusion is because he was sneaky and manipulative. He not only abused you physically, but he abused the trust you had in him. Does that make sense?"

Chloe nodded, "I feel so stupid. And dirty. Like maybe I did something to make him want to — or think he could. You know?"

"That's a very common feeling for survivors of sexual abuse. It's part of the manipulation of the offender. He already had your unconditional trust, and there was no reason for you not to trust him. We teach our children to be polite. He was a trusted person with authority, and he was slowly crossing lines. You knew it felt wrong, but you weren't sure why or what was happening. There's a name for what he was doing. It's called grooming."

"He was grooming me?"

"It sounds like it, yes. But you weren't compliant, and he backed off."

"Is that why Hannah went to him that night? Because she was jealous of me?"

"No. From what I've heard from the detective working on the case, he groomed Hannah when she was very young.

This was going on for a long time. I think Hannah knew he was harming her but was confused because he was her dad and she loved him. And he knew how to make her happy in other ways, so even though this felt like it was harming her, she didn't know how not to be a part of it."

Chloe's eyes filled with tears, but Dr. Schaeffer noted that her body was still relaxed. "Hannah told me she thought I would tell and it would stop. But I didn't. I let her down."

"Did she say you let her down?"

"She said it wasn't my fault."

"I think you should believe her."

"I can't."

"Well, the way I see it…" Dr. Schaeffer said.

Chloe watched Mel lean toward her. Without the cue, Chloe took a shaky breath in and exhaled.

Dr. Schaeffer continued, "Hannah needed it to stop. That's why she took the risk of you seeing them together. And when that didn't work, she found the courage to tell her mother. And her mother took measures to stop it."

"Is it bad that…"

"Is what bad, Chloe?"

"I'm glad he's dead."

"Being glad he's dead is just a feeling. It isn't bad or good. It's just the way you feel."

"But isn't it wrong?"

"Why would it be wrong? You didn't do anything to cause his death."

"Well, Hannah's sad."

"Are you glad Hannah's sad?"

"Of course not!"

"Right. You have compassion for your friend. You care about her."

"But I'm glad he's dead."

"What makes you glad about it?"

"Because…now I never have to see him again. And I know he can never hurt another girl."

"Well, that's certainly understandable. I'm glad you won't ever have to see him again, and I'm glad he can never hurt another girl again too."

"Does that mean you're glad he's dead?"

"No. It means I'm glad you never have to see him again and that he can never hurt another girl."

Chloe narrowed her eyes. "Maybe that's how I feel too."

"Maybe."

"But also, I hate him for what he did to Hannah, and I want him to burn in hell."

"That's understandable."

"Doesn't that make me a sinner?"

"Why would it?"

"Wishing a horrible thing on someone."

"Well, what's your idea about hell and how it works?"

"If you sin you go to hell and burn."

"Any sins? Sinful thoughts?"

"Well. No. That would be a venial sin. And if I repent I wouldn't go to hell."

"Do you want to repent for wishing Everret Calding will burn in hell?"

"No."

"Why not?"

"Because he belongs in hell."

"Why?"

"Because he knew what he was doing was evil."

"Then why do you feel bad about being glad he's dead and that he'll burn in hell?"

"Because I'm supposed to forgive."

"Do you have to forgive the act of evil?"

"I don't know — it's confusing."

"Let me see if I understand? Everett harmed Hannah, and he harmed you."

"Yes."

"And he knowingly committed evil acts. And he took his own life. And according to your understanding of Catholicism, this means he committed a mortal sin and that he will go to hell."

"Yes. My mom doesn't believe in hell."

"But you do?"

"Yes."

"Okay. So according to what you believe, Everett committed a mortal sin and will go to hell."

"Unless he repents and Jesus forgives him."

"Do you hope he didn't repent and Jesus doesn't forgive him?"

Chloe was silent for a long time. "Part of me does and part of me doesn't."

"Tell me about the part of you that hopes he does repent and get forgiveness."

"Well…that's how God works. And I want to be able to repent and receive forgiveness for my sins. So, it seems wrong to hope someone else doesn't."

"Ok. And what about the part where you hope he doesn't repent and get forgiveness."

"I don't want him to get off that easily. He should pay for what he did. He should pay for eternity."

"That's what you feel would be just?"

"Yes."

"Part of you wishes that he gets full retribution for what he did because it was so evil. Is that right?"

"Yes."

"I think that's completely understandable."

Chloe looked apprehensive. "Maybe it's understandable, but it feels wrong."

"Let me ask you something, Chloe."

"Okay."

"Do you hope that Everett wanted to repent and seek forgiveness and never had the opportunity to do so?"

Chloe thought about it for a long time. "No. I don't wish that. I hope he had the opportunity but was too selfish and stupid to take it."

"Because you want him to go to hell?"

"Yes, because that's where he belongs."

"If he did repent and get forgiveness, do you still wish that he goes to hell?"

"No. Then it's up to Jesus. But I'll be mad at God if he forgives Everett."

"And what happens if you're mad at God."

"I think it might be a sin. Maybe a mortal sin because it separates me from God."

"Hmmm. I'm not Catholic. But I studied theology in undergraduate school, and I have friends who are priests and we have many discussions."

"And?" Chloe asked.

"And, I don't agree that being angry at God separates you from him. I think God is strong enough and loving enough to handle your anger."

Chloe began to cry. "Like my mom? When I was mean to her and went to live with my dad? I was so angry, and I took it out on her."

"And she still loved you."

"But I separated myself from her."

"Yes, but only physically. And she never separated herself from you. Emotionally or spiritually."

"We were still connected."

"Yes."

"Does that mean I'm still connected to Jesus even though I'm mad at him."

"Exactly."

Chloe was silent for a long time. Dr. Schaeffer waited. When Chloe looked up, Dr. Schaeffer saw clarity and a determination that hadn't been there earlier.

"Okay."

"Okay?" Dr. Schaeffer asked.

"Okay. I believe you about God being able to take my anger. And I believe you that it's normal to want Everett to burn in hell. But I also don't want Hannah to feel sad. And she would feel sad if he burned in hell. So, if he did get the chance to repent and earn forgiveness, I hope he took it."

"For Hannah's sake?"

"Yes."

"That seems fair. And compassionate."

"Is our time up?"

"Yes, it is."

"K." Chloe got up as quickly as if a bell had just rung. "See ya next week, Mel!" she said before pulling the office door shut behind her.

Melanie Schaeffer inhaled, exhaled, leaned her head back against her chair, and listened to her heartbeat slow. The depth and complexity of children as well as their ability to access their feelings amazed Melanie. There were adults who struggled to articulate half of what Chloe had been able to do. Melanie fervently believed in the resilience of the human spirit. She just prayed it would be enough to see

Chloe through. And while she was at it, she hoped the same for Hannah.

Hannah sat with a therapist named Elena who had one of those faces that crinkled a lot when she smiled. Hannah watched Elena carefully. In her experience, people whose faces looked that happy when they smiled were tricky. They often smiled and then said something blistering right after, or smiled and made you think they were about to burst into laughter, but when they relaxed their faces, there was a kind of collapse that Hannah found disorienting and untrustworthy. Hannah allowed Elena to ask her as many questions as she wanted, answering politely, and trying to gauge whether Elena was genuine or just an authority figure. Hannah was well aware that as clinical as Elena was trying to be, and as much as everyone kept calling it the "Children's Advocacy Unit," they were in an office closely connected to the District Attorney's Office and that while they obviously couldn't arrest her father, there was a possibility her mother was in trouble.

Hannah appreciated the way Ivy had been straight with her on the ride over. Apparently, Alecia's friends were taking turns caring for Hannah. Thia had taken her to the stables as promised. Hannah was happy to see Mino, and it felt good to ride, but it was nothing like her dream. The cold air stung her cheeks and lifted the hair from her scalp, which for a while made her feel alive. But most of the ride felt flat and far away, as though she were watching someone else do it. Her body didn't feel like she was in sync with Mino, not the way she'd always felt before. Most of the time, she felt removed from her body and when she came back into it, she felt clumsy, like she'd been thrown onto a mechanical pony ride and couldn't find the right rhythm. The weak afternoon light turned everything dingy, tainting her mood even more.

Hannah made sure Mino was cooled down, properly watered, and blanketed after their ride. She let Mino nuzzle her hand before she left, but even that failed to stir any joy within her.

When Hannah left the stables, she saw Thia and Ivy huddled together. They stopped talking as soon as she appeared. Thia gave her a fake smile, and Ivy thrust a cup at her. "Hot chocolate," she said. She didn't smile, but when Hannah looked into Ivy's eyes she saw something. It wasn't pity, because that would have pissed her off and she would have refused the hot chocolate no matter how much she wanted it. It was something else. Not kindness exactly. She saw that in Thia. Hannah looked at Ivy and let several heartbeats go by before she reached her hand out for the hot chocolate. Understanding. That's what she saw in Ivy. Ivy understood, she knew.

Hannah took a sip and smiled. "Thanks, it's really good."

Ivy smiled back, "I got it from Mint on Main Street. It's pure chocolate melted and mixed with steamed milk."

Thia raised her paper-cup. "They know their hot chocolate over there."

"Mom loves their mint tea," Hannah offered.

"Of course she does," Thia said, "It's like crack!"

Hannah smirked.

"Not that I know what crack is like," Thia said, and Hannah forced herself not to roll her eyes.

Ivy took a sip of her hot chocolate as if she didn't notice the supreme awkwardness. "Hannah, I'm your ride to the Children's Advocacy Center, ok?"

"Sure."

"You ready to roll?"

"Yeah."

Thia leaned in and hugged Ivy. She stopped short at hugging Hannah when Hannah's body tensed, but she smiled at her. "Homemade lasagna for dinner, ok?"

"I hope Eric made it," Ivy teased.

"Obviously." Thia waved and sprinted off down the hill leaving Hannah and Ivy to make their way back to the car.

Now Hannah was subjected to Elena's crinkly-eyed smile and constant watchful gaze. She'd just finished giving Hannah the whole blah blah blah on survivors of sexual abuse. As if there was no Internet and Hannah hadn't googled it all herself.

Hannah ignored the small voice inside her reminding her that she'd never googled it previously. It was only once she'd gotten to Thia's that she'd read everything she could find on the Internet, holed up in Lila's smelly messy room. Hannah read and read, feeling alternately pissed off and relieved. She wondered what it must be like to be Lila. What it must have been like to be Chloe before Hannah's spite ruined her. That was how Hannah thought of that night and her actions, filled with spite and a desire to do two things, let Chloe know who was boss, along with a small flourish of hope that maybe Chloe would save her.

Hannah was an imaginative and creative child by nature. Yet try as she might, she wasn't able to conjure up a childhood for a girl without the stain of a father's hands, mouth, and warnings.

So, when Elena sat there parroting almost word for word what Hannah had read on the Internet and in countless chat rooms from a bunch of fucked up "survivors" (a "sisterhood" she wanted nothing to do with), she felt a rage bubble inside of her that felt almost impossible to extinguish. And she aimed it at this dumpy woman wearing big clunky wooden beads and hideous shoes that looked like some withered up old hippie's version of little-girl's Mary Janes.

Hannah was adept at hiding what she really felt. She was skilled at thinking one thing and saying another, feeling one way and looking another. So, she sat quietly, hands in her lap, listening to Elena and answering her questions in exactly the way she knew Elena expected her to.

Hannah waited, watched, and was finally rewarded when Elena got down to it. She softened her voice in a way meant (Hannah was sure) to evoke trust and said, "Tell me about the first time you told your mother what your father was doing to you."

Hannah felt her heartbeat race in spite of her determination to remain calm. She felt her pulse quicken. The idea that it was throbbing inside her wrist became almost unbearable and Hannah found it impossible to concentrate, which caused a panicky feeling inside her chest squeezing the place beneath her breastbone where her heart was trying to pump. She felt her throat constrict so that only a tiny pinprick hole allowed air into her lungs. Hannah could visualize the hole and if it grew any smaller, she wouldn't be able to breathe at all. She needed to concentrate. She needed to protect Alecia and maybe Everett too. Maybe it wasn't too late. Maybe her father hadn't really killed himself. Maybe the detective was lying. Maybe Elena was lying to trick her. Hannah felt her voice freezing inside her throat. Forming an icy block too hard and too big to get out. She should never have told. Look at what she'd done.

Ivy sat in the cramped overheated waiting room fighting the temptation to go out to the parking lot and for the first time ever break her one cigarette a day rule by bumming one from the circle of employees huddled under a tattered awning puffing away. She knew the group she'd seen on the way in would have dispersed back to their respective offices by now, bringing cold air and the stench of tobacco clinging to their clothes, hair, and probably breath, despite the mints that had undoubtedly been passed around. She also knew that a whole new circle would have formed by now. The realization that it was stress that created the desire to join them made her decide against it. That and the worry (as unfounded as it might be) that Hannah would need her sometime during her interview or "session" as the therapist had referred to it. Ivy's lawyer brain, however, had no doubt that it was indeed an interview.

Ivy was not someone who dwelled on the past, and when she thought about it at all, it was usually in response to someone else jogging her memory by telling a story. Or perhaps a sensory memory summoned by a song or a smell or an image of something she hadn't seen in a long time like those nostalgic Facebook posts of metal ice trays or car cigarette lighters, with the question DO YOU KNOW WHAT THIS IS in block letters.

Yet snatches of memory wove through her brain, interfering with her ability to concentrate on the emails in front of her. She'd been fourteen and underground on the subway. It was winter, and she was wearing a long coat and the platform became crowded and hot. She'd lingered too long at a friend's house on 72nd and Eighth Avenue and she'd had to switch trains in the middle of the rush hour crush. It was the mid-eighties and the subways were filthy, broke down frequently, and people no longer gave their seats to the elderly or pregnant women as a matter of course. So, when the six-foot 250-pound man with a beer gut began pushing against her and laughing as they got onto the train, throwing his hands up and yelling, "It's crowded here, girlie!" because she told him to back off, people threw nervous glances their way, but no one said anything. As the train lurched out of the station, Ivy kept one hand on the pole in front of her and used the other one to try and stop him from creeping his hand under her coat and climbing between her legs. Engaged in a mostly silent battle, she used all her energy to push his hand away. She had no-where to go and was obviously struggling. She knew the man next to her could tell what was happening, because his ears were bright red and he was staring straight ahead and studi-ously ignoring them. Ivy looked around and watched as men and women turned their faces, and she knew she was alone in the crush of people. The man would intermittently laugh and shout things like, "Relax girlie, it's just the moving train."

At one point Ivy wondered if she was imagining what was happening. As the train hurtled into the next station, she managed to choke out *stop!* and managed to elbow him in his hard fat stomach. But he just laughed and shrugged and said "Easy there, girlie." She got off the train shaking, fighting tears, and furious at herself that she hadn't managed to knee him in the balls.

An officer was standing on the station platform when she got off. He could see something had shaken her and asked, "You alright?"

"Some guy was putting his hand up my coat!"

"Ya gotta watch out for perverts."

"Can't you do something?"

He laughed, "Like what? The train's gone."

Ivy couldn't bear the thought of standing on the crowded platform and waiting for another train, so she headed up and walked home in the stinging cold, telling herself she'd never let anyone do that to her again. And promising herself, she'd never tell a soul how cowardly and weak she'd been letting that fat fuck feel her up in front of everyone, without consequence. She also swore to erase the entire incident from her mind, letting it get further and further away with every block she walked toward home.

And for the past thirty-three years she'd been successful at blocking it out. Yet now she could see his bloated, red, sneering face, hear his harsh laughter and the sarcastic way he said "girlie," and worse she could feel the creep of his fat fingers as he lifted her coat and pushed his way between her legs. Rage filled her, stealing her vision and her breath. Eventually, when it subsided and she was able to see the gray light behind the grimy waiting room window and feel the hard-plastic seat beneath her, she made a promise to herself that she'd fight for Hannah the way she hadn't fought for herself.

CHAPTER TWENTY-ONE
COMING TO

It took almost two weeks before Alecia was allowed to go home. It was important to leave Savannah without any questions or loose ends following her. Until Alecia could decide what to do, Everett's ashes were to be kept at the local crematorium. When the plane lifted off the ground from the Savannah airport, she felt like a molting bird leaving old feathers behind.

Alecia packed two suitcases, one with her clothing, make-up, and accessories, and one with Hannah's favorite clothes. The rest of their clothing and personal belongings had gone to a storage facility in Westchester. All of the furniture and household items arrived as an anonymous donation at a local woman's shelter in Georgia.

Money hadn't protected them, but it made it easier to move on. Alecia thought of all those children who didn't have that buffer, those who became homeless or institutionalized, marginalized by the adults around them simply because they were abused and there weren't funds to care for them.

She thought of the miserable rooms she'd rented throughout New York City in the short time between leaving her RA position at school and moving in with Everett. She thought how fortunate she was to have been a good student, to have caught the eye of a caring guidance counselor and received a scholarship and work-study, and the opportunity to be an RA. How little she'd cared about the isolation from her classmates, never invited to their rooms or to parties. She had no idea how to act around people her own age. Instead she watched and learned, incorporating aspects of them she admired and discarding the rest, reinventing herself so that when she met Everett she was ready to slip into a whole new life. For years, she'd congratulated herself on being an effective chameleon, yet all she'd done was exchange one viper's nest for another. This time though, she'd build her own nest, and it was with the money he'd earned. But it belonged to Hannah, and she'd use it to protect her from now on.

Alecia landed at JFK, rented a car, and retrieved her luggage. It was 3:30 and Hannah would be returning from school soon. According to Thia, Hannah had gone right back to her routine at school, catching up relatively easily.

She informed the school authorities that Everett had accidentally shot himself cleaning his gun. Of course, Detective Matthews had paid the school a visit during his investigation, but all they were able to tell him was what they knew — the family was considering relocating due to a change in Everett's job and that Hannah would likely return in a couple of weeks to finish the school term.

Alecia knew the staff and parents would gossip and speculate in hushed tones with a pretense of concern, that Hannah's classmates would hear all about it. There was nothing Alecia could do, but she hoped that having it happen out of state might minimize the chatter.

Many of the students had conservative parents who vigorously defended second amendment rights, so Alecia hoped Hannah would be spared any self-righteous "told-you-so" statements. Alecia could care less about gun reform or second amendment rights. She believed people, on the whole, were idiots, and would do stupid things with guns as long as they inhabited Earth. A podcast she listened to one day postulated that people were a virus on the earth and that while we may destroy life on earth, we would never destroy the planet. Earth would be here long after we eradicated ourselves. Alecia liked to imagine Earth, like a meadow growing back after a forest fire in all of its splendor and none of the animus shadows.

Alecia would have to wait a few more hours before picking Hannah up and taking her to the two-bedroom condo apartment she'd quietly rented in her maiden name before leaving town. She'd had it fully furnished using the help of a discreet and exclusive service, which helped corporate families relocate. She'd gone for a minimalist tasteful look, which she knew Hannah admired. Alecia had bored Hannah to death on the airplane ride to Savannah, showing her magazine pictures and asking her which rooms she liked and what she liked about them. Hannah had complied — Alecia knew — because it distracted her from where they were going and why. She hoped Hannah liked the apartment. It was closer to her school in a luxury building with a pool. Alecia found it soulless, but she hoped it had amenities Hannah would appreciate.

Susan Goldstone, Attorney-at-Law, was not what Alecia was expecting. For one thing, she had a kind face, large blue eyes, and a smile that made you want to smile back. In her sixties, wearing a bright red jacket and matching beaded earrings, she looked approachable, and Alecia wondered if she'd have the steel necessary to represent her. Alecia's fears on that score were assuaged, however, when Susan ushered her into her office, gestured to a chair on one side of the massive wood desk, then positioned herself behind the desk, and said in a straight forward voice, "I can help you, but I'm going to ask you some tough questions. Are you ready for that?"

Alecia looked straight into Susan's eyes and saw a laser focus and intelligence that made her feel for the first time in a long time, that maybe everything would be all right, and that while she would never relinquish control, she could let someone else take the wheel for a bit.

"Ask me anything you want."

"How did you not know?"

"I've asked myself that every day. And I don't know if I have an answer."

"Try."

"I guess — I just never thought he was capable of something like that. And Hannah seemed so normal, so well-adjusted it never even occurred to me something was wrong. They did spend time alone together, usually in the evenings, I go to bed early...."

"What's early?"

"8:00. 8:15."

"Weekends as well?"

"If we were home, yes. We had an active social calendar, so most Saturday evenings we were home by 11:00 or 11:30, and Hannah was asleep by then."

"Who was primarily responsible for Hannah in the evenings when she was younger?"

"I mean — I was the stay-at-home-parent, so I was...."

"But?"

Susan watched as Alecia flushed. It was an ugly flush that mottled her neck and crept over her face, leaving red welts on her otherwise smooth forehead.

"Everett said he wanted to spend quality time with Hannah and give me a break…."

"And?"

"He always did bath and bed time while I…."

"While you?"

"Cleaned up the kitchen and prepared everything for the next morning."

"What was their routine?"

"It varied. Every other night was a bath, or else he just had her wash up and put on pajamas, then he read her bedtime stories and tucked her in. He was a bit of a sucker, reading her more books than I ever would, sometimes staying until she fell asleep. I always thought…."

"What?"

"That she had him wrapped around her finger. It irritated me, but I never saw the harm…he was her father…and she never had difficulty waking up in the morning — so."

"What time did he typically come to bed?"

"I don't — I didn't pay much attention. Sometimes he would fall asleep reading to her, or he would work in his office. The only time he went to bed earlier than me was when I was hosting book club or having a PTA meeting at the house."

"How was your sex life?"

"I don't — why? Is that important?"

"We need to be prepared for these kinds of questions."

"From whom?"

"Alecia, the DA will be considering charges. I'm hoping this won't get anywhere close to a trial, and if I was a betting woman, I'd lay odds that we won't get there. But they are going to question you, and I don't want any surprises."

Alecia sighed. "I didn't think anything of it then."

"Anything of what?"

"Many couples aren't sexually — don't have — frequent sex. It can't possibly mean all the husbands are perverted child rapists."

Susan leaned forward. "Correct. But your husband *was* a perverted child rapist. So please try and answer the question, because, believe me, as difficult as it is to talk about it with me, it's going to be worse with the prosecutor."

"We had infrequent sex. Back then I was relieved. And I assumed he was taking his cues from me. But the truth is, one of the reasons I fell for him...."

"Go on."

"He was romantic — but never — pushy; sex didn't seem as important to him. I thought he was a true gentleman. It made me believe...."

"What?"

"That my hopes had come true. That there were two kinds of men, perverts and gentleman."

"That's an odd world view."

Alecia stared at Susan coldly, "That's rather judgmental."

Susan shrugged. "I'm your attorney, not your therapist."

They stared at one another for a while until Alecia sighed, "I realize of course, given everything that happened, my entire thinking was skewed. Obviously."

Susan leaned forward again, "Were you sexually abused as a child?"

"Yes."

"By your father?"

"Yes."

"Have you ever told anyone else?"

"No."

"Nobody? A counselor? A therapist? A friend?"

"I've never told anyone."

"That's unfortunate."

"Yeah, well, who knew I'd need that horror show as evidence to protect myself."

Susan leaned forward, "There was nothing wrong with letting your husband bathe your child and put her to sleep. That's what good fathers do."

"But I should have known — I should have sensed something was wrong."

"It will be difficult to believe that you didn't just turn a blind eye."

"Is that what you think I did?"

"I think denial is a powerful defense mechanism."

Alecia twisted her mouth into a smirk. "I thought you weren't a therapist."

Susan smirked back, "I'm not. But a good defense attorney will always have a shrink on speed dial."

"I'll never forgive myself."

Susan leaned forward, "I'm not a rabbi or a priest either. Granting forgiveness isn't in my job description. But as your lawyer, I'm telling you I need you to fight for yourself and your daughter. And I'll tell you something else as a mother. I'd love to think I know everything I need to in order to protect my children. But guess what? That's a lie mothers tell themselves to get through the day."

Alecia looked at her, "Except my daughter paid a terrible price for the lies I told myself."

"That's true. So now what?"

Alecia looked at her, "That's what I'm here to find out."

"To fight for yourself?"

"What are my chances?"

"I need to discuss things with the DA's office, but my guess is they are not inclined to prosecute. I think they will mandate therapy for you and Hannah."

"I would do that anyway."

"And they may mandate community service."

"I'm ready for that."

"I'd like to get a little ahead of it."

"What do you mean?"

Susan reached into her drawer and pulled out a card, sliding it across the shiny surface of her desk.

Alecia picked it up, "My Sister's Place?"

"It's a shelter for battered women and their children."

"I know what it is."

"Good. The director is a friend of mine, that's her number, she's expecting your call."

"I don't understand."

"I want you to volunteer there. Start the community service on your own."

"Wait — why this — I thought I'd be cleaning highways or bathrooms or…?"

"Would you prefer that?"

"Actually, yes."

"Why is that?"

"Because, I don't know the first thing about dealing with domestic violence — and talking to people about it."

"They'll train you."

"I don't see why I need to…."

"It will look good to the DA's office."

"I don't know if I can."

"You would rather clean highways and bathrooms because that's in your comfort zone?"

Alecia thought about all those nights Everett took Hannah upstairs, and she spent the evening making the kitchen sparkle. She slid the card into her bag.

Susan looked at her. "If you want me to work with you, I need you to follow my advice. Otherwise I'm happy to bill you for my time and return the rest of your retainer."

Alecia looked skeptical, "You won't work with me if I don't do this?"

"I will not."

"I'll call. If they let me volunteer, I'll do it."

Susan stood up. "Let me know as soon as that's in place. Meanwhile I'll contact the district attorney's office and make arrangements for us to go in."

Alecia walked briskly to the car. She knew there was nothing she could do to tamp down the simultaneous feelings of longing and terror she felt. In a few minutes, she would have Hannah back, and they would begin the jigsaw puzzle of fitting into their new life together.

Hannah had to see Elena two more times and each was worse than the last. Hannah gave stock answers she knew Elena wanted to hear and was in turn dismayed and furious when Elena just seemed to accept them. It was as if nothing had changed. Hannah still had to put up a front, acting one way while feeling another. She alternately missed and hated her mother and didn't know how she felt about Everett. There were times she missed him so much she thought she would die from it, and there were times she was glad she would never have to face him again. She felt grateful to Thia and Eric and even the kids for taking her in and making her feel welcome and keeping her distracted. Yet there were times she hated them. For being so normal, for yelling at each other and then just as easily saying I love you. For their messiness and chaos and freedom. For feeling welcome yet not belonging, for needing them and being repulsed by them. She longed for Alecia and dreaded seeing her. All of it made her exhausted, and she craved sleep, yet when she got into bed at night she was afraid to sleep because she was afraid of her dreams and even more afraid of waking the next morning and remembering. She was drained from pretending.

Ivy stood when Elena escorted Hannah out to the waiting room. She watched as Hannah nodded politely and said good bye, but she could see how dull and flat Hannah's eyes looked, how her shoulders drooped, and Ivy couldn't help wondering if this supposed therapy was doing more harm than good.

They walked in silence to the car, once Hannah buckled up Ivy looked over at her and spoke. "Your mom called. She's on her way to Thia's."

Hannah grew still. After a while she nodded.

"I can't tell how you're feeling about that."

Hannah looked at her. "I don't how I feel about it."

"Huh." Ivy started the car but made no move to put it in drive. "I get that."

Hannah gave her a skeptical look.

"I get that part of you wants to get on with your life, see your mom, and be as normal as possible. But another part of you is afraid."

"I'm not afraid."

"Guess I got that wrong. Guess I'm thinking *I'd* be afraid."

Hannah looked at Ivy. She didn't think Ivy was afraid of anything. "Why? Why would you be afraid if you were me?"

Ivy shrugged. "Everything's different. People are afraid of change. Even when it's for the better or something they want. Change can be scary."

"Do you think my mom will go to jail?"

Ivy looked at her. "It's possible that the DA will press charges for child endangerment. But I sincerely doubt it."

"Why?"

"Because you aren't in danger any more. Because your mom did what she could once she found out. We'll have to wait and see."

Hannah nodded.

Ivy looked up at the sky through the driver's side window. It was growing dark and the moon was visible. She imagined her own home. The boys would be there by now, dropped off from their various activities. James had rearranged his calendar to be home for them. He'd promised his famous Spaghetti Bolognese, and she imagined the four of them cooking in the kitchen, the steam from the pot fogging his glasses. She wanted desperately to be with them. She wanted equally to be away from the heaviness of Hannah. She knew that in twenty minutes she would be dropping Hannah at Thia's, that Alecia would be there soon after if not before, that Thia would smooth the reunion, and that Hannah would be sleeping in a new bed in a new apartment with her mom that night. It took everything she had not to throw her car in reverse and peel out of the parking lot toward Thia's.

"Hannah?" Ivy waited for Hannah to look at her. "What happened to you is terrible." Ivy saw the glazing of Hannah's eyes. "You might think you had some choices about what happened to you. But you didn't."

Hannah looked more carefully at Ivy now.

"You may have thought you were a participant. But you weren't. None of it was in your control. And that is probably what would have scared me the most."

Hannah looked at her for a while. Almost imperceptibly, she nodded, but Ivy saw it.

"But Hannah, the thing is, while none of what happened was something you could control, you can control what you do from here on out."

"What do mean?"

"I mean, you're in control of you now."

"I don't always feel like I am. My thoughts — the memories — I can't control them."

"Okay. Fair enough. But you can control what you do about it. How you think about it. You don't need to let this define you."

Hannah glared at her. "Yeah, well, it's not like I'm announcing it to the world, My dad's a pervert and so am I."

"You aren't a pervert. He abused you. But you aren't broken."

"I feel broken."

"But you aren't. So, get the help you need. Do the work. I see you. You're a hard worker."

"Are you talking about therapy? Because Elena sucks at it."

"She won't be your therapist forever. You can choose a different one. But I'm talking about you. You need to decide you're worth something. And you need to do something about that."

Hannah rolled her eyes.

"How much pot are you smoking?"

"Huh?"

"Thia said you go for walks and come home high."

"Wow."

"So how often?"

Hannah shrugged. "Whenever I can."

"If I told you how bad it is for you would you believe me?"

"Maybe."

"Would you stop doing it?"

Hannah looked at her. One of the things she wanted to stop doing was pretending. "Probably not."

"Why not?"

"Because it's the only thing that makes me forget."

"There are other healthier ways to do that."

"Yeah, well I haven't found them."

"Fair enough."

They were silent for a while. "Are you going to tell Alecia?"

"Do you want me to?"

"Not really."

"Why not?"

Hannah looked impatient. "Obviously she'll have a bird."

Ivy shrugged. "So?"

"I don't want to hear her."

Ivy looked at her,. "This is what I mean about choices. You had a choice to lie to me or tell the truth. You told me the truth."

"I'm sick of pretending."

"Then don't."

"Oh, okay. I'll say, hey Alecia, guess what, I get high, and I like it so I'm not gonna stop. She'll lock me in my room for the rest of my life."

"That's a risk you take. Or you try talking to your therapist about it."

"I don't trust Elena."

"Then get a different one."

"Not sure the Children's Advocacy Center will appreciate that." Hannah said it in a sarcastic tone that would make the girls at school wither away, but Ivy just stared her down.

"Fair point. You probably have to wait until the DA has finished investigating before changing therapists. Maybe you can consider holding off on the weed until then. See how you do?"

Hannah thought about it. She wasn't sure she could get through a day without it. Although, she never got high when she was in Savannah. So maybe. Just until the court thing was settled. "I'll think about it."

"Good."

"That's it?"

Ivy looked at her. "I appreciate your honesty. So, for now that's it. I'm hoping you'll stay away from weed for the time being and that you'll address it with a new therapist when the time comes."

"You aren't going to say anything to Alecia?"

"Not for the time being. But if I think you're in danger, I will."

"Ha. Alecia would never be this cool."

"I'm not cool, Hannah. But I trust you to start making choices for yourself. And if they aren't the right ones, then I hope you come to me and tell me. I'll always be here for you. And so will your mom."

Hannah looked away. "She wasn't. Before. When Everett...."

"You're right."

"But when I told her she helped me."

"Yeah."

"It's confusing."

"I know."

"Sometimes I think it will never get better."

"Hannah, it's going to be a long hard road, but you've got it in you. I believe in you. Even if you don't believe in yourself."

"Why?"

Ivy looked at her and Hannah saw the conviction in her eyes. "I see your strength."

Hannah nodded.

Ivy's phone pinged, and she looked at it automatically.

"Your mom's at Thia's."

Hannah nodded. "I'm ready." And this time she was.

Hannah's new building had a rooftop garden. It had a swimming pool on the roof covered with a tarp, but Hannah couldn't imagine summer time ever replacing this interminable winter.

The morning broke cold, crisp, and clear. Hannah went up to the rooftop before school. She and Alecia planned to go up that night to watch the blood moon rise. Hannah knew a bunch of random people from the building would seek that location as well. She wished she could watch the moon rise by herself, but she also knew how to create space in her mind even when other people were around.

This morning, however, the rooftop was all hers. Hannah watched the mound of gray clouds move and separate in the sky, revealing streaks of blue pink and gold. She found a spot where she could sit comfortably and pulled her journal out of her backpack. She opened it to the last entry and read her words.

If everyone has a secret, I am hers. She'd written it first about Chloe, then about Alecia. Now she was no one's secret but her own.

She began to write.

Sometimes I don't know what to do with the rage inside me. Thia told me to give it to whatever I think God is.

Chloe said her therapist told her God can hold our anger.

I don't think Alecia believes in God. When Everett was alive we went to church for all the big stuff, and sometimes on Sunday when it was Alecia's turn to be refreshment lady. But I don't think she really liked it. I think it was something she thought she had to do. Maybe I'll ask her about it. I can ask her things now that I never could before.

I'm not sure what I think about God, but I feel something. Some other presence, and I think it's good.

At school, we're studying memoir. Wikipedia says memoir is a collection of memories about moments or events. So, in a way, I guess this journal is my memoir.

It is not a story of forgiveness. Neither is it a story of revenge. Sometimes, I wonder if it is a story of love, because I will always love them. He was my father. She is my mother. The "literature" says I will always have difficulties with trust. I laughed when I read that. No one needs a PhD to figure that out. This isn't a story of learning to trust because that would be a story beyond my lifetime.

Maybe it's a story of faith. In myself, and whatever connection I have made in the sky. Maybe that connection is God, maybe it isn't. But I'll decide it for myself, because I will never again let anyone tell me how or what to think.

Today, I will look for the cracks between the clouds and that's where the moon will rise. The sky will darken and clear and my new story will begin, along with the blood moon.

Hannah snapped her journal shut, buried it in her backpack, and left the rooftop to begin her short walk to school.

By the time Hannah got to school, Alecia was sitting in the small intake office of My Sister's Place. When she first went in, she told them she wanted to volunteer by doing odd jobs such as cleaning out the employee refrigerator (she told herself she'd literally be saving lives since she was pretty sure people could still die from botulism), or running clothing and furniture drives. They already had a cleaning team and a whole group of volunteers dedicated to obtaining clothing and furniture donations. They needed intake workers. Alecia, with great trepidation, began her training. She felt wobbly doing the first few and was terrified that she'd come across as cold or off-putting and that the women wouldn't stay and their (or their children's) lives would be at risk because of it. Yet none of the women left. They came in and, for that moment in time anyway, were safe.

Alecia looked up to welcome her first new client of the day, a slight woman holding an infant and a diaper bag. The thought flashed through her mind, *if only I'd have known about Everett when Hannah was this young. If only I'd taken her away then.* But then she looked at the fear in the woman's eyes and knew she didn't have the luxury of wondering anymore about what could have been — she had a job to do.

Alecia stood up and ushered the woman to a seat, "How can I help you?"

She waited while the woman took a shaky breath, then began to tell her story.

Epilogue

Just like moons and like suns,
with the certainty of tides,
just like hopes springing high,
Still I'll rise.
        ~Maya Angelou

April book club was on a Saturday morning at Thia's house and they were discussing *Little Fires Everywhere* by Celeste Ng.

Thia moved the brown bag of bagels over and placed a plastic container of fruit salad on the coffee table, "Pre-cut from the supermarket. Fight me."

"Who cares?" Alecia said graciously. "You made bloody marys and mimosas, so I love you."

"Cheers to that," Ivy said raising her glass.

Fiona looked around at her girlfriends then down at the book. "The way this book tackled race and class and how it shapes motherhood…."

Alecia caught Fiona's eye and held it, "and friendship. The way friendship shapes motherhood."

Thia smiled. Inadvertently her hand went to the blue Lapis stone nestled in the hollow of her throat. She pressed it gently. "The power of speaking out and speaking up."

Fiona thought about the cuts etched into the skin of her daughter's thighs. Each scar an unspoken word. Fiona felt the sting of them against her own skin.

The Daniels' back garden had become a mud pit from the heavy spring rains. Hannah and Chloe were entertaining Thia's children with a violent game of soccer. Lila had just scored and was doing a victory dance in the goalie's (her brother) face, causing him to shove her, earning him a slide tackle from his older brother. This, of course, ensued in a full-on brawl with Lila on top. Chloe was pulling them all apart. Hannah ran over from the opposite goal to help but slid on a streak of mud and landed on her back.

The ground was soft and she was unhurt. She allowed the shouting of the others to recede in her mind and watched the budding cherry branches above her sway. She wondered if she would be able to capture the layers of color with her set of pastels, the varying greens of the buds shooting from the rich brown of the branches. Cherry trees, Hannah thought, had a particular richness to the bark. Tiny horizontal lines like raised scars on the trunk — a texture that set them apart from the other trees. Hannah wondered if layering ink over pastel would give her that effect. She felt a sudden urgency to try it. She tried to take a picture in her mind of the precise composition of leaves, branches, and the scuttle of clouds revealing a bruised sky beyond.

Chloe successfully separated the children then sent them on a mission to collect sticks from the woods behind their yard and promised to help them build a fort if they gathered enough. Then she ran over to Hannah.

"You ok?"

Hannah nodded. "Where did the brats go?"

"I sent them into the woods."

Hannah smirked.

Chloe stuck her hand out, and Hannah grasped it, jumping up in a fluid motion. "I need a bagel."

Chloe nodded, and they walked together toward Thia's kitchen door.

The End